Powers of Attorney

Trevor M. Aldridge
M.A. (Cantab.), Q.C. (Hon.), Solicitor

10th edition

LONDON
SWEET & MAXWELL
2007

Ninth Edition   2000
Tenth Edition   2007

Published in 2007 by
Sweet & Maxwell Limited of 100 Avenue Road,
http://www.sweetandmaxwell.co.uk
Typeset by LBJ Typesetting Ltd of Kingsclere
Printed and bound in Great Britain by Athenaeum Press Ltd

No natural forests were destroyed to make this product;
only farmed timber was used and re-planted.

British Library Cataloguing in Publication Data

A CIP catalogue record for this book
is available from the British Library

ISBN 978-1-84703-193-8

1005504419

Powers of Attorney

AUSTRALIA
Law Book Co.
Sydney

CANADA AND USA
Carswell
Toronto

HONG KONG
Sweet & Maxwell Asia

NEW ZEALAND
Brookers
Wellington

SINGAPORE and MALAYSIA
Sweet & Maxwell Asia
Singapore and Kuala Lumpur

Preface to 10th edition

The role of powers of attorney has been significantly extended by the Mental Capacity Act 2005. Lasting powers of attorney, which became available from October 1, 2007, allow a donor to grant a power which not only survives the loss of mental capacity but also gives an attorney authority relating to the donor's personal welfare. Until now, enduring powers of attorney have been restricted to the traditional area of the donor's property and affairs. This is now covered by a separate form of lasting power of attorney. The 2005 Act has also broken new ground in spelling out how an attorney appointed under a lasting power of attorney should discharge his responsibilities, and a Code of Practice has been published.

A lasting power of attorney must be granted on a prescribed form. There are separate forms for one relating to the donor's personal welfare and for one relating to his property and affairs. Each form incorporates a certificate, which must be provided by a suitably qualified third party to confirm that, after discussion, the donor understands the meaning of the power. A lasting power must be registered by the Public Guardian. The procedure differs from the arrangements which applied to enduring powers of attorney, principally because a lasting power must be registered as soon as it is executed, rather than waiting until the donor ceases to have capacity.

No new enduring powers of attorney can be granted, but those granted earlier continue to be valid. The attorney's authority continues if the power has already been registered, and if the time comes to register other powers this can still be done, although with the Public Guardian rather than the Court of Protection.

This new edition has integrated lasting powers of attorney into the text of the book, to provide guidance to those directly concerned—people wishing to grant them, attorneys whom they appoint and those who deal with the attorneys—and to their advisers.

Trevor M. Aldridge

July 2007

Contents

Table of Cases

Table of Statutes

Table of Statutory Instruments

Citations

In this book the following abbreviations are used for frequently cited sources:

Statutes
   "1925 Act": Trustee Act 1925.
   (References to s.25 of the 1925 Act are to that section as re-enacted by s.5 of the 1999 Act, except in Ch.16.)
   "1971 Act": Powers of Attorney Act 1971.
   "1996 Act": Trusts of Land and Appointment of Trustees Act 1996.
   "1999 Act": Trustee Delegation Act 1999.
   "2000 Act": Trustee Act 2000.
   "2005 Act": Mental Capacity Act 2005.

Statutory instruments
   "2007 Regs": Lasting Powers of Attorney, Enduring Powers of Attorney and Public Guardian Regulations 2007 (SI 2007/1253).

Code of practice
   "Code of practice": *Mental Capacity Act 2005 Code of Practice* (Department of Constitutional Affairs, 2007).

Chapter 1

Introduction

1. Definition: power of attorney

A power of attorney is a document by which one person **1-01**
("donor") gives another person ("attorney") the power to act on
his behalf and in his name. It may be completely general, entitling
the attorney to do—almost—everything the donor could himself
do, or it may be limited to certain defined objects.

The practical purpose of a power of attorney is not only to invest
the attorney with power to act for the donor, but also to provide
him with a document defining the extent of his authority, which he
can produce as evidence to the third parties with whom he is to
deal.

There is no statutory definition of a power of attorney. The 1971
Act provides that "an instrument creating a power of attorney shall
be executed as a deed by the donor of the power" (s.1(1)). This
makes it clear that, in general, instruments which are not deeds can
no longer validly be powers of attorney as they once could.
Formerly, it was only strictly necessary for the power to be granted
by deed if authority was required to execute another deed.
Nevertheless, the 1971 Act does not invalidate forms of proxy
signed by shareholders which, in giving the proxy the power to
exercise the shareholder's voting rights, are clearly in the nature of
powers of attorney.

2. Types of power of attorney

In summary, there are four distinct types of power of attorney: **1-02**

Ordinary (traditional) powers
A power of attorney was originally granted to authorise the
attorney to manage the donor's property and financial affairs or for
commercial purposes. The attorney's authority comes to an end if
the donor ceases to have mental capacity.

Trustee powers

The general rules forbid a trustee to delegate his functions and responsibilities to anyone else. Statute authorises a trustee to grant a power of attorney in certain circumstances.

Enduring powers

An enduring power of attorney, which could be granted from March 10, 1986, until September 30, 2007, enabled the donor to give the attorney authority to manage the donor's property and financial affairs even after the donor had lost mental capacity. No further enduring powers can be granted, but those validly granted earlier continue to be effective.

Lasting powers

A lasting power of attorney, which was introduced by the 2005 Act on October 1, 2007, can be used in the same way as an enduring power. In addition, a lasting power can give the attorney authority in relation to matters of the donor's personal welfare. This class of power of attorney is effectively sub-divided, because there are separate prescribed forms for powers dealing with the donor's property and affairs and for those deal with his personal welfare. A donor wishing to grant a comprehensive power, giving both types of authority, must execute two powers.

3. Sources of law

1–03   The two statutes that deal in any comprehensive way with powers of attorney are the 1971 Act, which made provision for traditional commercial and personal powers, and the 2005 Act, which introduced lasting powers of attorney and preserved the rules relating to existing enduring powers of attorney. Both are reprinted in Appendix 1 (the 1971 Act as since amended).

The law authorising an individual trustee to grant a power of attorney is now s.25 of the 1925 Act (which was amended and re-enacted by the 1999 Act), s.9 of the Trusts of Land and Appointment of Trustees Act 1996 and other provisions of the 1999 Act. They are also reprinted in Appendix 1. The Trustee Act 2000 deals with delegation by trustees as a body, which may be by power of attorney but need not be.

Certain other statutes relate to powers of attorney for specific purposes, but the source of much of the law in this field is still the common law.

4. Extending scope of personal powers of attorney

1–04   Before statute intervened, every power of attorney granted by an individual was automatically revoked if the donor became mentally incapable, and powers could only be granted to give the attorney authority to deal with the donor's property and conduct his affairs. This gave rise to two major inconveniences, which were dealt with first by the introduction of enduring powers and then by their replacement with lasting powers.

(a) Revocation when donor incapable

The revocation when the donor became incapable led to consid- **1–05** erable uncertainty. It was often not possible to be certain when this occurred, particularly in the case of a donor gradually failing with the onset of old age or progressive disease. This made it unclear whether a power was still valid. There was also the criticism that a power of attorney ceased to be effective at precisely the time when it was most needed.

The automatic revocation of a power of attorney when the donor ceased to have mental capacity also meant that a person could not privately arrange in advance who would have authority to handle his affairs when, at a later date, he was unable to do so. The Court of Protection could appoint a receiver, but that procedure was unnecessarily cumbersome and expensive, and did not give the donor the ability to choose who would have responsibility for his property and affairs.

(b) Property and affairs only

Limiting the scope of powers of attorney to property and affairs **1–06** meant that many decisions of a personal nature which needed to be taken for a person who had ceased to have capacity were beyond the scope of the authority which could be granted to an attorney. There could be property and welfare aspects of a single decision, e.g. where someone should live, and dividing the two made for difficulties.

(c) New forms of power

Enduring powers of attorney, introduced by the Enduring **1–07** Powers of Attorney Act 1985 which came into force on March 10, 1986, tackled the first problem. They remained valid even though the donor had ceased to have mental capacity, but they were still confined to dealing with his property and affairs. They were superseded by lasting powers of attorney, introduced by the 2005 Act, which not only survive the donor's mental incapacity, but may also give authority to deal with his personal welfare.

Because both enduring powers and lasting powers were designed for use when the donor would no longer be in a position to control or appreciate what was being done on his behalf, the Acts which introduced them required that safeguards be put in place. The 2005 Act went further, laying down principles which the attorney must observe in exercising his authority.

It is still open to a donor to grant a traditional power of attorney, to which the statutory safeguards do not apply. Such a power will cease to be effective if the donor loses mental capacity and cannot extend to personal welfare matters.

The Court of Protection retains its jurisdiction in relation to patients who have lost mental capacity, and can appoint deputies to act as their agents. The court can also make a declaration as to whether a person has or lacks capacity to make a specified decision or to make decisions on specified matters, and as to the lawfulness of an act done or to be done (2005 Act s.15). This jurisdiction allows the court to determine whether the donor is or was capable of granting a power of attorney, whether a traditional or a lasting power.

5. Lasting powers of attorney

(a) Procedure in outline

1–08　　This is, in barest outline, the procedure for creating a lasting power or attorney. It must be granted in a prescribed form, which makes clear its purpose and effect. The donor or the attorney must apply to the Public Guardian to register the power, after notifying anyone the donor may have nominated in the power for that purpose.

(b) Advising on granting a lasting power

1–09　　The Law Society published guidelines for solicitors advising a client who wished to grant an enduring power of attorney (*Enduring Powers of Attorney: Guidelines for Solicitors*, revised September 1999). This guidance is currently being revised in the light of the replacement of enduring powers by lasting powers. The following is a summary of the earlier edition, adapted to the new circumstances.

The donor of the power is the solicitor's client. If a third party purports to give the client's instructions, the solicitor should obtain the client's written confirmation. A solicitor should not accept instructions if there is a suspicion that the client has been under duress or undue influence. In case of doubt, he should obtain medical advice to satisfy himself of the donor's mental capacity to grant the power. A doctor who is satisfied about the donor's capacity should record that opinion and witness the donor's signature on the power (*Kenward v Adams, The Times*, November 29, 1975).

There are cases in which a solicitor may advise that a lasting power of attorney relating to property and affairs is not appropriate; the guidance, which was limited to enduring powers of attorney, necessarily did not deal with powers relating to the donor's personal welfare. The alternative to a power of attorney would be a recommendation that in due course a deputy should be appointed by the Court of Protection. Examples of such cases are: where there are persistent family conflicts (which does not necessarily render a particular relative unsuitable to act as attorney: *Re F, The Times*, April 29, 2004), where the assets are more substantial and complex than members of the family are accustomed to handle and where litigation may result in substantial personal injury damages.

6. Enduring powers of attorney

Since October 1, 2007, it has not been possible to grant an **1–10** enduring power of attorney, as the 1985 Act has been repealed. However, existing enduring powers remain effective, whether or not they have yet been registered (2005 Act Sch.4, para.1), see Ch.15, p.113.

7. Attorney's authority

(a) Ordinary powers of attorney

An ordinary power of attorney not only defines the limits of the **1–11** attorney's authority but it can also specify how he is to exercise his powers. Without more, a power of attorney does not oblige the attorney to take any action, it merely authorises him to do so if he chooses. It has been called a

"one-sided instrument, an instrument which expresses the meaning of the person who makes it, but is not in any sense a contract"

(*Chatenay v Brazilian Submarine Telegraph Co.* [1891] 1 Q.B. 79 at 85 *per* Lindley L.J.). This emphasises that the consent of the attorney is not required when a power of attorney is executed in his favour. He has the option not to exercise the authority it confers. An ordinary power of attorney is normally granted by deed poll.

The attorney's position may well change as soon as he takes action pursuant to a power. He then often assumes an obligation, for example, after selling part of the donor's property he may be bound to deposit the proceeds of sale in a particular bank account. This duty is more in the nature of a trust than a contract. The attorney has the discretion of a trustee whether or not to act, but must exercise the discretion in the interest of the donor.

Contractual duties may arise in connection with a power of attorney. The donor normally agrees to ratify the attorney's act under the power, and that is a matter of contract. The power itself may be granted as part of a contract, as in the case of a power incorporated into an equitable mortgage. Also, the attorney may independently have contracted to exercise the powers granted, as in the case of a solicitor who becomes his client's attorney to conclude a transaction in which he has accepted professional instructions.

(b) Lasting power of attorney

1–12   The fact that an attorney appointed by a lasting power of attorney executes the instrument, which contains a statement that he understands the duties imposed on an attorney (2005 Act Sch.1, para.2(1)(d)), strongly suggests that he has agreed to undertake the duties. This is reinforced by the fact that the attorney must notify the Public Guardian on a prescribed form before he can effectively disclaim the appointment, which may revoke the power (2005 Act s.13(5), (6)(a), (7); 2007 Regs reg.20).

It may well be, therefore, that the attorney has an enforceable duty to act, albeit in the exercise of his discretion, and this may be of particular concern where the attorney's appointment relates to the donor's personal welfare.

8. Power coupled with an interest

1–13   A power of attorney may be used as part of a contractual arrangement between the donor and the attorney, to conclude the transaction in the agreed manner, either conditionally or without conditions. The grant of the power by the donor is part of the consideration that he provides in exchange for that provided by the attorney. This contractual arrangement is a power coupled with an interest.

In this case, the interest of the attorney is essentially a proprietary and beneficial one. That has two consequences. First, it will often be part of the bargain that the power of attorney is not revoked for a specified period, or that it is irrevocable. Such a restriction on the donor's normal power of revocation is binding. Secondly, the power is expressly granted to enable the attorney to obtain a benefit for which he has contracted. He therefore exercises the power in his own interest, rather than in the donor's interest.

9. Trustees

Trustees have limited statutory rights to appoint attorneys to carry out their functions, summarised below. They may be supplemented by powers expressly given in the instrument creating the trust. **1–14**

(a) Delegation by individual trustees

Generally, individual trustees are entitled to delegate their functions for up to 12 months. When doing so, they must notify their fellow trustees and anyone entitled to appoint new trustees to the trust. **1–15**

(b) Trustees who are also beneficiaries

A trustee who has a beneficial interest in land, or in the income from it, can freely delegate by power of attorney. Typically, this might be a joint owner of property, where the joint owners are technically trustees holding the property for themselves as beneficiaries. **1–16**

(c) Delegation by trustees as a body

Trustees, acting as a body, now have wide powers to delegate their functions, and the delegation does not have to be by power of attorney (Trustee Act 2000 s.11). Trustees of land have power, by power of attorney, to delegate to one or more of the beneficiaries of full age any of their functions relating to the land. **1–17**

10. Limits on powers of attorney

There are limits on the powers that can be delegated by a power of attorney. The general form of power prescribed by the 1971 Act confers "authority to do on behalf of the donor anything which he can lawfully do by an attorney" (s.10(1)). The Act does not define the limits of the authority. However, bearing in mind the state of the law when it was enacted, it must exclude matters of personal welfare. **1–18**

Other restrictions on the scope of the delegation may stem either from the donor's position or from the nature of the action to be performed. There may also be practical limitations. It seems unlikely, for example, that a life assurance company would accept a proposal and medical history form signed by an attorney, even though the prospective assured could validly authorise the attorney to complete it.

(a) Agents

1–19   The maxim *delegatus non potest delegare* means that an attorney cannot further delegate his authority, by appointing an attorney to carry out those functions in his stead, unless the terms of the appointment permit it. An enduring power of attorney cannot give the attorney the right to appoint a substitute or successor (1985 Act s.2(9)). There is however, a limited statutory exception to this rule (1925 Act s.25).

(b) Appointments

1–20   Those who have appointments of a personal nature cannot delegate their functions to an attorney. This applies, e.g. to a director of a company, although the articles of association of some companies expressly allow directors to appoint alternate directors (e.g. Table A, arts 65–69: Companies (Tables A to F) Regulations 1985). It also applies to those elected or appointed to public office, and to those employed whether under a contract of service or a contract for services.

(c) Statutory authority

1–21   Statutory authority granted to a particular person cannot be delegated. This applies, for example, to the right to practise as a doctor or a solicitor on duly qualifying, and to the rights conferred on the grant of a licence. However, a distinction must be drawn between a licensee's privileges and administrative collateral matters. A person licensed to sell alcoholic liquor cannot appoint an attorney to sell drink on his behalf. Yet it is common in leases and tenancy agreements relating to licensed premises for the tenant to appoint the landlord or his nominee as attorney to make or concur in an application to renew, vary or transfer the premises licence.

(d) Statutory rights

1–22   Whether statutory rights may be exercised by an attorney on behalf of the donor depends upon the wording of the Act, e.g. it may require a personal signature or it may permit an agent to sign on his principal's behalf. In one case, it was held that a tenant under a long lease of a flat who wished to claim a new extended lease (Leasehold Reform, Housing and Urban Development Act 1993 s.42) could not do so by a notice signed by an attorney (*St Ermins Property Co v Tingay* [2002] 3 E.G.L.R. 53).

(e) Personal privileges

Where individuals are given statutory privileges or concessions, **1–23** it may not be possible to delegate them by granting a power of attorney. This applied to the exemption from excise duty on tobacco imported for personal use from elsewhere in the European Union (*R. v Customs and Excise Commissioners Ex p. Emu Tabac s.à.r.l.* [1998] Q.B. 791 (ECJ); *Customs and Excise Commissioners v Newbury* [2003] 1 W.L.R. 2131).

(f) Wills

A will must be "signed . . . by the testator or some other person **1–24** in his presence and by his direction" (Wills Act 1837 s.9, as substituted by Administration of Justice Act 1982 s.17), except in the case of certain soldiers and sailors. This is a formality which cannot be delegated. Exceptionally, the Court of Protection, or a deputy appointed by the court, may execute a will on behalf of a testator who lacks capacity (2005 Act s.18(1)(i)). A lasting power of attorney probably cannot give that authority, as the attorney's power to make gifts is limited and, except in relation to charities, clearly only contemplates gifts *inter vivos* (2005 Act s.12).

(g) Gifts

An attorney appointed under a lasting power of attorney or an **1–25** enduring power of attorney has limited authority to make gifts from the donor's estate. The fact that this statutory authority was needed suggests that an attorney under an ordinary power has no such authority unless it was expressly included in the power.

(h) Litigation

A party to proceedings has a right of audience before the courts **1–26** and the right to conduct litigation (Courts and Legal Services Act 1990 ss.27, 28). This right cannot be delegated by power of attorney (*Gregory v Turner* [2003] 1 W.L.R. 1149). Lay representation is, however, allowed in small claims proceedings, at the discretion of the district judge. A litigant could use a power of attorney to appoint a representative, but need not do so. In one case, the Court of Appeal noted, without comment, that proceedings had been conducted by an attorney in the county court hearing below (*Credit & Mercantile Plc v Marks* [2005] Ch. 81 at [2]); that case may have been an example of this.

(i) Voting

1–27   The authority which may be given by a lasting power of attorney expressly excludes voting at an election for any public office or in a referendum (2005 Act s.29). It seems unlikely that an ordinary power of attorney could give that authority, although an elector may appoint a proxy under the statutory procedure (Representation of the People Act 2000 s.12, Sch.4).

11. Charging for preparation

1–28   A power of attorney is not one of the deeds which solicitors have a monopoly on drawing for profit, even though it relates to property or legal proceedings (Solicitors Act 1974 s.22(3)(c)). Anyone may therefore prepare a power and charge for doing so.

Chapter 2

Scope of Power

1. Principles

What acts a power of attorney authorises the attorney to do is a **2–01**
question of construction of the document.

"Where an act purporting to be done under a power of attorney
is challenged as being in excess of the authority conferred by the
power, it is necessary to shew that on a fair construction of the
whole instrument the authority in question is to be found within
the four corners of the instrument, either in express terms or by
necessary implication"

(*Bryant, Powis and Bryant Ltd. v La Banque du Peuple* [1893]
A.C. 170 at 177 *per* Lord Macnaghten).

A transaction entered into by an attorney is not valid if it falls
outside the scope of the power of attorney. The possibility of
invalidity can, however, be removed, if the person intended to
benefit from the obligation in question waives the rights which it
purports to confer. If that doubt related only to certain terms, the
waiver ensures that the remainder are enforceable (*Hawksley v
Outram* [1892] 3 Ch. 59).

In considering the extent of powers to be granted, the intending
donor should be warned of two contradictory dangers. On the one
hand, in conferring unnecessarily wide powers there is the risk that
an attorney who turns out to be untrustworthy, or merely one
whose judgment is faulty, will exercise his authority in areas which
he could and should have left alone. On the other hand, a very
restrictive definition of the powers can prevent an attorney from
satisfactorily completing the main object of the grant, because he
lacks authority to perform necessary acts.

These considerations are obviously more acute in the case of a
lasting power of attorney, which will operate after the donor is
powerless to change the identity of the attorney or the scope of his
authority.

2. Ordinary powers of attorney

(a) Wide powers

2–02   A donor who wishes to invest his attorney with full powers can seek to itemise and define all the acts that the attorney may do for him, or he may adopt the brief statutory form set out in Sch.1 to the 1971 Act. The second course is now normally adopted.

The statutory form describes itself as a "general power of attorney" and simply appoints one person, or more than one, to be the grantor's attorney "in accordance with section 10 of the Powers of Attorney Act 1971". A form "to the like effect", also expressed to be made under the Act, can be used (1971 Act s.10(1)).

The statutory form of power authorises the attorney "to do on behalf of the donor anything which he can lawfully do by an attorney" (1971 Act s.10(1)). To this, there are certain exceptions. The power does not extend to the functions that the donor has as a trustee or personal representative, or as tenant for life or statutory owners under the Settled Land Act 1925 (1971 Act s.10(2)). There seems no reason against incorporating into a single document both the statutory form and authority to perform any of the excluded acts that are required in any particular case.

Where an attorney is likely to have to act abroad under the power, it may be more satisfactory to set out the attorney's authority in full. Those to whom it has to be exhibited to establish the validity of the attorney's acts may not be aware of the terms of the 1971 Act and may not have the facilities for referring to it.

(b)   Limited authority

2–03   An ordinary power of attorney may restrict the authority of the attorney to only one, or some, of the matters which a general power could cover. Examples are dealt with below, paras 2–09—2–12.

3. Lasting powers of attorney

(a)   Property and affairs

2–04   A lasting power relating to the donor's property and affairs may give general authority over such matters to the attorney, or it may be limited to specified matters. The prescribed form (form LPA PA: 2007 Regs Sch.1) requires the donor to state whether or not he wishes to restrict or place a condition on the attorney by completing one of two tick boxes, Yes or No. If he ticks Yes, details must be given. The prescribed information, which is part of the form, cautions against imposing restrictions which would result in nobody having authority to take particular decisions, so that it would become necessary to apply to the Court of Protection.

The 2005 Act does not specify the matters covered by this form of lasting power of attorney, but the extent of the authority is assumed to be the same as that covered by an ordinary power of attorney.

(b) Personal welfare

The authority given to an attorney by a lasting power of attorney 2–05 relating to the donor's personal welfare can only be exercised if the donor lacks capacity, or the attorney reasonably believes that he lacks it (2005 Act s.11(7)(a)).

There is no statutory definition of how far the authority given by a lasting power of attorney relating to the donor's personal welfare can extend, although the power may restrict the authority to particular areas. As this form of power of attorney is an innovation, so that there is no established body of law, its extent remains to be defined. The matters which may be covered by Court of Protection decisions, or the authority given to a deputy, may offer some guidance. They include, as they would be expressed in the context of a power of attorney (2005 Act ss.11(7)(c), (8), 17(1)): where the donor is to live; the donor's contact with specified persons; giving or refusing consent to health care treatment (but not life-sustaining treatment, unless the power expressly provides) and deciding who is responsible for it. If the donor has made an advance decision to refuse treatment (2005 Act ss.24–26), the attorney's authority is subject to it (2005 Act s.11(7)(b)).

The following matters are expressly excluded from an attorney's authority (2005 Act ss.27, 28):

  (i) consenting to marriage or civil partnership;

 (ii) consenting to sexual relations;

(iii) consenting to a divorce or the dissolution of a civil partnership based on two years' separation;

(iv) consenting to a child being placed for adoption or to an adoption order;

 (v) discharging parental responsibilities, other than in relating to a child's property;

(vi) giving consent under the Human Fertilisation and Embryology Act 1990;

(vii) consenting to medical treatment for mental disorder.

As in the case of a lasting power relating to the donor's property and affairs, a lasting power relating to personal welfare may limit the attorney's authority. The prescribed form (form LPA PW: 2007 Regs Sch.1) requires the donor to state whether or not he wishes to restrict or place a condition on the attorney by completing one of two tick boxes, Yes or No. If he ticks Yes, details must be given. Here again, the prescribed information, which is part of the form, cautions against imposing restrictions which would result in nobody having authority to take particular decisions, so that it would become necessary to apply to the Court of Protection.

(c) Restraining the donor

2–06 There is a conditional restriction on the attorney's authority to do something intended to restrain the donor, or to authorise someone else to do it. Restraint means using or threatening force to do something which the donor resists, or restricting his freedom of movement, whether or not he resists. This is intended to go further than depriving the donor of his liberty within the meaning of the European Convention on Human Rights, Art.5(1) (2005 Act s.11(1), (5), (6)).

The donor may be restrained if three conditions are satisfied (2005 Act s.11 (2)–(4)):

(i) The donor lacks capacity in relation to the matter in question, or the attorney reasonably believes that he does,

(ii) The attorney reasonably believes that it is necessary to act in that way to prevent harm to the donor, and

(iii) The act is proportionate both to the likelihood of harm to the donor and the severity of that harm.

4. Other powers of attorney

(a) Trustee powers of attorney

2–07 A trustee who uses the general power of attorney, prescribed by the 1925 Act for use by trustees, delegates "all the trusts, powers and discretions" vested in him under the identified trust (1925 Act s.25(5)). The effect is the same if he uses a form to the like effect which is expressed to be made under s.25(5) of that Act.

(b) Enduring powers of attorney

2–08 See Ch.15, p.113.

5. Limited Authority

(a) Generally

An attorney's authority can be limited in a variety of ways: to a **2–09** particular transaction, e.g. buying an identified house; to one type of action, e.g. to collecting rents; to dealing with one named person, e.g. operating an account at a specified bank; to a limited period of time. Precedents for clauses to give a power in a variety of specified circumstances are set out in Appendix 4.

A power of attorney given for limited purposes is strictly interpreted by the courts, so that forethought in deciding what is needed and precision in drafting are more important. Examples of reported restrictive interpretations are given below.

A donor is in a vulnerable position. Although he may hedge the attorney's authority about with restrictions, third parties are entitled to rely upon the attorney's ostensible authority.

One way in which the donor can seek to protect himself is to require the attorney always to act explicitly as the donor's agent, and not in his own name. This draws to the attention of third parties the fact that the attorney's authority may be limited. It has express statutory consequences in the case of bills of exchange (para.8–04). The donor must necessarily still rely on the attorney following his instructions.

Another way in which the donor may seek to safeguard his position is to impose the requirement that the attorney obtain the consent of a named person before acting or before taking any more important steps. But this may cause practical difficulties. A third party dealing with the attorney will require the consent of the person named to be proved, and there is no established routine for that. Again, the power of attorney may effectively be invalidated by the death or incapacity of the named person.

A donor who considers that the concurrence of a named person is essential might just as well appoint that person as joint attorney, but not a joint and several attorney. This will immediately make clear to third parties that his concurrence is necessary.

It is quite possible for the donor to make it a condition that the attorney obtain his (the donor's) concurrence before doing either anything or specific acts. That gives him close control, but defeats the normal purpose of granting a power of attorney which is to allow the attorney to attend to the donor's business without troubling him.

(b) Borrowing

A particular example of the court's policy of construing powers **2–10** of attorney restrictively is provided by powers to borrow on the donor's behalf. They tend to lean against interpreting a clause as allowing the attorney to borrow and give security from the donor's property (e.g. *Jacobs v Morris* [1902] 1 Ch. 816). If the donor wishes the attorney to have this power, it should be expressly stated.

(c) Bank accounts

2–11   There is a temptation when a power of attorney is granted for limited purposes to give authority to operate the donor's bank account "for the purposes aforesaid". This may result in grave practical inconveniences. The bank may require the attorney to provide strict proof of the purposes for which he wishes to draw money, on each occasion that he does so (*Reckitt v Barnett, Pembroke and Slater Ltd.* [1929] A.C. 176).

The easiest way to give the attorney limited access to the donor's bank balance without the inconvenience of additional formalities is usually to open a special account as the only one on which the attorney is entitled to draw.

(d) Examples

2–12   The following are examples of powers that have been interpreted restrictively.

POWER CONFERRED	HELD NOT TO AUTHORIZE
"To act on my behalf in all matters relating to my property . . . and to mortgage . . ."	Mortgage to secure past debt of donor for that would amount merely to voluntary gift.
Re Bowles' Mortgage Trust (1874) 31 L.T. 365.	
"In connection with my business to make, draw, sign, accept or indorse bills of exchange . . ."	Borrowing money on donor's behalf and giving bills therefor,
Jacobs v Morris [1902] 1 Ch. 816.	
"To settle accounts, pay all debts due from me as executrix of *A* decd, and to act for me as executrix of *A*."	Accepting bill of exchange for debts due by testator, for that would charge the executrix in her own right.
Gardner v Baillie (1796) 6 Term. Rep. 591.	
"To transact all business" (following powers principally to recover specific debts).	Indorsing bill of exchange for discounting,
Hay v Goldsmidt (1804) 1 Taunt. 349; and see *Hogg v Snaith* (1808) 1 Taunt. 347; *Esdaile v La Nauze* (1835) 1 Y. & C. Ex. 394.	

"To sign acceptances . . . negotiate, make sale, dispose of, assign and transfer" Government promissory notes.	Pledging the notes

Jonmenjoy Coondoo v Watson (1884) 9 App. Cas. 561, PC, distinguishing
Bank of Bengal v Macleod (1849) 7 Moo. P.C. 35, where a similar power
included the word "indorse" and this was held to authorise a pledge.

"To draw cheques without restriction."	Drawing cheques for donee's private debt.

Reckitt v Barnett, Pembroke and Slater Ltd. [1929] A.C. 176.

"For the purpose of exercising for me all . . . powers of privileges conferred by" a partnership deed "to do anything whatsoever in or about my concerns."	Dissolving the partnership.

Harper v Godsell (1870) L.R. 5 Q.B. 422.

"To sell, or concur in selling, any of my real, leasehold, or personal property . . .".	A restraint of trade clause in the contract to sell, as a going concern, a business carried on by a partnership in which the donor was a partner.

Hawksley v Outram [1892] 3 Ch. 359.

"To sell all or any of my lands."	Sale of land previously settled voluntarily on trustees.

General Meat Supply Assocn, Ltd v Bouffler (1879) 41 L.T. 719.

"To sell any real or personal property . . . belonging to me."	Sale of land of which donor was mortgagee.

Re Dowson & Jenkins' Contract [1904] 2 Ch. 219.

"To sell and convey my property at *B*, whether owned solely or jointly with any other person."	Conveyance of land held by donor as trustee for sale.

Green v Whitehead [1930] 1 Ch. 38, CA.

6. Gifts

(a) Ordinary powers of attorney

An attorney under an ordinary power of attorney can make gifts **2–13**
out of the donor's estate, to the extent that he honestly considers
that in doing so he is implementing the purposes for which the
power was granted. However, that does not mean that he can make
gifts in his own favour, unless the donor expressly authorises it. An
attorney's position is in some ways fiduciary, and there is a general

rule that a trustee may not benefit from his trust. An attorney is not in every way equated with a trustee—it is accepted practice, e.g. for professional attorneys to pay their own fees from the donor's estate, without express authority in the power—yet it is assumed that he cannot make voluntary payments in his own favour.

(b) Lasting powers of attorney

2–14   An attorney under a lasting power of attorney relating to the donor's property may only make gifts from the donor's estate in certain circumstances, and even then the power may restrict this authority or impose conditions (2005 Act s.12).

Subject to the overall condition that each gift is not unreasonable, having regard to all the circumstances, particularly the size of the donor's estate, the attorney may make gifts:

  (i) to people related to or connected with the donor, including the attorney himself, on customary occasions. Those occasions are a birthday, marriage or civil partnership, and other occasions when families, friends or associates customarily give presents;

 (ii) to a charity to which the donor had donated or might have been expected to contribute.

(c) Enduring powers of attorney

2–15   See Ch.15, p.113.

7. Interpretation

2–16   To ascertain the extent of the authority granted by a power of attorney, the words of the document must be construed. The donor's intentions are relevant only to the extent that they are expressed in the deed's terms. As with the interpretation of other documents, this is a matter of law rather than fact.

(a) Donor's ability to perform

2–17   No one may delegate the performance of an act which he is not himself entitled to perform. A power of attorney cannot validly authorise the attorney to do a criminal act, nor to perform a contract that is illegal, e.g. by being in restraint of trade. The first

question to be asked, therefore, to determine whether an attorney
has the right to do a particular act, is whether the donor has the
right to do it (*Shrewsbury & Birmingham Railway Co. v NW Railway
Co.* (1857) 6 H.L. Cas. 113).

(b) Ostensible authority

Because, in dealings with third parties, the attorney's powers **2–18**
extend as far as his ostensible authority, the donor cannot suc-
cessfully claim to restrict their scope by relying on private instructions to the attorney (*Bryant, Powis and Bryant Ltd. v La Banque
du Peuple* [1893] A.C. 170, 180). However, a restriction brought to
the attention of third parties is valid (*Overbrooke Estates Ltd. v
Glencombe Properties Ltd.* [1974] 1 W.L.R. 1335: printed particu-
lars of a property to be sold by auction gave notice that the
auctioneers had no authority to make representations or give
warranties about the property). This argues for spelling out, on the
face of the power, any restriction to which the attorney is to be
subject.

This rule may be modified where the circumstances put the third
party on enquiry. He cannot rely on the attorney's ostensible
authority to extend his actual authority as a defence against the
consequences of his own negligence. A bank was affected with
notice of a donee's abuse of powers when it did not enquire into
the circumstances in which he paid into his own account cheques
which showed on their face that the money was not his (*Midland
Bank Ltd. v Reckitt* [1933] A.C. 1).

(c) Ultra vires

Clearly, if an act which the attorney purports to do is outside the **2–19**
scope of the authority granted by the power of attorney, it will be
ultra vires and void. However, if the act is within the scope of the
power, albeit part of a fraud to which the attorney is not a party, it
is initially valid but voidable (*Norwich Building Society v Steed*
[1993] Ch. 116). The distinction is important to innocent third
parties deriving title from the voidable transaction.

(d) Recitals

Where a power of attorney contains recitals, which is not now **2–20**
usual, they may limit the scope of the authority that the operative
part of the deed grants. A power of attorney that recited the
donor's intention of going abroad was held to be effective only
during the donor's absence, notwithstanding that the clause confer-

ring the powers contained no such limit (*Danby v Coutts & Co.* (1885) 29 Ch. 500).

(e) General rides of construction

2–21   In the interpretation of a power of attorney as for other deeds, statute applies general rules of interpretation. "Month" means calendar month; "person" includes a corporation; the singular includes the plural and vice versa; the masculine includes the feminine and vice versa. These meanings can be excluded or modified expressly or by implication if the context requires (Law of Property Act 1925 s.61). However, "person" and "individual" are not synonymous. The latter only refers to a human person.

(f) Land

2–22   A power of attorney granted after March 1, 2000 which gives authority to do an act relating to land (widely interpreted: 1925 Act s.68(6)) has a broad effect, albeit subject to anything to the contrary in the power. It extends to doing the act in question with respect to any estate or interest in it which the donor then holds, whether alone or jointly (1999 Act s.10).

This provision prevents undue technicality interfering with the intention of a donor. So, e.g. a power granting authority "to sell my house" when the house was jointly owned, would cover the attorney selling the donor's interest in the legal estate (as trustee/beneficiary of land) and his equitable interest.

(g) Ejusdem generis

2–23   The *ejusdem generic* rule, that general words at the end of a list of items in an identifiable category are construed so as not to extend the category so identified, has been applied to limit the effect of a clause in a power of attorney giving general powers following a series of limited powers (*Bryant, Powis and Bryant Ltd. v La Banque du Peuple* [1893] A.C. 170). A general power that stands alone is not affected. A donor who wishes to spell out certain express powers and to follow with a comprehensive power can ensure that the latter is effective by expressing it to be unrestricted by the limitations in previous clauses.

In applying the rule, the court may be affected by the purpose for which the power was granted.

"The power of attorney appoints [the attorney] the purchasing agent for the business carried on by [the donor], and gives him

certain particularised powers in connection with purchases, and
then goes on to give him this power of accepting bills and
making notes in connection with the said business. In my
judgment the later words are intended merely to cover such
powers beyond the mere power to purchase, which is expressly
given, as are necessarily implied by the appointment of [the
attorney] as purchasing agent"

(*Jacobs v Morris* [1902] 1 Ch. 816 at 828 *per* Vaughan Williams
L.J.).

(h) Ambiguity

If a power is ambiguous, the donor is bound when the attorney 2–24
bona fide places a reasonable interpretation on it and acts accordingly. However, if he acts in a way that does not comply with either
possible interpretation, the donor is not bound by the attorney's
acts (*Weigall & Co. v Runciman & Co.* (1916) 115 L.T. 61).

(i) Proper law

What is the proper law of a power of attorney may depend on 2–25
the question to be addressed. The Contracts (Applicable Law) Act
1990 determines the law applying to its effect on the relations
between the donor and the attorney, but it does not apply to the
issue of the attorney's ability to bind the donor in dealings with
third parties (Sch.1, art.1, para.2(f)).

The statute allows the parties to choose the law which is to apply
(Sch.1, art.3, para.1), unless all the other relevant elements connect
the transaction to another particular country. In that case, that
country's law applies (Sch.1, art.3, para.3). If the parties do not
choose a system of law, the law of the country most closely
connected applies, with a presumption in favour of the country of
the attorney's habitual residence (Sch.1, art.4, paras 1, 2).

Where the common law is not superseded by the statute, the
proper law is that of the country where the power is used or that of
the transaction in which it is to be employed (*Sinfra Akt v Sinfra
Ltd.* [1939] 2 All E.R. 675). That rule may be modified by the
intention of the parties, whether express or implied, derived from
the instrument.

The complications inherent in a proposal to grant a single power
of attorney for use in a number of different jurisdictions are
obvious. It will often be simpler to prepare a series of separate
documents, each for a different country.

8. Later extensions

(a) Ordinary powers of attorney

2–26   A question arises whether, once a power of attorney has been granted, the donor can subsequently informally extend the attorney's authority simply by giving him written instructions.

Section 1 of the 1971 Act casts some doubt on the efficacy of this procedure. That section requires every instrument creating a power of attorney to be executed as a deed. Can it be said that a letter of extension is not a power of attorney, a term not defined by the Act? Although such a letter would not purport to be a power of attorney, it is suggested that any document purporting to confer a new power of this nature should come within the meaning of the term, even though informal. If that is correct, the informality of a letter would render it ineffective, unless it was saved by the doctrine of estoppel preventing the donor from denying that the extension of the authority was effective.

A later letter can estop the donor from denying that the attorney has authority to do what it requests. If a power gives express authority to do a particular act, and that is followed by general words which would not normally authorise the attorney to go beyond what was necessary for the specified act, a letter from the donor indicating what he wants done can prevent his later denying that the attorney has authority to do it (*Perry v Hall* (1860) 2 De. G. F. & J. 38).

An alternative way to achieve an extension of the attorney's authority is to notify a third party that the power is to be treated as extended. In *Reckitt v Barnett, Pembroke and Slater Ltd.* [1929] A.C. 176, the donor wrote to his bank saying that they were to treat a power of attorney, which did not expressly refer to drawing cheques, as authorising the attorney to draw on the donor's bank account without restriction. That letter was construed as one with the power and interpreted to mean that cheques could freely be drawn only for the purposes for which the power was given.

A similar letter would clearly still be effective, notwithstanding the 1971 Act, because a bank has a contractual duty to act on its customer's instructions. However, whether a valid estoppel can still be based upon such a letter, if the recipient is not bound to act at the donor's direction, is open to question. If the statement is, on the face of it, invalid in form—as a power of attorney not a deed now is—it seems unlikely that anyone changing his position in reliance upon it would be entitled to protection in the absence of some degree of deceit.

As to the use of subsequent communications to restrict rather than to extend, the attorney's authority, see para.12–13.

Chapter 3

Donor

1. Capacity

The donor's capacity is relevant at two separate times: first, when **3–01** the power of attorney is granted, and secondly, when the attorney exercises the authority granted by the power.

(a) Granting the power

A person who lacks the mental capacity to grant a power of **3–02** attorney cannot grant a valid power. However, a purported power granted by someone who lacks capacity can later be validated, if he regains capacity and then ratifies it. In effect, the original power is a nullity and the power if first effectively granted on the later ratification. The details of the power then granted are ascertained by referring to the original document.

(b) Exercising authority

An attorney appointed by an ordinary power cannot validly **3–03** exercise his authority at a time when the donor lacks capacity. This is not merely a question of whether the donor understands the attorney's role. An attorney can only validly do an act that, at the time he does it, the donor has the capacity to do (*Drew v Nunn* (1879) 4 Q.B.D. 661).

The common law rule is that subsequent mental incapacity terminates the authority granted by a power of attorney. The exact nature of the lack of capacity is not defined; the 1971 Act refers to the donor's "incapacity" (s.4(1)(a)(ii)), but adds no further detail. The power is revoked despite the attorney's ignorance of the change in circumstances (*Yonge v Toynbee* [1910] 1 K.B. 215). To this general rule, there are now a number of exceptions. The donor's mental incapacity will not prejudice the authority of an attorney appointed under a lasting power, an enduring power (provided it is registered) or a power coupled with an interest. An attorney acting under a power which, without his knowledge, has been revoked by the donor's loss of capacity has statutory protection (1971 Act s.5(1)). Opposite third parties, an attorney's ostensible authority under a revoked power may continue.

(c)   Nature of capacity

3–04   The legal capacity to grant a power of attorney generally coincides with the donor's ability to enter into a binding contract. One must ask, "Was he or she capable of understanding the nature of the contract which he or she entered into?" (*Boughton v Knight* (1873) L.R. 3 P. & D. 64 at 72). The rule is that the donor must, with the assistance of whatever explanation he was given, have the mental capacity to understand the nature and effect of the transaction (*Re K, Re F* [1988] Ch. 310). This is a common law rule, and none of the statutes dealing with powers of attorney has addressed the point.

For the purposes of lasting powers of attorney, a person lacks mental capacity and therefore the capacity to grant a power of attorney when, by reason of a permanent or temporary impairment of the mind or brain or a disturbance with its functioning, he cannot make a decision for himself in relation to the matter. Inability to make a decision means being unable to understand, retain, use and weigh relevant information, or communicate the decision. The following cannot alone establish a lack of capacity: a person's age, appearance, or a condition or behaviours which may lead others to make unjustified assumptions (2005 Act ss.2(1)–(3), 3(1)).

For an enduring power, Hoffman J. accepted this summary of what the donor must understand when granting it (*Re K, Re F*, above, at 316):

> "First, if such be the terms of the power, that the attorney will be able to assume complete authority over the donor's affairs; second, if such be the terms of the power, that the attorney will in general be able to do anything with the donor's property which he himself could have done; third, that the authority will continue if the donor should be or become mentally incapable; fourth, that if he should be or become mentally incapable, the power will be irrevocable without confirmation by the court."

In judging a donor's mental capacity, guidance issued jointly by the British Medical Association and the Law Society (*Assessment of*

Mental Capacity: Guidance for Doctors and Lawyers, 1995) suggests that questions to test understanding which can be answered "Yes" or "No" may not be adequate. This draws on an analogous decision in *Re Beaney (deceased)* [1978] 1 W.L.R. 770, which concerned the capacity of someone who subsequently died to execute a valid transfer of a house. Mr Martin Nourse Q.C., sitting as a deputy judge of the Chancery Division, said (at 777):

> "She was physically capable of signing her name and she was capable of understanding simple things, although she quickly forgot them. This enabled her to give the appearance of understanding things which were not so simple, particularly if the questions she was asked could be given a 'Yes' or 'No' answer, being the answer which was obviously wanted."

This capacity to grant a valid power must not be confused with the requirement of mental capacity in the donor at the time when the attorney acts under the power (except in the case of lasting or enduring powers), see below under *Mental Patients*, para.3–08.

2. Partners

As a normal partnership is unincorporated, a firm which wishes **3–05** to appoint an attorney to act on its behalf must do so by means of a joint appointment by all the partners. Their capacity to appoint an attorney jointly is the same as their capacity as individuals. One partner has no implied authority to bind the other partner by deed (*Marchant v Morton Down & Co.* [1901] 2 K.B. 829), and as a power of attorney must be given by deed (1971 Act s.1), one partner cannot grant a valid power of attorney on behalf of the firm.

In relation to any real property which the partners own as partnership property, they (or some of them) will necessarily hold the legal estate as trustees (Law of Property Act 1925 s.34). The rules relating to trustees granting powers of attorney therefore apply (Ch.13, p.93).

If one partner grants his copartner a power of attorney to do something which each partner is already entitled to do individually on behalf of the firm—e.g. in the case of a trading partnership, to draw and indorse bills of exchange—it is construed as authority to do the act in respect of the partner's personal estate (*Attwood v Munnings* (1827) 7 B. & C. 278).

A partner may be able to delegate his functions as such, although that could well depend on the nature of the partnership and whether it should be inferred that personal performance is one of the partnership obligations. Authority to exercise the donor's powers and privileges under a partnership deed does not permit the attorney to dissolve the partnership (*Harper v Godsell* (1870) L.R. 5 Q.B. 422).

3. Corporations

3–06 A body corporate—a company or a limited liability partnership—can create an ordinary power of attorney. No act of a company can be called into question by reason of its lack of capacity, and anyone dealing with a company in good faith may assume that the board of directors are free to bind the company (Companies Act 1985 ss.35, 35A). A limited liability partnership has unlimited capacity (Limited Liability Partnerships Act 2000 s.1(3)). A corporation cannot, however, create a lasting power of attorney (2005 Act s.10(1)) nor, formerly, an enduring power of attorney (Enduring Powers of Attorney Act 1985 s.1(1)).

The directors of a company may appoint an agent to execute any agreement or instrument which is not a deed in relation to any matters within its powers. This appointment need not be by a formal power of attorney but can be by resolution or otherwise (Law of Property Act 1925 s.74(2)).

A company has a general power to appoint an attorney to execute deeds on its behalf outside the United Kingdom. A deed which the attorney has executed takes effect as if it were executed under the company's common seal (Companies Act 1985, s.38; Companies Act 1989 Sch.17, para.1). Article 71 of Table A gives the directors a general power to appoint agents, which may be exercised by power of attorney (Companies (Tables A to F) Regulations 1985).

The Companies Act 2006 will, when brought into force, expressly authorise companies to empower, by deed, an attorney to execute deeds or documents on its behalf, generally or in respect of specified matters. The deeds or documents which the attorney executes on its behalf bind the company as if executed by the company (Companies Act 2006 s.47).

4. Minors

3–07 The extent to which a minor (under the age of eighteen: Family Law Reform Act 1969 s.1) can validly grant a power of attorney is still somewhat doubtful. Certainly, it is no longer the case, as Lord Mansfield held, that a power of attorney granted by a minor is void (*Zouch d Abbot and Hallet v Parsons* (1765) 3 Burr. 1794). Lord Denning M.R. said,

"The correct proposition is that an infant cannot appoint an agent to make a disposition of his property so as to bind him irrevocably. A disposition by an agent for an infant is voidable just as a disposition by the infant himself would be so long as it is avoided within a reasonable time after attaining full age"

(*G(A) v G(T)* [1970] 2 Q.B. 643 at 652).

A power of attorney which a mother granted on behalf of her children aged 12 and 10, used to bring foreign litigation which was not in their best interests, was set aside (*Black v Yates* [1992] Q.B. 526). The judge noted that "there was no evidence before me that the children, at the time that the power of attorney was given, were aware of any of the steps being taken on their behalf, let alone able to give them independent consideration or to give any informed consent as to the power of attorney or the authority of their mother to give it on their behalf" (at 553, *per* Potter J.).

There is also the question whether a power of attorney granted by a minor is for that reason revocable in circumstances in which it otherwise would not be. The act of appointing an agent, as distinct from the act of entering into the proposed contract, could itself be an imprudence from the consequences of which the law should protect a minor. However, if the power is coupled with an interest in a transaction that fully binds the minor, there seems no ground for suggesting that it can be revoked. In other cases, the power of attorney itself may be revocable within a reasonable time after the minor comes of age, but without prejudice to the acts already performed under its authority.

5. Mental patients

The fact that a person has been diagnosed with, or is receiving 3–08 treatment for, some mental illness does not of itself mean that he does not have capacity to grant a power of attorney. What is relevant is the donor's understanding when executing the power. An otherwise incapable patient may have a lucid interval and be able to grant a power. A person who is unfit to manage his affairs may nevertheless be able to grant a valid power (*Re K, Re F* [1988] Ch. 310).

This principle has received statutory recognition is relation to lasting powers of attorney. The question whether a person lacks capacity is to be answered in relation to the matter in question and there is a general presumption that a person has capacity unless it is established that he lacks it (2005 Act ss.1(2), 2(1)).

6. Drunkards

It seems that if a person who is so drunk that he cannot 3–09 appreciate what he is doing contracts with another who realises his state, the contract is voidable by the drunkard when he is sober again (*Matthews v Baxter* (1873) L.R. 8 Exch. 132).

"There ought to be no distinction between a person so drunk as not to know the nature of the transaction, and a person of unsound mind to the same extent"

(*Hart v O'Connor* [1985] A.C. 1000 (PC) at 1005). Presumably, the rule would be extended to incapacity because of the influence of narcotic drugs. This should apply on the grant of a power on attorney, on the basis that the capacity to grant a power follows the capacity to contract.

It would scarcely be practical for the authority of an attorney to be cancelled, or even suspended, at any time when the donor happened to be drunk. Yet, in principle, the donor should be of full capacity both when the power is granted, and when authority under it is exercised. The point does not seem to have been decided.

7. Enemy aliens

3–10   An enemy alien in time of war cannot validly contract, and therefore is incapable of granting a power of attorney. A power existing when war is declared is automatically revoked when one of the parties becomes an enemy alien (*V/O Sovfracht v NV Gebr Van Udens* [1943] A.C. 203).

An irrevocable power of attorney for the sale of land is an exception (*Tingley v Muller* [1917] 2 Ch. 144). It is suggested that the exception would extend to all powers coupled with an interest, because in such cases the attorney is not really the donor's agent, but acts independently of him.

8. Attorneys

3–11   A person who is appointed to be someone else's attorney normally has no power to grant a further power of attorney, to authorise someone else to carry out his functions under the first power of attorney. The rule *delegatus non potest delegare* makes a subsequent delegation invalid.

Nevertheless, an ordinary power of attorney may authorise the attorney whom it appoints to appoint a substitute. A precedent for a clause for that purpose is given in Appendix 4. However, neither a lasting power of attorney nor an enduring power of attorney can authorise the attorney to appoint a substitute or successor (2005 Act s.10(8)(a), Sch.4, para.2(6)). But a lasting power may appoint a person to replace the attorney whose appointment is automatically terminated on his death, bankruptcy, divorce from or dissolution of a civil partnership with the donor or loss of capacity (2005 Act s.10(8)(b)).

The statutory powers given to trustees as a body to appoint an attorney can include conferring authority to appoint a substitute if, but only if, it is reasonably necessary to do so (2000 Act s.14(2), (3)(a)).

With one exception, the statutory provision authorising individual trustees to delegate their powers for up to twelve months contains no reference to substitutes. It does not seem appropriate for a power of attorney granted thereunder to contain such a clause. It would undermine part of the purpose of the statutory notice of the grant of the power, which has to name the attorney. The exception is to permit the delegation of the power to transfer inscribed stock (1925 Act s.25(8)).

9. Personal representatives

Once a grant of representation has been made, personal repre- **3–12** sentatives have the powers of delegation, both as individuals and collectively, that are enjoyed by trustees generally (1925 Act s.25(1)(a); 2000 Act, s.35). See Ch.13, p.93.

The powers of attorneys to obtain grants of representation are dealt with separately in Ch.18, p.137.

10. Tenants for life and statutory owners

The statutory powers that trustees enjoy to delegate as individ- **3–13** uals apply equally to tenants for life and to statutory owners (Ch.13, p.93). There are special provisions about the notice that must be given when granting a power of attorney. In the case of a tenant for life, it goes to the trustees of the settlement and to any other person who, jointly with the donor, constitutes the tenant for life. A statutory owner must give notice to any other person who, with the donor, constitutes the statutory owner (1925 Act s.25(10)(b), (c)).

11. Bankrupts

While a bankrupt is not barred from granting an ordinary power **3–14** of attorney, it is not of practical importance, at least as far as disposing of property is concerned, because his property is vested in his trustee in bankruptcy.

Upon the donor of an earlier power of attorney becoming bankrupt, the power is automatically revoked (*Markwick v Hardingham* (1880) 15 Ch. 339). A power coupled with an interest is an exception to this rule, and is not affected (*Barclays Bank Ltd. v*

Bird [1954] Ch. 274). It is also possible for an attorney to perform ministerial acts, merely carrying into effect a contract entered into before the bankruptcy (*Dixon v Ewart* (1891) Buck. 94). So far as a lasting power relates to the donor's property and affairs, it is revoked by the donor's subsequent bankruptcy (or, if the donor is merely subject to an interim bankruptcy restrictions order, it is suspended while the order is in effect) (2005 Act s.13(3), (4)). It follows that a bankrupt cannot grant a lasting power of attorney relating to his property and affairs.

12. Trustees in bankruptcy

3–15   A trustee in bankruptcy is empowered to execute any power of attorney needed for carrying into effect the provisions of the Insolvency Act 1986 (Sch.5, para.14(f)). He does so using the title "the trustee of the estate of [the bankrupt] a bankrupt" (s.305(4)).

13. Liquidators

3–16   A liquidator in a winding up has power "to appoint an agent to do any business which the liquidator is unable to do himself". The power extends to acts which the liquidator is "unable" rather than "unwilling" to do (Insolvency Act 1986 Sch.4, para.12).

14. Patrons of a benefice

3–17   A registered patron of a Church of England benefice may delegate the discharge of his patronage functions by power of attorney (Patronage (Benefices) Measure 1986 s.5; Patronages Measure Rules 2000 s.4).

Chapter 4

Attorney

1. Capacity

(a) Freedom of choice

Generally, the donor of a power of attorney has complete **4–01** freedom of choice in deciding who shall act as his attorney. In practice, the selection is obviously important, but, except in the case of an enduring power, the law does not take any special steps to restrict the capacity to act as an attorney to those who might be considered suitable.

(b) Suitability

An objection can be made to the proposed registration of an **4–02** enduring power of attorney on the ground that the attorney is unsuitable (para.15–11). The position is different in respect of a lasting power of attorney: the grounds for objection to registration are not spelled out. The unsuitability of the attorney could rarely apply to a lasting power, because registration takes place soon after the power is granted, when the donor would recently have selected the attorney.

2. More than one attorney

(a) Joint or joint and several

If more than one attorney is appointed, the grant of the power **4–03** may be to them jointly, or to them jointly and severally. There is an essential difference. The authority of attorneys who are appointed jointly can only be exercised by all of them collectively. On the other hand, when attorneys are appointed jointly and severally, one or some of them may act alone, or they may all act together. The result is that a joint power must necessarily come to an end when any one of the attorneys ceases to have the capacity to act, or dies, because it is then impossible for all of them to act together as their appointment required.

An ordinary power could vary the arrangements by making express provision. It could, e.g. specify that any two of a greater number of attorneys should act on any occasion. A joint and several power granted to fifteen people was validly exercised by four of them (*Guthrie v Armstrong* (1822) 5 B. & A. 628).

If one of a number of attorneys disclaims the power, he ceases to be able to exercise it, but that does not prejudice the authority of the remaining attorneys, unless the power of attorney provides to the contrary (Law of Property Act 1925 s.156). A provision that the power is to be exercised by all the attorneys jointly would preclude the remaining attorneys acting after one had disclaimed; presumably a power of attorney conferring joint authority, but not making any further express provision, would have the same effect.

(b) Statutory forms of power of attorney

Ordinary power of attorney

4–04   The statutory form of general power can be used to appoint more than one attorney in which case it allows, and indeed requires, the donor to choose whether the appointment is joint or joint and several (1971 Act Sch.1).

Trustee power of attorney

The statutory general trustee power of attorney assumes that only one trustee is appointed (1925 Act s.25(6)). It will not normally be convenient to appoint more than one attorney, although the trustee donor may wish to appoint a second attorney to act as an alternative. There seems to be no impediment in the way of this for a power granted under s.25 of the 1925 Act if the statutory form is not used.

Lasting power of attorney

Attorneys may be appointed under a lasting power of attorney to act jointly or jointly and severally. They may also be appointed jointly in respect of some matters and jointly and severally in respect of others. Where nothing is said, the appointment is assumed to be joint (2005 Act s.10(4), (5)). The effect of one out of several attorneys failing to qualify to act, not executing the power or not complying with registration requirements varies depending on the nature of the appointment. If the attorneys are to act jointly, no lasting power of attorney can be created. If the appointment is joint and several, it does not take effect in the case of the defaulting attorney, but the power of attorney is created to appoint the others (2005 Act s.10(6), (7)).

Enduring power of attorney

A power of attorney granted to more than one person must appoint them to act either jointly or jointly and severally. If it does not, it cannot be an enduring power (2005 Act Sch.4, para.20(1)). Until the donor loses mental capacity, it can take effect as an ordinary power of attorney.

3. Substitutes

It is not normally possible for an attorney to appoint a substitute **4–05** to act in his stead. Exceptionally, an ordinary power may give the attorney express authority to do so or may appoint a different attorney to take over in certain circumstances. A power of attorney coupled with an interest may enure to the benefit of successors in title.

The statutory provisions governing lasting powers of attorney make limited provision. The power itself may appoint someone to replace the attorney, or any of them, on the happening of certain events which terminate an attorney's appointment and might otherwise revoke the power (2005 Act s.10(8)(b)). The prescribed forms of lasting power of attorney allow the donor to impose restrictions on the substitution, and point out that without a restriction the nominated substitute will automatically replace the first attorney to go (Forms LPA PA and LPA PW, para.5: 2007 Regs Sch.1). So, if the two attorneys which a power appoints are a member of donor's family and a professional adviser, and it nominates a second professional adviser as substitute, the donor can ensure that the substitute does not replace the family member. If a substitution is made, the Public Guardian must attach a note to that effect to the instrument and give the other attorneys notice (2005 Act Sch.1, paras 23, 25).

A substitute attorney has the same authority as the original attorney, unless the power of attorney provides otherwise.

4. Minors

A minor can be appointed an attorney and can bind the donor of **4–06** an ordinary power (*Re D'Angibau* (1880) 15 Ch. 228 at 246), but only in relation to property other than land (*Hearle v Greenbank* (1749) 3 Atk. 695). It is not clear whether an attorney who is a minor can merely be appointed to carry out ministerial powers, or to what extent discretion can be delegated to him.

Although a minor cannot own a legal estate in land (Law of Property Act 1925 s.1(6)), there seems no reason why someone under age should not be appointed attorney to deal with land. This could be done before 1926, provided the minor had no interest in the property (*King v Bellord* (1863) 1 H. & M. 343 at 347), but there seems to have been no decision since.

An attorney appointed by a lasting power of attorney must have reached the age of 18 (2005 Act s.10(1)(a)).

An attorney appointed by an enduring power of attorney only has to be 18 when he executes the power, which he must do before it can be registered (2005 Act Sch.4, para.2(5)(a)). The attorney could therefore be under that age when appointed. While still a minor and before the donor loses capacity, he could exercise authority under the power while it can still be treated as an ordinary power of attorney.

There is no express requirement that an attorney appointed by a trustee under the Trustee Act should be of full age. However, as a minor cannot be appointed as a trustee (Law of Property Act 1925 s.20), it must be doubtful whether a power of attorney can validly delegate a trustee's discretionary powers to a minor. Such a grant would be repugnant to the statutory restriction on under age trustees.

An attorney appointed to take a grant of letters of administration must be of full age.

5. Bankrupts

4–07 It has been said that the bankruptcy of an attorney under an ordinary power of attorney automatically revokes the power (*Hudson v Granger* (1821) 5 B. & Ald. 27). But that is not universally the case, even where the attorney receives money on the donor's behalf (*McCall v The Australian Meat Co. Ltd.* (1870) 19 W.R. 188). It now seems that a power is revoked only if the nature of the attorney's duties is such that his bankruptcy renders him unfit to carry them out.

A bankrupt may not be appointed an attorney under a lasting power of attorney in relation to the donor's property and affairs. A bankrupt can be appointed in relation to his personal welfare. If an attorney becomes bankrupt later, his appointment is terminated and the power revoked (or, in both cases, suspended if he is bankrupt merely because he is subject to an interim bankruptcy restriction order) so far as the appointment relates to the donor's property and affairs. The bankruptcy has no effect on the attorney's authority in relation to the donor's personal welfare. There are two other cases in which the power of attorney is not revoked: first, where the attorney is replaced under the terms of the instrument; secondly, if the power appointed more than one attorney to act jointly and severally, and after the bankruptcy there remains at least one attorney (2005 Act ss.10(2), 13(5)–(9)).

In the case of an enduring power of attorney, see Ch.15, p.113.

6. Corporations

(a) Generally

A corporation can act as attorney if it is authorised to do so by **4–08** its memorandum of association or other constitution document. In appointing a large corporation, it is common to provide for the attorney to nominate one of its officers to carry out the functions. Or, the power can actually appoint "such of the officers of . . . Ltd/ Plc as the company shall appoint" (*cf.* the power cited in *Barclays Bank Ltd. v Bird* [1954] Ch. 274).

A corporation cannot act as an attorney under a lasting power of attorney in relation to the donor's personal welfare, and only a trust corporation may be appointed attorney in respect of the donor's property and affairs. A trust corporation is similarly the only type of corporation which may execute an enduring power as attorney, and therefore continue to act after the donor losses mental capacity (2005 Act s.10(1)(b), Sch.4, para.2(5)(b)).

(b) Trust corporations

A trust corporation is designated by statute or statutory instru- **4–09** ment. Disregarding those designated for limited purposes only, they include (Law of Property (Amendment) Act 1926 s.3(1); Supreme Court Act 1981 s.128:

(1) the Official Solicitor, the Treasury Solicitor, the solicitor to the Duchy of Lancaster;

(2) a corporation complying with the following conditions:

    (i) it is incorporated under the law of the whole or any part of a member state of the European Union;

    (ii) its constitution empowers it to undertake trust business in England and Wales;

    (iii) it has at least one place of business in the United Kingdom;

    (iv) its constitution comes into one of three categories. First, it is incorporated by special Act of Parliament or Royal Charter. Or, secondly, it is a company, either limited or unlimited, registered in a European Union member state with an issued capital of not less than £250,000 of which at least £100,000 has been paid up in cash. Or, thirdly, it is an unlimited company registered in a European Union member state, and one of its constituent members is a company within one of the first two categories.

7. Partners

(a) Individual appointment

4-10   The appointment of a partner in a firm as attorney is personal to him and confers no authority on any other partner. If the appointment is not in connection with the business of the firm, the other partners are not liable for any breach of duty or misconduct on the attorney's part.

But if the power of attorney is granted in respect of something within the scope of the firm's business—e.g. appointing a partner in a firm of solicitors to executer a transfer and complete a sale of land, when the firm was representing the donor professionally—the whole firm is responsible for the attorney's acts. Indeed, if the circumstances make it clear that the power is granted in connection with the firm's business, all the partners are liable for any money received under it, whether or not in the ordinary course of business (*St Aubyn v Smart* (1868) L.R. 3 Ch. App. 646 at 649 *per* Page Wood L.J.).

(b) Appointment of firm

4-11   There is doubt whether a power of attorney can appoint an unincorporated firm, by its firm name, as attorney, so that the partners for the time being are the donor's attorneys. In the case of a lasting or enduring power, it is necessary for the attorneys to execute the instrument creating it, so it is probably impractical on that ground.

In the case of an ordinary power, however, the appointment should be perfectly valid if the reference to the firms' name identifies the individual partners with certainty. By analogy, the appointment of a firm of solicitors as executors of a will was construed as referring to the partners in the named firm at the date of the testator's death (*Re Horgan decd* [1971] P. 50). As an ordinary power of attorney normally takes effect immediately, if the appointment is construed as referring to the partners at that date, there will normally be no complication arising from changes of partners. But the question would arise, as a matter of construction, whether the partners were attorneys only so long as they remained partners in firm and whether new partners were to be treated as substitute attorneys.

If the donor intends that the attorneys are to be the partners in the firm for the time being, and that the appointment is to continue in relation to the then current partners despite changes in the firm's constitution, it is recommended that the deed should refer to the partners in the firm (although not by name) rather than to the firm itself. This type of appointment is subject to considerable drawbacks. An attorney might at any time be called upon to prove that he is a member of the firm in question. Further, the firm may be dissolved, or it may split so that it is not clear which new entity, if any, is the successor to the original partnership.

A power of attorney of this type should appoint the partners to act jointly and severally, rather than jointly. Even if the firm is originally small, it may grow to a point where the involvement of all the partners in joint decisions under the power of attorney is impracticable.

A precedent of a clause to appoint as attorneys the partners for the time being in a named firm is included in App.4, but its use is subject to the reservations expressed here.

8. Successors in title

A power of attorney coupled with an interest, given to secure a **4–12** proprietary interest, may be granted to the person entitled to that interest and those deriving title to it under him. Those successors in title automatically become attorneys under the power, by virtue of their title to the property in question (1971 Act s.4(2)).

A case in which a grant in this form is useful is where the purchaser of land for resale takes a power to execute conveyances in favour of ultimate purchasers.

Chapter 5

Contents of Power

1. Recitals

A power of attorney may recite the circumstances in which it **5–01** comes to be executed. This is not usual, and it is rarely advisable. The interpretation of the main provisions of the power can be affected by the recitals, which can reduce the scope of the attorney's authority (*Danby v Coutts & Co.* (1885) 29 Ch. 500). This may mean that those dealing with the attorney have to make more extensive enquiries than usual to assure themselves of the validity of what he proposes to do.

2. Attorney's powers

The extent of the authority of the attorney should be set out in **5–02** the power, unless either statutory short form of power of attorney is adopted. The extent and definition of the powers is discussed in Ch.2, p.11.

3. Substitution

(a) Ordinary power of attorney

A donor granting an ordinary power of attorney who wants to **5–03** empower his attorney to appoint a substitute to act instead of him must include provision to that effect in the instrument.

The statutory form of general power does not refer to appointing a substitute. The authority it confers on the attorney is "to do on behalf of the donor anything which he can lawfully do by an attorney" (1971 Act s.10(1)). The act of appointing a substitute is an act which the attorney does by authority of the donor, but not on his behalf. For that reason, it is considered that the general power does not of itself authorise the attorney to appoint a substitute.

The donor can limit the choice of a substitute, e.g. to another member of the firm in which the attorney is a partner or to a person qualified as a chartered surveyor. But this does involve the difficulty that a third party dealing with the substitute attorney could demand proof that he qualified for appointment. A compromise is for the power of attorney to provide that a third party may assume that a substitute is qualified. This prevents the donor from repudiating any of the substitute's acts on the ground that he should not have been appointed, but the donor would have a right of recourse against the original attorney if he suffered loss as a result of an improper appointment.

A form of clause for this purpose is included in Appendix 4, para.A4–04.

(b) Power of attorney coupled with an interest

5–04 A power coupled with an interest and securing a proprietary interest can be granted to the person entitled to that interest and his successors in title. Those successors become the attorneys, by a form of substitution. However, if the power also includes a clause entitling the attorney to appoint a substitute, that remains effective (1971 Act s.4(2)).

(c) Lasting power of attorney

5–05 A lasting power of attorney cannot empower the attorney to appoint a substitute. But it may name a person to replace the attorney if his appointment is automatically terminated by one of certain specified events: death, loss of capacity, divorce from or the dissolution of civil partnership to the donor or, in the case of a power granted in relation to the donor's property and affairs, bankruptcy or the winding-up of a trust corporation (2005 Act s.10(8)).

4. Duration

5–06 The power of attorney can define the period for which the attorney's authority is to last. This is discussed further in relation to the different types of power: ordinary and lasting powers, Ch.7, p.53; trustee powers, Ch.13, p.93; enduring powers, Ch.15, p.113.

5. Remuneration of attorney

(a) Ordinary powers of attorney

5–07 It is doubted whether the rule that a trustee may not profit from his trust unless expressly authorised to do so is applicable to attorneys. Certainly, a power of attorney can provide for remuneration for the attorney (*Frith v Frith* [1906] A.C. 254). Although there does not seem to be authority on the question whether an attorney can claim payment *quantum meruit* in the absence of express terms about remuneration, it is suggested that he could. If the attorney acts under a contract that he will provide that service, he will have a claim for a reasonable charge under the Supply of Goods and Services Act 1982 s.15.

That would certainly accord with practice. Many powers are granted to professional advisers, without express terms about payment. The understanding, which is fulfilled, is that the attorney will be paid for what he does.

The view that no charging clause is required in an ordinary power is supported by an opinion of the Council of the Law Society given in 1958. This states that a solicitor who is appointed an attorney under a power without any express provision about his remuneration is entitled to charge both for his professional work, including the preparation of the power of attorney, and for non-professional work undertaken as attorney (1 *Law Society Digest*, 4th cum. supp.96). A form of clause expressly entitling the attorney to charge is included in Appendix 4, para.A4–02.

(b) Lasting powers of attorney

The prescribed forms of lasting power of attorney require the **5–08** donor to state whether or not he has agreed that his attorney(s) may charge. There is a box for recording "additional information about fees that I have agreed with my attorney(s)", which would be an appropriate place to insert a professional charging clause (form LPA PA, para.8; form LPA PW, para.9).

(c) Enduring powers of attorney

See Ch.15, p.113.

6. Ratification

(a) General

A power of attorney often contains an undertaking by the donor **5–09** to ratify what the attorney does or purports to do under the power. The scope of this provision is in some doubt. A clause undertaking to ratify "whatsoever" the attorney did or purported to do was held not to extend the scope of the authority granted by the power (*Midland Bank Ltd. v Reckitt* [1933] A.C. 1: the attorney had improperly paid into his own bank account cheques drawn on the donor's account).

It is suggested that the true meaning of the clause is to prevent the donor from denying the attorney's authority to do anything which the power appears to permit, even though, because of some irregularity, the attorney was not effectively invested with the necessary powers. In other words, the clause merely reinforces the power, but does not extend it.

It may not even be able to go that far. True ratification is always retrospective. If therefore the donor was not legally capable of performing the act at the date of its performance, so that he could not have delegated the power to perform it, there can be no ratification (*Boston Deep Sea Fishing and Ice Co. Ltd. v Farnham* [1957] 1 W.L.R. 1051). The attorney must also have done the act ratified on behalf of the donor, and not on his own account.

"The first essential to the doctrine of ratification . . . is that the agent shall not be acting for himself, but shall be intending to bind a named or ascertainable principal" (*Imperial Bank of Canada v Begley* [1936] 2 All E.R. 367 at 374 *per* Lord Maugham).

Usually only the principal for whom an act was purported to be done can ratify it. But a receiver for debenture holders has been held capable of ratifying a transaction carried out by an earlier receiver, as no third party rights had intervened (*Lawson v Hosemaster Co. Ltd.* [1966] 1 W.L.R. 1300).

There may be ratification even though the donor has not undertaken to ratify. It can extend to validating acts that were in fact beyond the attorney's authority. Ratification may be deduced from the donor's conduct.

(b) Lasting or enduring power of attorney

5–10   A donor who has lost capacity cannot effectively ratify acts by the attorney. An express covenant to ratify is therefore of limited use in a lasting or an enduring power of attorney.

The Court of Protection has relieving powers which can be used as a substitute for ratification. It has jurisdiction to relieve the attorney in whole or part from liability on account of a breach of duty as attorney. This jurisdiction only applies after the donor has lost capacity, but can apply to past breaches which would include those committed while the donor still had capacity (2005 Act s.23(3)(d), Sch.4, para.16(2)(f)).

7. Proper law

5–11   A power of attorney may expressly declare which is to be the proper law of the power. This will be effective, at least in English law, to designate the law governing the relations between the donor and the attorney. Whether the power is acceptable in the country in which it is to be used must depend on the law of that country.

Chapter 6

Form of Power

1. Deed

(a) Newly granted powers

A power of attorney must now be granted by deed (1971 Act **6–01**
s.1). This general rule, which was new in 1971, is unqualified. But it
does not extend to other documents in the nature of powers of
attorney that are expressly authorised, for instance, delegation of
powers by charitable trustees, appointment of an agent to sign a
contract on behalf of a company, or a proxy granted by a
shareholder in a company.

The need for a power of attorney to be granted by deed may
influence the form of an instrument to which a power is incidental.
So, a deed must be used to grant a short tenancy of licensed
premises if the instrument incorporates a power of attorney for
dealing with the premises licence, although it would not otherwise
be needed.

(b) Older powers

Before 1971, a power of attorney had to be a deed under seal if **6–02**
it authorised the attorney to execute a deed on the donor's behalf
or if it was giving more general authority which would necessarily
involve that (*Berkeley v Hardy* (1826) 5 B. & C. 355). Similarly, a
power to deliver a deed already signed and sealed had to be under
seal (*Windsor Refrigerator Co. Ltd. v Branch Nominees Ltd.* [1961]
Ch. 88; rvsd on other grounds). However, a verbal authority
sufficed to allow an attorney to execute a deed in the donor's
presence (*R. v Longnor (Inhabitants)* (1833) 4 B. & Ad. 647).

In one case, a guarantee was effectively executed by an attorney,
even though the power had not been sealed. The power stated that
it had been "signed, sealed and delivered" in the presence of the

witness, and the seal (which was then required) had apparently been omitted by an oversight. A bank advanced money on security of a debenture, supported by the guarantee. It was held that the guarantee was effective, because there had been an estoppel: the bank had relied on the statement about execution, and had changed its position to its detriment by advancing the money (*TCB Ltd v Gray* [1986] Ch. 621; issue not decided on appeal).

2. Lasting powers of attorney

(a) Prescribed forms

6–03   A lasting power of attorney must be in one of the prescribed forms (either form LPA PA in relation to the donor's property and affairs, or form LPA PW in relation to the donor's personal welfare: 2007 Regs reg.5, Sch,1). This requirement is satisfied by the use of a Welsh language version of the relevant form (2007 Regs reg.3(1)). If the power differs in an immaterial respect from the prescribed form, the Public Guardian may treat it as sufficient and the Court of Protection has power to declare that an instrument not in the prescribed form is to be treated as if it were, if satisfied that those executing it intended to create a lasting power of attorney (2005 Act Sch.1, paras 1(1)(a), 3). Otherwise, an instrument which is not in the prescribed form does not confer any authority (2005 Act s.9(3)). Accordingly, it cannot be treated as an ordinary power, even before the donor loses capacity.

The power must include the following, which are provided for by the prescribed forms (2005 Act Sch.1, para.2):

(a) the prescribed information, which differs in the two prescribed forms;

(b) statements by the donor that—

    (i) he has read the prescribed information, or a prescribed part of it, or has had it read to him;

    (ii) he intends the authority conferred by the power to include taking decisions on his behalf when he no longer has capacity;

    (iii) naming one or more persons (maximum, five: 2007 Regs reg.6) whom he wishes to be notified of any application to register the power ("named person'), or a statement that there is none;

(c) statements by the attorney that—

    (i) he has read the prescribed information, or a prescribed part of it, or has had it read to him;

    (ii) he understands an attorney's statutory duties concerning the principles governing lasting powers of attorney and acting in the donor's best interests;

(d) a certificate ("LPA certificate")—
not to nominate any named person (≥ donor opts
independent verification the validity ʰe ᵉg.7(a))—as
below). ᵒwer (see

(b) LPA certificates: contents

An LPA certificate must state that in the opinion of the persc **6–04**
giving it when the donor executes the instrument—

(i) he understands the purpose of the power of attorney and
the scope of the authority it grants,

(ii) no fraud or undue pressure is being used to induce the
donor to create a lasting power of attorney, and

(iii) there is nothing to prevent a lasting power being created.

The prescribed form of certificate, which is Part B of each of the
prescribed forms of lasting power of attorney, identifies the person
giving the certificate and requires him to show that he is eligible to
give the certificate. He must declare that he has read the parts of
the power completed by the donor and by him and the prescribed
information. He must also state that he has discussed the contents
with the donor in the absence of the attorney, and say who was
then present, although preferably there should be nobody. Finally,
he must confirm that he completes the certificate immediately after
discussing the power with the donor.

(c) LPA certificates: who may give

There are two classes of people from whom the donor of a **6–05**
lasting power of attorney may choose the person who gives an LPA
certificate, but in every case that person must fall outside the list of
people who are disqualified. The eligible classes are: first, someone
who has known the donor personally for at least two years before
the certificate is signed; secondly, a person whom the donor
reasonably considers has the professional skills and expertise to
give the certificate (2007 Regs reg.8(1)). Only examples are given
of the second category, they fall into two groups: medical/social
and legal.

In the medical/social group are: a registered health care professional (i.e. a member of a regulated profession: National Health
Service Reform and Health Care Professions Act 2002 s.25(3)), a
social worker (registered by the General Social Care Council, the
Care Council for Wales, the Scottish Social Services Council or the

ocial Care Council), and an independent mental
Northern ~ (2005 Act s.35). The legal group comprises a
capacity icitor or an advocate called or admitted in any part
barriste d Kingdom (2007 Regs reg.8(2), (4)).
of the owing are disqualified from giving a certificate (2007
Tg.8(3)):
Re

(i) a member for the donor's family, and his business partner or
employee,

(ii) the attorney, a member of his family, his business partner or
employee, a director or employee of an attorney trust
corporation and an attorney appointed by the donor under
any other lasting power of attorney or an enduring power of
attorney (whether or not since revoked),

(iii) the owner, director, manager or employee of a care home
(defined: Care Standards Act 2000 s.3) where the donor
lives when the power is executed, or a member of their
family.

3. Execution

(a) Witnesses

6–06   For the valid execution of a deed by an individual at least one
witness is essential. The donor must sign the deed (or make his
mark on it) in the presence of a witness who attests the signature,
or it can be signed on his behalf in his presence and that of two
witnesses who attest the signature (Law of Property (Miscellaneous
Provisions) Act 1989 s.1(3), (4)). There is no requirement as to the
competence or the independence of the witnesses.

(b) Lasting power of attorney

6–07   A detailed procedure is laid down for executing lasting powers of
attorney. There are five successive steps, each to be taken as soon
as reasonably practical after the preceding one (2007 Regs
reg.9(1)—(7), (10)).

Step 1 The donor must read the prescribed information, or have
it read to him.

Step 2 The donor must complete part A of the prescribed form,
or direct that it be done. He must sign, or make his mark,
in the presence of a witness. If it is signed at his direction,
there must be two witnesses.

Step 3 The person giving the LPA certificate (or each of them, if two certificates are required) must complete part B and sign it.

Step 4 Each attorney must read the prescribed information, or have it read to him.

Step 5 Each attorney must complete part C, or direct that it be done. He must sign, or make his mark, in the presence of a witness. If it is signed at his direction, there must be two witnesses.

In each case, a witness must sign, or make his mark, and give his full name and address. The donor may not act as a witness of anyone else's signature. An attorney may witness another attorney's signature, but nobody else's (2007 Regs reg.9(8), (9)).

(c) Companies

A company need no longer have a common seal, and may **6–08** execute a power of attorney in accordance with the rules governing all deeds. The document must be signed by a director and the secretary or by two directors and be expressed to be executed by the company (Companies Act 1985, s.36A(4); Companies Act 1989 s.130(2)). Companies may still nevertheless use seals.

A power of attorney executed by a company under seal must be witnessed as the articles of association of the company require. Table A prescribed under the Companies Act 1985 requires that an instrument which is sealed be signed by a director and the secretary of the company or by two directors. The directors may vary this (Companies (Tables A to F) Regulations 1985 art.101). Under the Companies Act 1948, the second signatory could be some other person appointed by the directors for the purpose (Table A, art.113).

It is often convenient to take advantage of the provision that, in favour of a purchaser, a deed purporting to be sealed by a company in the presence of and attested by a director and secretary, or other permanent officer or his deputy, is deemed to be duly executed and to take effect accordingly (Law of Property Act 1925 s.74(1)). A similar provision applies where a company executes without a seal (Companies Act 1985 s.36A(6); Companies Act 1989 s.130(2)).

Some foreign companies do not have a seal, because none is required by the law of the country of their incorporation. It seems that until now such a company has been incapable of executing a deed recognised by English law, and therefore it could not grant a power of attorney. In practice, however, a declaration or affidavit confirming the validity under the law of the company's incorpora-

tion of the procedure adapted may be accepted. There is power for
the Secretary of State to make regulations applying to companies
incorporated outside Great Britain the rules for execution without
a seal (Companies Act 1989 s.130(6)), but none has yet been made.

(d) Attorney

6–09   An attorney appointed by a lasting power of attorney is required
to execute the power (para.6–07).

In the case of an enduring power of attorney, the attorney (or all
attorneys who are appointed to act jointly) must execute it if it is to
survive the donor's incapacity (2005 Act Sch.4, para.2(1)(b)), but, if
appropriately worded, it can take effect as an ordinary power of
attorney without that execution. Where attorneys are appointed to
act jointly and severally and one who does not sign, he has no
authority one the donor ceases to have capacity, but that does not
prejudice the position of the other attorneys.

There will be some cases, particularly on the grant of a power
coupled with an interest, where the power is part, and often a
subsidiary part, of a contract. In such a case, it is often essential,
because of the other contents of the document, that both parties
execute it. The fact that even on the grant of a simple power of
attorney there may be reciprocal obligations does not mean that
the attorney must execute it. The authority is offered to the
attorney on conditions, for example, that he exercises it in a certain
way, and in return he has the benefit of the donor's covenant to
ratify his acts. These conditions are activated upon the attorney
exercising the powers granted to him.

(e) Physically incapable donor

6–10   Where the donor is incapable of signing, but is nevertheless
mentally capable of granting a power of attorney, it is suggested
that the following form would be appropriate. The signatory should
not be the attorney,

[Signature]

SIGNED as a deed by [signatory] at the direction and on behalf
of [donor] in his/her presence and in the presence of both of the
following witnesses.

If appropriate, a statement could confirm that the signatory had
read the power of attorney, and/or explained its significance, to the
donor before signing.

4. Stamp duty

(a) Duty abolished

Granting a power of attorney does not, of itself, attract stamp **6–11** duty land tax. No stamp duty was payable on powers of attorney executed on or after 19 March 1985, and not stamped before March 26.

(b) Duty formerly charged

Stamp duty was previously charged on powers of attorney under **6–12** the head, "Letter or Power of Attorney, and commission, factory, mandate or other instrument in the nature thereof". Immediately before abolition, the general rate of duty was 50p. (Stamp Act 1891 Sch.1). This head covered more than mere powers of attorney. Any written delegation by one person to another to act in the first's name was covered (*Walker v Remmett* (1846) 2 C.B. 850). However, a donor who gave his attorney further instructions did not attract any further duty (*Parker v Dubois* (1836) 1 M. & W. 30).

The fact that a power was granted by more than one donor, or to more than one attorney, did not of itself attract more than one charge to duty. That was so, even though the powers conferred by the document related to more than one matter (Finance Act 1927 s.56).

Certain specified types of power of attorney were exempt from stamp duty and others were charged at a reduced rate.

Chapter 7

Duration of Power

1. Period of authority

The period for which authority is granted by a power of attorney **7–01**
is of importance to all concerned. For the donor, it defines for how
long he has granted the attorney the ability to deal with his
property or affairs; it informs the attorney when he will cease to
have the right to bind the donor, after which he would lay himself
open to claims for breach of warranty of authority; it limits the
time during which a third party may safely deal with the attorney as
representing the donor. In some circumstances, a third party may
be protected when dealing with the attorney even though the
power is no longer valid (see Ch.12, p.85).

A power may come to an end by effluxion of time, by operation
of law, by the donor revoking it, or by the attorney releasing or
disclaiming it. Some powers are irrevocable, or may only be
revoked by the donor with the attorney's consent. They may in fact
come to an end, but they could theoretically be permanent.

Statutory provision relating to enduring powers of attorney are
dealt with in Ch.15 at p.113.

2. Terms of the power of attorney

(a) Specified period

A power of attorney may be expressed to be granted for a stated **7–02**
period. When that period comes to an end, the power expires
without further formality. A prime example of this type of power is
one granted by an individual trustee under the Trustee Act which
cannot be for longer than twelve months (1925 Act s.25(2)).

In interpreting a power of attorney, "month" means calendar
month (Law of Property Act 1925 s.61), and references to a time of
day refer to Greenwich mean time or summer time as the case may
be (Interpretation Act 1978 ss.9, 23(3)).

(b) Purpose specified

7–03   If a power of attorney is granted to authorise a single act, or in connection with one specified venture, it necessarily comes to an end when that purpose is achieved. This applies to a power granted to allow an attorney to execute a transfer to complete a specified sale of land. Once the transfer is executed, the power is spent. Similarly, a power of attorney delegating a partner's powers under a partnership agreement comes to an end if the partnership is dissolved.

(c) Until incapacity

7–04   A person making provision for incapacity in the future may well wish to retain decision making powers in his own hands until he lacks capacity. A lasting power of attorney relating to the donor's personal welfare only gives the attorney authority to act and make decisions when the donor lacks capacity, or the attorney reasonably believes that he lacks it (2005 Act s.11(7)(a)).

However, as a general rule a lasting power of attorney relating to the donor's property and affairs comes into force as soon as it is registered, even though the donor still has full capacity. This contrasts with the position of an enduring power of attorney which can only be registered when the donor is losing or has lost capacity, so that it is not difficult to suspend its operation until then. Nevertheless, the effectiveness of a lasting power of attorney can, in principle, be suspended while the donor retains capacity. The prescribed information on the form of power suggests this possibility (para.4).

The donor must insert an appropriate restriction on the donor's powers. This could straightforwardly say that no powers were to be exercised while the donor retained capacity, but that could make it very difficult for the attorney, and indeed third parties, to know at what precise moment the power of attorney became effective. It is probably more satisfactory to restrict the attorney to cases where he reasonably believes that the donor lacks capacity.

In such a case, judging whether the power of attorney can or should be used requires the application of the fundamental statutory principles for judging want of capacity. In particular, a person is assumed to have capacity unless it is established that he lacks it, and he is not to be treated as unable to make a decision unless all practicable steps have been taken to help him to do so, but unsuccessfully (2005 Act s.1(2), (3)). The code of practice emphasises that an assessment of capacity must relate to the specific decision to be made, and a lack of capacity must be shown on the balance of probabilities (paras 4.4, 4.10).

(d) Future period

A power of attorney need not be granted to take effect **7–05** immediately. It may come into force on a future date specified in the document. Or, it may be triggered by a future event, for example when the donor leaves the country. In the case of an enduring power, it could commence on the donor becoming incapable. The only requirement is that the time the power become effective can be identified with certainty.

3. Termination by operation of law

(a) Want of capacity

If the donor ceases to have the capacity to do the acts for which **7–06** a power of attorney delegates authority, that power comes to an end by operation of law. This is the common law rule, to which there are major statutory exception in that both lasting powers of attorney and enduring power of attorney remain in force even though the donor loses mental capacity (2005 Act s.9(1), Sch.4, para.1(1)(a)).

If the attorney appointed by a lasting power of attorney loses capacity the power is revoked unless there is another attorney appointed to act jointly and severally or the attorney is replaced under the terms of the power (2005 Act s.13(5)(b), (6)(d), (7)). There are other exceptions in the case of irrevocable powers coupled with an interest. Subject to those exceptions, such disabilities as the death, dissolution or mental incapacity of the donor terminate the attorney's authority. The disability does this automatically, and it makes no difference that the attorney is unaware of what has happened (*Yonge v Toynbee* [1910] 1 K.B. 215). However, the attorney incurs no liability if he acts under the power in ignorance of its revocation (1971 Act s.5(1)).

(b) Destruction of subject matter

Some earlier editions of this book suggested that the destruction **7–07** of the subject matter of a power of attorney brought the power to an end. Although it would clearly render the power ineffective, there seems no ground to suppose that it would actually be terminated. This distinction might be important if after the destruction there was a reconstruction or the donor acquired something else to which the power could be construed to refer.

4. Revocation: lasting powers of attorney

While the donor of a lasting power of attorney retains capacity, **7–08** he may at any time revoke it (2005 Act s.13(2)). He must notify the Public Guardian and the attorney, or all of them if more than one.

The Public Guardian, on being satisfied that the power has been revoked, cancels the registration and notifies the donor and the attorney(s) (2007 Regs reg.21).

In addition, certain events revoke a lasting power of attorney. However, they are all subject to two exceptions. First, the power remains in force if the attorney in question is replaced under a provision in the power. Secondly, if more than one attorney was appointed to act jointly and severally—but not merely jointly—and at least one remaining attorney is not affected by the event in question, the power will continue to give him (or them) authority (2005 Act s.13(5)(b), (7)).

(a) Death of donor

7–09   The death of the donor revokes a lasting power of attorney. When the Public Guardian is satisfied that this has happened, he must cancel the registration of the power and notify the attorney, or all the attorneys if more than one (2007 Regs reg.22).

(b) Divorce or dissolution

7–10   If the donor and the attorney under a lasting power of attorney were married or in a civil partnership, the power is revoked by divorce, annulment or dissolution of the marriage or partnership. This does not apply if the power provides that this should not happen (2005 Act s.13(6)(c), (11)).

(c) Bankruptcy

7–11   The bankruptcy of the donor of a lasting power of attorney relating to his property and affairs, revokes the power (2005 Act s.13(3)). That form of power of attorney is revoked by the bankruptcy of the sole attorney, one of attorneys appointed to act jointly or the survivor of attorneys appointed to act jointly and severally (2005 Act s.13(6)(b)). In either case, the bankruptcy of the donor or that of the attorney, if it is merely because an interim bankruptcy restrictions order applies, the effect is only to suspend the power of attorney (2005 Act s.13(4), (9)).

Bankruptcy has no effect on a lasting power of attorney relating to the donor's personal welfare (2005 Act s.13(8)).

In the case of the revocation which is limited to the donor's property and affairs, but not in relation to other matters, or of a suspension of a power, the Public Guardian must attach a note to that effect to the instrument and give notice to the attorney (2005 Act Sch.1, paras 21, 25).

(d) Attorney's capacity

If the attorney under a lasting power of attorney ceases to have **7–12** capacity or dies, the power is revoked (2005 Act s.13(6)(b), (d)). The same applies if the attorney is a trust corporation and it is wound up or dissolved.

As in the case of a donor, the attorney's lack of capacity means that at the material time he is unable to make a decision for himself, as a result of his mind or brain being impaired, or its functioning being disturbed. Crucially, it does not matter whether the impairment or disturbance is permanent or temporary (2005 Act s.2(1), (2)). Accordingly, even if an attorney only temporarily lacks capacity, the power of attorney is revoked and is not revived by the attorney recovering capacity.

(e) Disclaimer

An attorney who disclaims his appointment (para.7–24) brings it **7–13** to an end and revokes the power of attorney (2005 Act s.13(6)(a)).

(f) Consequences of revocation

When a lasting power of attorney has been revoked in any of the **7–14** circumstances outlined in paras 7–10—7–14 above, the Public Guardian must cancel the registration of the instrument and notify both the donor and all the attorneys. The original power and any office copies of it must be delivered up to the Public Guardian to be cancelled (2005 Act Sch.1, paras 17, 20).

5. Revocation: other powers of attorney

(a) Consent of attorney

Normally the revocation of a power of attorney is a unilateral act **7–15** by the donor. Just as he does not need the attorney's consent to grant the power, he does not need that consent to end it. However, the attorney's consent may be made a condition precedent to the revocation of a power coupled with an interest in circumstances in which it can be irrevocable. A power given as security, stated to be irrevocable and protected by statute, can only be revoked with the attorney's consent.

The donor may contract that he will not revoke the power for a particular period. That would be unusual. It may be that in other cases where the power of attorney is part of a commercial relationship, and "especially those involving mutual trust and confidence", the donor is only entitled to revoke it where it is reasonable to do so (*Martin-Baker Aircraft Co. Ltd. v Canadian Flight Equipment Ltd.* [1955] 2 Q.B. 556). Nevertheless, a donor can revoke a power in defiance of such restraints. That may render him liable to damages, but the power is effectively revoked.

(b) Express revocation

7–16   An express revocation of a power of attorney should be by deed. A precedent is set out in Appendix 3, para.A3–10. After an enduring power of attorney has been registered, there are formalities to be completed before any revocation can be valid.

If the donor considers that there is a danger that the attorney will continue to act under the power of attorney notwithstanding its revocation, thereby continuing to bind him opposite third parties, he should take all the steps he can to ensure that the revocation comes to the attention of third parties. There is no prescribed general way to notify them.

Where the danger concerns a limited number of third parties—e.g. the donor's bank—the surest course is to notify each of them individually. Some earlier editions of this book recommended endorsing a memorandum of the notification on the power of attorney. This presupposes that it is in the hands of the donor, which is unlikely. However, now that the contents of a power can be proved by the production of a photocopy, an endorsement would be no guarantee against misuse: a copy made earlier, before the memorandum was on it, could be used.

(c) Implied revocation

7–17   If the donor of a power of attorney does an act which is incompatible with the continued operation of the power, it is revoked. An example of implied revocation is provided by a shareholder who appoints a proxy for attending a particular meeting. He revokes the instrument of proxy by attending in person and voting (*Cousins v International Brick Co. Ltd.* [1931] 2 Ch. 90). Suitably drawn articles of association for the company concerned could reverse that effect.

There are few cases in which such an act by the grantor will be unequivocal. The authority that a power of attorney grants is normally concurrent with that of the donor. The fact that the donor himself does something that the attorney could have done under the power does not, therefore, prejudice the power. A power of attorney allowing the attorney to draw cheques on the donor's bank account may, for example, result in both the donor and the attorney drawing on the account.

It is unwise for a donor to rely upon an implied revocation. It should be confirmed by an express revocation without delay. An attorney who comes to hear of an act on the donor's part that might be construed as an implied revocation should immediately ask the donor for clarification of the position.

(d) Grant of subsequent power of attorney

A donor does not necessarily revoke an earlier power of attorney **7–18** by granting another one. This is an example of an act which may revoke the earlier power by implication, but it only does so if its continuation is inconsistent with the existence of the second power. The onus of proof is on the person claiming that the earlier power has been revoked, who must show that it was the donor's intention (*Re E* [2001] Ch. 364).

6. Irrevocable powers

(a) At common law

A power of attorney coupled with an interest is irrevocable at **7–19** common law while that interest subsists (*Walsh v Whitcomb* (1797) 2 Esp. 565). Lord Romilly M.R. referred to "the ordinary case of a power of attorney given for value, which, as everybody is aware, is not revocable" (*Oldham v Oldham* (1867) L.R. Eq. 404 at 407). This applies to a power given to a creditor to sell land and to retain the proceeds to repay himself (*Gaussen v Morton* (1830) 10 B. & C. 731). A power linked to a mortgage remains irrevocable until the money has been repaid (*Barclays Bank Ltd. v Bird* [1954] Ch. 274).

A distinction must be drawn between a power coupled with an interest, and a case in which the interest is only collateral to the power. The latter does not render the power irrevocable (*Chinnock v Sainsbury* (1860) 30 L.J. Ch. 409). An example of a collateral interest is a solicitor's lien for his costs over the deeds of property in respect of which his client has given him a power of attorney.

(b) Powers given as security

Section 4 of the 1971 Act gives express statutory power to make **7–20** powers of attorney given as security irrevocable. This overlaps with the common law power. The powers to which this applies are those given to secure either a proprietary interest of the attorney, or the performance of an obligation owed to the attorney. This definition seems to make the class coextensive with powers coupled with an interest. In addition, the power must be expressed to be irrevocable.

The section does not require that the power be given for valuable consideration, as did earlier provisions now repealed (Law of Property Act 1925 s.126(1)). Giving sufficient consideration has sometimes been equated with coupling an interest with a power.

> "What is meant by an authority coupled with an interest being irrevocable is this,—that where an agreement is entered into on a sufficient consideration, whereby an authority is given for the purpose of securing some benefit to the donee of the authority, such an authority is irrevocable"

(*Clarke v Laurie* (1857) 2 H. & N. 199 at 200 *per* Williams J.).

The attorney must have a proprietary interest, or some obligation must be owed to him. An example was a power of attorney which the registered shareholder gave to a company which was buying his shares, but not immediately taking a transfer of them, so also allow the purchaser to vote, etc. (*Re Kilnoore Ltd* [2000] Ch. 289). But a company which gave a power of attorney to a receiver under a debenture did not create a power given as security, because that requirement was not satisfied (*Barrows v Chief Land Registrar* [1977] C.L.Y. 315).

This is the effect of the section on a power that qualifies. So long as the attorney has the proprietary interest, or the obligation to him remains undischarged, the power cannot be revoked by the donor unilaterally. Nor do the death, incapacity or bankruptcy of the donor affect it. Similarly, a power granted by a corporation is not revoked by the donor's being wound up (*Sowman v David Samuel Trust Ltd.* [1978] 1 W.L.R. 22), or dissolved.

This provision applies to powers whenever they were created (1971 Act s.4(3)). The earlier statutory provisions are explained in connection with dealings with land, para.17–06.

(c) Other powers expressed as irrevocable

7–21   The 1971 Act tackles the problem that a third party dealing with an attorney appointed by a power purporting to be given as security and expressed to be irrevocable cannot know whether it does truly come into the category dealt with in the last section. It does so by giving the third party equivalent protection, while not making the power irrevocable.

If on the face of it a power is expressed to be given as security and to be irrevocable, a third party who does not know that it was not in fact given as security can assume that it is only revocable with the attorney's consent (1971 Act s.5(3)).

As between the donor and the attorney, such a power is not irrevocable. An attorney who continues to purport to exercise his authority once it has been revoked runs the risk of liability to the donor for any loss he causes.

The problems arising in earlier powers of attorney which were expressed to be irrevocable are dealt with in relation to dealings with land, because their importance in practice is now mostly confined to powers forming part of the title to land.

(d) Seamen's wages

A power of attorney which gives authority to receive the wages **7–22** of a seaman on a United Kingdom ship cannot be made irrevocable (Merchant Shipping Act 1995 s.34(1)(d)). This effectively prevents wages which have yet to be paid being given as security. The prohibition does not apply to the wages of a seaman engaged in a foreign port (*Rowlands v Miller* [1899] 1 Q.B. 735, construing Merchant Shipping Act 1894 s.163, now repealed, which was in similar terms).

7. Disclaimer

(a) General

The attorney may renounce or disclaim the authority which a **7–23** power of attorney grants to him. This ends the authority (Law of Property Act 1925 s.156(1)). The renunciation should be communicated to the donor, who is then entitled to rely on the attorney not exercising the authority.

A precedent for a formal deed of disclaimer is included in Appendix 3, para.A3–09.

(b) Lasting powers of attorney

An attorney appointed by a lasting power of attorney who **7–24** effectively disclaims his appointment brings it to an end and may revoke the power of attorney (2005 Act s.13(6)(a)).

In order to disclaim, the attorney must complete the prescribed form LPA 005 (2007 Regs Sch.6). It must be sent to the donor, with copies to the Public Guardian and any other attorney appointed under the power (2007 Regs reg.20).

8. Presumption of non-revocation

7–25   In certain circumstances, there is a presumption in favour of a purchaser that a third party dealing with an attorney had no knowledge of any revocation of the power. This makes the transaction with the attorney as valid as if the power were still subsisting.

Chapter 8

Exercising a Power

1. Using donor's name

It is generally advisable and convenient for an attorney to **8–01**
exercise the powers granted to him in the donor's name. If he
contracts in his name, and he can generally choose that
alternative, the third party with whom he is dealing will not be put
on notice that the attorney is contracting on the donor's behalf.
The attorney then runs the risk of incurring personal liability. But
even if he signs on behalf of the donor, the attorney can also be
personally liable if the evidence is that he also intended to sign in
his own right (*Young v Schuler* (1883) 11 Q.B.D. 651).

An attorney has express statutory power to execute instruments
with his own name. He may do any other thing in his own name.
This is as effective as if the instrument was executed or the act
done in the donor's name (1971 Act s.7(1)).

The normal form of execution of a deed by an attorney is:

AB [donor]
by his attorney
CD [attorney]
An alternative is:
CD [attorney]
as attorney for and on behalf of
AB [donor]

Where there are joint attorneys, both should sign, but no
particular wording is required, other than referring to "attorneys"
in the plural. Where more than one attorney is appointed to act
jointly or severally, one or more of them can sign, but no reference
to the position is needed on the face of the document.

2. Powers granted by corporations

8–02   An attorney acting under a power granted by a corporation may act in his own name or in the corporation's name, as is the case with powers granted by other donors (1971 Act s.7(1),(2)). There are special statutory provisions covering this case, which may be used as an alternative.

A conveyance of property in the name of the corporation (including a corporation sole) may be signed by the attorney in the name of the corporation in the presence of at least one witness (Law of Property Act 1925 s.74(3); Law of Property (Miscellaneous Provisions) Act 1989 Sch.2). In this context, "conveyance" includes a mortgage, charge, lease or any other assurance of property, which would include a Land Registry transfer (Law of Property Act 1925 s.205(1)(ii)).

Execution of a deed under this provision would be in this form:

SIGNED ON BEHALF OF   XYZ Limited [donor]
XYZ LIMITED FOR   by its attorney
DELIVERY AS A DEED in
the presence of: AB [attorney]
    CD [witness]

A similar, but not identical, provision applies to an attorney appointed by a registered company to execute deeds outside the United Kingdom (Companies Act 1985 s.38; Companies Act 1989 Sch.17, para.7).

In this case the attorney must "execute" the deed, rather than merely signing it. The following form should be used:

SIGNED AS A DEED AND
DELIVERED BY AB [attorney]
AB
ON BEHALF OF XYZ LIMITED
in the presence of:
    CD [witness]

Alternatively, a company which has a common seal may have a facsimile of it—called an official seal—for use outside the United Kingdom. The seal has on the face of it the name of every territory, district or place where it is to be used. The company may empower attorneys to affix that seal. That authority need not itself be under seal. It would be necessary expressly to authorise sealing officers if no directors were available overseas for that purpose. To verify the validity of a sealing under this provision, the person affixing the seal must certify on the deed the date and place at which the seal is affixed (Companies Act 1985 s.39; Companies Act 1989 Sch.17, para.2). The following is a form of execution which complies with these provisions:

THE OFFICIAL SEAL OF XYZ LIMITED was
hereunto affixed in the presence of AB and
CD (duly authorised in that behalf by an
instrument under the common seal of XYZ   Official
Limited dated   seal
at   on the
as the said AB and the said CD
hereby certify:
    AB
    CD

3. Corporation as attorney

Where a corporation is appointed attorney, it may execute deeds **8–03**
on the donor's behalf under its own common seal (or by the
signatures of a director and the secretary or two directors: Companies Act 1985 s.36A(4); Companies Act 1989 s.130(2)) as
attorney. This procedure will often be inconvenient, and an
alternative is provided by statute. The board of directors, council
or other governing body of the corporation may, by resolution or
otherwise, appoint someone to execute deeds and other instruments in the donor's name. An instrument to convey an interest in
property that appears to be executed by an officer so appointed is
deemed, in favour of a purchaser, to have been executed by an
officer who was duly authorised (Law of Property Act 1925
s.74(4)). "Purchaser" here means a purchaser in good faith for
valuable consideration and it includes a lessee and a mortgagee
(s.205(1)(xxi)). It is therefore useful for the document to show the
officer's authority on the face of it. The testimonium could read:

IN WITNESS whereof AB [the officer] an officer of XYZ
Limited [the attorney] duly appointed by the board of directors
of XYZ Limited by resolution dated   to execute
deeds in the name of CD [donor] in exercise of the power in that
behalf granted by CD to XYZ Limited by a Power of Attorney
dated   has hereunto set the hand of
CD the day and year first before written.
The deed would then be executed:
CD [donor]
by authority of his attorney XYZ Limited
AB [officer]

The statutory procedure for delegation to an officer of the
attorney corporation applies equally if the donor, as well as the
attorney, is a corporation.
The memorandum and articles of association of a company
acting as an attorney, or the charter or other governing instrument

of a corporation, may lay down some other way for it to delegate the execution of documents on the donor's behalf. The general statutory provisions do not supersede any such other arrangements (Law of Property Act 1925 s.74(6)).

4. Bills of exchange

8–04 A power of attorney may authorise the drawing, accepting and endorsing bills of exchange and promissory notes on the donor's behalf. A registered company may authorise any person to sign bills and notes on its behalf (Companies Act 1985 s.37).

The donor is expressly protected by statute if the attorney makes it clear that he signs on behalf of the donor.

"A signature by procuration operates as notice that the agent has but a limited authority to sign, and the principal is only bound by such signature if the agent in so signing was acting within the actual limits of his authority"

(Bills of Exchange Act 1882 s.25). This means

"that a person who takes a bill or note so accepted or indorsed ['per pro'] is bound at his peril to inquire into the extent of the agent's authority"

(*Bryant, Powis and Bryant Ltd. v La Banque du Peuple* [1893] A.C. 170 at 177 *per* Lord Macnaughten).

For this reason, there is a clear advantage to a donor in requiring, in the power, that the attorney always signs in such cases explicitly on the donor's behalf.

5. Proving authority

(a) General

8–05 An attorney may establish his authority by producing the original power, but he also has the alternative of doing so by producing a copy. A person with whom he deals is not entitled to require that the original power be surrendered to him (*Lancashire and Yorkshire Reversionary Interest Co. v Burke* [1907] 1 Ch. 486).

If a copy is to prove the contents of a power of attorney it must meet the following requirements (1971 Act s.3(1),(3)):

(1) It must be reproduced photographically or by some other device for reproducing documents in facsimile.

(2) It must bear a certificate at the end that the copy is a true and complete copy of the original. There has been no reported

dispute about the positioning of the certificate—unlike the litigation over the positioning of the signature "at the foot or end" of a will (Wills Act 1837 s.9 (as substituted by the Administration of Justice Act 1982 s.17))—but it should be noted that a copy certified in any other position does not satisfy the statutory condition.

(3) If the original consists of two or more pages, it must bear a certificate at the end of each page to the effect that it is a true and complete copy of the corresponding page of the original. This precludes copying a power of attorney in such a way that there is a change in pagination, either by reproducing more than one page of the original on one page of the copy or by showing only part of an original page on a sheet of copy.

(4) Every certificate must be signed by a solicitor, notary public or by a stockbroker who is a member of any stock exchange within the meaning of the Stock Transfer Act 1963 or the Stock Transfer Act (Northern Ireland) 1963.

As well as a copy of the original, the contents of a power of attorney may be proved by a copy of a copy, which itself satisfies the four conditions set out above. In that case, the copy of the copy must also comply with the conditions, but the certificates will refer to the first copy instead of to the original.

These provisions were novel when introduced by the 1971 Act. They replaced the former practice of filing powers in the central office of the Supreme Court, which enabled office copies to be obtained to prove the contents of the power when it was necessary to produce proof to a number of people simultaneously. The old provisions are dealt with in Ch.16 (p.123), as they may still be of importance in matters of title.

Two points should be noted. First, the provisions about facsimile copies apply equally to powers created before October 1, 1971, when the 1971 Act came into force. Secondly, it is still possible to bespeak office copies of some powers filed while that facility remained available.

(b) Lasting and enduring powers of attorney

Once a lasting or an enduring power of attorney has been **8–06** registered, an office copy of it can be obtained from the Public Guardian. An office copy is evidence both of the contents of the instrument and of the fact that it has been registered (2005 Act Sch.1, para.16, Sch.4, para.15(3), (4)). Before October 1, 2007, office copies of enduring powers of attorney were issued by the Court of Protection, and they may be used in the same way. In addition, a certified copy complying with the 1971 Act may still be used to prove the contents.

(c) Court of Protection orders

8–07   The Court of Protection has a wide jurisdiction in connection with lasting and enduring powers of attorney, including their interpretation. If it is necessary to establish the contents of an order of the court, an office copy is admissible in all legal proceedings as evidence of the original (2005 Act s.47(3)).

6. Custody of power

(a) Ordinary powers of attorney

8–08   As a power of attorney is the instrument giving an attorney his authority, which he will be called upon to exhibit to those with whom he deals on the donor's behalf, he normally is given custody of it.

Before the enactment of the 1971 Act, a donor who wished to revoke a power gained considerable protection against the unauthorised further exercise of the authority it granted, by retaking custody of the power. At that time, the power's contents had to be proved by production of the original, or of an office copy of it. A formal deed of revocation could be filed in court, which would cause the filed power to be marked as revoked, and prevent the issue of further office copies of an apparently valid power. The donor was at risk from any earlier office copies which were extant, but no further. Now that privately produced copies can prove the contents of a power, or even a copy of a copy, there is little or nothing the donor can do to prevent a fraudulent attorney pro-liferating them.

(b) Lasting powers of attorney

8–09   If the registration of a lasting power of attorney is cancelled—because it is revoked, or the Court of Protection determines that a requirement for creating the power was not met or that it contains a provision which is ineffective or prevents its valid operation—the instrument must be delivered up to the Public Guardian (2005 Act Sch.1, para.20).

(c) Enduring powers of attorney

8–10   In certain cases, the Court of Protection must direct the Public Guardian to cancel the registration of an enduring power of attorney. The instrument must then be delivered up to the Public Guardian for cancellation, unless the court otherwise directs. This applies: on confirmation of revocation by the donor, on revocation by direction of the court or the mental incapacity of the attorney, when the power has expired, if it was not a valid and subsisting enduring power when registered, if fraud or undue pressure induced the donor to grant it, or having regard to all the circumstances, in particular the attorney's relationship with the donor, the attorney is unsuitable to act (2005 Act Sch.4, para.16(4), (6)).

7. Legal proceedings

An attorney who sues on behalf of a donor should do so in the **8–11** donor's name (*Jones and Saldanha v Gurney* [1913] W.N. 72). When the donor is abroad, and indeed that is the reason for granting the power of attorney, the fact that he is the only plaintiff may result in his being ordered to give security for costs.

Chapter 9

Duties of Donor

1. Warranty of ability to delegate

It is for the donor of a power of attorney to establish that he is **9–01**
entitled to grant the power which he purports to do. The attorney
is generally entitled to rely on its validity. Circumstances may put
an attorney on notice that the power may not or cannot be validly
granted.

In normal cases, where there is no reason for the attorney to
doubt the power granted to him, he is not bound to make
investigations to assure himself that any of his actions under the
power will be valid.

The attorney may find himself personally at risk. If the donor has
contracted with a third party not to compete in a particular field,
an attorney who knows nothing of that restriction may make
competitive arrangements on the donor's behalf. The third party
could be in a position to seek an injunction to restrain both the
donor and his attorney. In such a case, the attorney may seek an
indemnity from the donor. He is entitled to damages on breach of
what amounts to a warranty that the donor validly granted to the
attorney the authority stated in the power of attorney.

2. Indemnity

In addition to cases arising because the donor has empowered **9–02**
the attorney to do more than he was entitled to delegate, the donor
is generally liable to indemnify his attorney against expense and
liability that he properly incurs in the performance of acts under a
power (*Westropp v Solomon* (1849) 8 C.B. 345). This duty does not
extend to a case where the attorney exceeds his authority and the
act is not ratified by the donor (*Barron v Fitzgerald* (1840) 6 Bing.
N.C. 201).

3. Ratification

9–03   Notwithstanding the undertaking on the part of the donor to ratify whatever the donor does, commonly found in ordinary powers of attorney, ratification is rarely appropriate. Ratification is the subsequent validation of an act done by the attorney which was not authorised at the time it was done. It should not be necessary, or indeed possible, in respect of acts done pursuant to the power. As they are authorised at the time they are done, they are immediately valid, and need no ratification. If, on the other hand, an attorney exceeds his powers, his acts do not, in the absence of ostensible authority, bind the donor. The donor is not obliged to ratify such an action, which would involve his widening the scope of the authority that he delegated (*Midland Bank Ltd. v Reckitt* [1933] A.C. 1).

In a case where the power is defective, either for some want of formality not apparent on the face of it or because of some collateral arrangement with a third party, there is a duty on the donor to stand behind the attorney and ratify the acts he does which would have been valid and within the power, but for the circumstances of which the attorney was ignorant. In those circumstances, it is considered that the donor has a duty to ratify the attorney's acts—or to put the attorney in the same position as if he had ratified—and that he has that duty whether or not it is expressly stated in the power.

Chapter 10

Duties of Attorney

1. General principles

(a) Act within authority

An attorney has a duty to the donor of the power of attorney **10–01** which appointed him to act only within the limits of the authority conferred by the power. The scope of the attorney's authority may be defined expressly—by the actual words of the power—or impliedly, for example, by circumstances as where the principal object of the power carries with it authority to do necessary ancillary acts.

(b) Duty to act

The question arises whether the attorney has a duty to do what **10–02** he has authority to do. Does he have a positive obligation to do what he is authorised to do, or merely a negative obligation not to exceed his authority? A distinction must be made between a gratuitous attorney and an attorney who is paid. An unpaid attorney need not do anything. An attorney for reward has an obligation to carry out any duties which he undertakes to perform, and is liable for non-feasance.

2. Lasting power of attorney

(a) General

Statutory provisions govern the conduct of an attorney **10–03** appointed by a lasting power of attorney. They relate principally, but not exclusively, to a lasting power relating to the donor's personal welfare. He must follow certain basic principles (2005 Act s.1) and have regard to the code of practice (2005 Act s.42(4)(a)).

The basic principles are:

  (i) a person must be assumed to have capacity unless the contrary is established;

  (ii) a person is not to be treated as incapable of making a decision unless practicable steps to help him have proved unsuccessful;

  (iii) a person is not to be treated as unable to make a decision because he makes an unwise decision;

  (iv) an act or decision on behalf of a person lacking capacity must be done or made in his best interests.

(b) Donor's capacity

10–04 If the attorney is only to make decisions when the donor lacks capacity—and sometimes a power will be granted on the basis that the attorney will exercise his authority whether or not the donor could himself have acted—the attorney is required to make the statutory presumption that the donor has the necessary capacity, unless it is established that he lacks it. In each case, the question is whether the donor has capacity in relation to the particular decision in question. It must be decided on the balance of probabilities (2005 Act s.2(4)).

He is unable to make a decision if he cannot (2005 Act s.3(1), (3)):

  (i) understand and retain, at least for a short period, the relevant information;

  (ii) use and weigh the information as part of the decision making process;

  (iii) communicate his decision.

However, the conclusion that the donor lacks capacity should not be reached because of his (2005 Act s.2(3)):

  (i) age,

  (ii) appearance (which can include physical manifestations of a medical condition, dress or body adornments e.g. tattoos: code of practice, para.4.8),

  (iii) condition (e.g. physical disabilities, learning disabilities, drunkenness: code of practice, para.4.9), or

  (iv) behaviour (e.g. exaggeratedly extrovert or introvert: code of practice, para.4.9) which could lead to unjustified assumptions.

The question may be whether the attorney reasonably believes that the donor lacks capacity. To establish reasonable belief the attorney must take reasonable steps to establish the position. This will not normally require involving a professional to make an assessment, but may involve considering earlier difficulties and making efforts to help the donor to make a decision (code of practice, paras 4.44, 4.45).

(c) Donor's best interests

In order to act in the donor's best interests, the attorney must **10–05** consider all the circumstances, including whether and when the donor is likely to have capacity in relation to the matter. The decision should not be based on what the attorney would want had he been the person lacking capacity (code of practice, para.5.7). Rather, he must (2005 Act s.4(2)–(4), (5)–(8)):

(a) consider, so far as reasonably ascertainable—

    (i) the donor's past and present wishes and feelings;
    (ii) the donor's beliefs and values and other factors he would likely to consider if he had capacity;

(b) permit and encourage the donor to participate, and improve his ability to do so, so far as reasonably possible; and

(c) consult and take into account the views of anyone named by the donor as someone to be consulted, anyone caring for the donor or interested in his welfare.

Nevertheless, the attorney's decision must not be taken merely on the basis of the donor's age or appearance, or his condition or aspects of his behaviour which might lead others into making unjustified assumptions about his best interests. There is also a restriction relating to a decision concerning life-sustaining treatment, which can only be taken if the instrument gives express authority: the attorney must not be motivated by a desire to bring about the donor's death (2005 Act s.4(1), (5)).

3. Enduring powers of attorney

After an enduring power of attorney has been registered, the **10–06** Court of Protection may give directions relating to the management or disposal by the attorney of the donor's property and affairs (2005 Act Sch.1, para.16(2)(b)(i)). This appears to give a jurisdiction to extend the attorney's authority, but it is restricted to administrative affairs (*Re R* [1990] Ch. 647).

It is not entirely clear whether the statutory provisions governing the conduct of attorneys appointed under lasting powers of attorney (paras 10–03—10–05) also govern attorneys under enduring powers. The general principles laid down by the 2005 Act are said to "apply for the purposes of this Act" (2005 Act s.1(1)). An enduring power which was registered after October 1, 2007, is registered under the 2005 Act, and the attorney's actions might therefore be described as for the purposes of the Act. However, that reasoning could not be applied to earlier registrations.

An argument against any application of these principles to attorneys under enduring powers—except to the extent that they apply at common law—is the limit on the duty to have regard to the code of practice. It is imposed on an attorney under a lasting power (2005 Act s.42(4)(a)), but not on an attorney under an enduring power, unless acting in a professional capacity or for remuneration (2005 Act s.42(4)(e), (f)). Nevertheless, the code of practice itself states that the best interests principle applies to attorneys under registered enduring powers of attorney (para.5.2).

4. Standard of care

10–07   The standard of care that an attorney must bring to carrying out his duties varies depending whether or not he is paid. If paid, he must exercise the care, skill and diligence of a reasonable man. Further, if he undertakes those duties in the course of a profession, he must exercise proper professional competence. A volunteer attorney must use such skill as he possesses, and show such care and skill as he would display in conducting his own affairs. Here again, even though he is not paid, if the attorney holds himself out as having the necessary skills, he must come up to the standard he has set himself.

5. Good faith and disclosure

10–08   The attorney must not put himself in a position where his duty to the donor conflicts with his duty to someone else. There will be cases where the donor is himself aware of a conflict. If he knows before making the appointment, the attorney is not at fault. But once the attorney has accepted the appointment, he must make a full disclosure to the donor before accepting any conflicting employment.

The position of an agent serving two different principals was examined by Donaldson J. in *North and South Trust Co. v Berkeley* [1971] 1 W.L.R. 470, in the context of Lloyd's insurance brokers whose practice was to represent the insured in effecting the policy, and both the insured and the underwriters in negotiating settlement of a claim. He said (at 484):

"Fully informed consent apart, an agent cannot lawfully place himself in a position in which he owes a duty to another which is inconsistent with his duty to his principal."

The principal's consent can be derived from a common usage, but such usage "must at least be notorious, certain and reasonable" (at 482). An attorney with a conflicting interest is liable to compensate the donor for any resulting loss.

The question arises whether the attorney who is in breach of this duty to the donor can validly contract on the donor's behalf and bind him. If the contract is with a third party, the normal principles apply, and the donor is bound to the extent of the attorney's ostensible authority. However, if the contract is made on the donor's behalf with the attorney's second principal, the donor can avoid it. Further, if the second principal knew of the existing relationship between the donor and the attorney, the court will assume that the consideration he gave as his part of the bargain would, but for the arrangement with the attorney, have been greater by the amount of any payment he made to the attorney.

The attorney is under a duty to account to the donor for any profit he makes from a third party. Similarly, the donor has a right to any secret profits or bribes that the attorney receives.

The donor's rights are not all cumulative. Where the attorney is guilty of a fraud that results in the disposal of one of the donor's assets at an undervalue, or the acquisition on his behalf of something at too great a price, and the attorney receives a bribe for his connivance, the donor has a choice. He can either recover damages for fraud—which in this example would be the difference between the price and the value of the asset—or he may require the attorney to account for the bribe. He is not entitled to both. The donor is put to his election, but does not have to choose until the time that judgment is entered in his favour on one of the two causes of action (*Mahesan S/O Thambiah v Malaysia Government Officers' Co-operative Housing Society Ltd* [1979] A.C. 374).

6. Criminal responsibility

An attorney who misuses his authority may be guilty of a **10–09** criminal offence. In one case, attorneys who appropriated for their own use the proceeds of assets belonging to a 99–year old donor who lacked the mental capacity to manage her own affairs, were convicted of conspiracy to steal (*R. v Kendrick and Hopkins* [1997] 2 Cr. App. R. 524).

Land cannot normally be stolen, but there is an exception in the case of an attorney. If he is authorised to sell or dispose of the donor's land, the attorney commits the crime of theft if he appropriates it by dealing with it in breach of the confidence reposed in him (Theft Act 1968 s.4(2)).

7. Accounting

(a) General

10–10   The attorney has a duty to keep the donor's money separate from his own, and from any other people's that he has in his hands. Complying with accounting requirements such as those imposed on solicitors for clients' money generally is presumed to satisfy this requirement, without the need to keep the money in a separate bank account. The attorney's duty extends to keeping up-to-date records of the state of account between the two parties. If the donor entrusts his books to his attorney, they must be produced to the donor on demand.

The attorney holds the donor's money as trustee (*Burdick v Garrick* (1870) L.R. 5 Ch. App. 233: money paid by a solicitor attorney into his firm's account, before professional accounting rules were imposed). The trust stems from the obligation to keep the money apart.

> "It is clear that if the terms upon which the person receives the money are that he is bound to keep it separate, either in a bank or elsewhere, and to hand that money so kept as a separate fund to a person entitled to it, then he is a trustee of that money and must hand it over to the person who is his *cestui que trust*"

(*Henry v Hammond* [1913] 2 K.B. 515 at 521 *per* Channell J.). The trust extends to any interest earned by the money. It arises without the donor being informed that the money has been set aside (*Re Chelsea Cloisters Ltd.* (1980) 41 P. & C.R. 98).

The result of the money being held on trust is that the statute of limitations does not run against the donor to prevent his claiming the money. It also saves the donor's money from forming part of the attorney's estate if the attorney goes bankrupt.

(b) Enduring powers of attorney

10–11   The Court of Protection may make an order that the attorney appointed by an enduring power of attorney which has been registered should render accounts and produce records which he kept for that purpose (2005 Act Sch.1, para.16(2)(ii)).

8. Personal performance

An attorney is only entitled to delegate his powers and duties **10–12** where he has authority to do so, whether expressly or by implication. There is an implied power to delegate purely ministerial acts. In other cases, the position has been summed up this way,

> "an authority . . . may and should be implied where, from the conduct of the parties to the original contract of agency, the usage of trade, or the nature of the particular business which is the subject of the agency, it may reasonably be presumed that the parties to the contract of agency originally intended that such authority should exist, or where, in the course of employment, unforeseen emergencies arise which impose upon the agent the necessity of employing a substitute"

(*De Bussche v Alt* (1878) 8 Ch.D. 286 at 310 *per* Thesiger L.J.).

Some of the reasons why an attorney, like any other agent, can only delegate where specially authorised, were illustrated in the case of an estate agent appointed to sell a house.

> "The reason is because an estate agent holds a position of discretion and trust. Discretion in his conduct of negotiations. Trust in his handling of affairs . . . Furthermore, he is at liberty in the course of the negotiations to receive a deposit as stakeholder"

(*John McCann & Co. v Pow* [1974] 1 W.L.R. 1643 at 1647 *per* Lord Denning M.R.).

Nevertheless, it is possible for the donor to give the attorney power to delegate and to create privity of contract between the donor and the substitute. This would be unusual. It requires that the donor contemplated that certain acts would be done by a substitute, and that he gave the attorney power to create privity of contract between him and the substitute (*Calico Printers' Association v Barclays Bank Ltd* (1931) 145 L.T. 51 at 55).

Generally, there is no contract between the donor of a power and his attorney's substitute. They will not therefore be able to sue each other for breach of contract, unless the Contracts (Rights of Third Parties) Act 1999 applies. In an appropriate case the donor would be able to take action in tort.

9. Confidentiality

An attorney, like other agents, is under a duty to keep the **10–13** donor's affairs confidential, unless the donor authorises him to disclose them (*LS Harris Trustees Ltd v Power Packing Services*

(Hermit Road) Ltd [1970] 2 Ll. Rep. 65). He is also limited in the extent to which he is entitled to use the knowledge he acquires as attorney. He may not put what he learns in the course of his duties to his private benefit, nor may he solicit the donor's customers (*Julien Praet et Cie. S.A. v HG Poland Ltd.* [1962] 1 Ll. Rep. 566).

These duties continue after the power comes to an end (*Amber Size and Chemical Co. Ltd. v Menzel* [1913] 2 Ch. 239).

10. Registration

10–14   The attorney appointed by a lasting power of attorney may register the power with the Public Guardian when it has been granted. The donor may also register. The lasting power is not effective until it is registered (2005 Act s.9(2)(b)). For details, see Ch.14, p.105.

The attorney appointed by an enduring power of attorney has a duty to register it, as opposed to being empowered to do so, and he must apply as soon as practicable if he has reason to believe that the donor is or is becoming mentally incapable (2005 Act Sch.4 para.4(1), (2)). For details, see Ch.15, p.113.

11. Court of Protection jurisdiction: enduring powers of attorney

10–15   The Court of Protection has an extensive jurisdiction over the attorney appointed under an enduring power which has been registered. It has powers (2005 Act Sch.4, para.16(2)):

(i) to give directions as to the management or disposal by the attorney of the donor's property and affairs;

(ii) to direct the rendering of accounts by the attorney, and the production of the records he keeps for that purpose;

(iii) to give directions regarding the attorney's remuneration or expenses, whether or not they are mentioned in the instrument, including the power to make orders to repay excessive remuneration, or to pay additional sums;

(iv) to require that the attorney furnish information or produce documents or things which he has in his possession in his capacity as attorney;

(v) to give any consent or authority which the attorney would have had to obtain from a mentally capable donor;

(vi) to authorise the attorney to benefit himself, or persons other than the donor, in some way beyond the general statutory authority.

Chapter 11

Protection of Attorney

1. General

(a) Nature of liability

An attorney who purports to act under a power of attorney **11–01** which is invalid—either because it was not validly granted, so that it never conferred any authority, or because it has ceased to be valid, either through expiry or revocation—can be liable for any loss which his act causes to others. In the absence of statutory intervention, there are three possible types of claim he may face. First, the donor of the power may claim for the wrongful disposal of his property, or other loss caused by unauthorised interference in his affairs. Secondly, a person with whom the attorney contracts, purportedly on behalf of the donor, will have a claim for breach of warranty of authority. Thirdly, there could also be a claim from a third party more remotely affected, for instance, taking property from the person who bought from the attorney, and finding himself without proper title.

If the attorney is aware that his authority under the power of attorney is at an end, but nevertheless continues to act under the power, he is justifiably liable.

However, if the power is revoked without his knowledge, he can find himself unwittingly liable. It is possible for the donor to revoke a power of attorney without notifying the attorney. Further, and probably more seriously, there are cases in which the law impliedly revokes a power. The moment the donor dies, any power he granted ceases to have effect. An ordinary power, although not a lasting power or an enduring power, is revoked when the donor ceases to have mental capacity. Not only is that revocation automatic, but it is frequently impossible to say precisely when it occurs.

(b) Statutory protection

11–02   Statute has recognised the difficulty in which these rules may place an honest attorney, and has provided protection. An attorney who acts in pursuance of a power when it has been revoked incurs no liability provided he did not at the time know that it had been revoked (1971 Act s.5(1)). This protection applies to all forms of power of attorney. It is extended to the case of a lasting power of attorney which ceases in relation to the donor's property and affairs, even though it continues in effect in relation to the donor's personal welfare (2005 Act s.14(5)).

Certain points should be noted. First, the attorney must act "in pursuance of the power", which means that his act must be one which, had the power still been in force, it would have authorised. No protection is afforded to an attorney doing an act for which he would not have had authority in the first place, or continuing to act after a time limit expressly imposed by the original instrument. Secondly, the attorney is protected against liability both to the donor and to others. Thirdly, knowledge of the revocation removes the protection. It does not matter from what source he learns that the power has been revoked.

Where a registered enduring power of attorney is revoked by the donor, the knowledge which removes the attorney's protection is knowledge that the revocation has been confirmed by the Court of Protection, but not knowledge of the unconfirmed revocation (2005 Act Sch.1, para.18(5)).

When a lasting power of attorney is revoked or suspended because of one of the statutory causes, the Public Guardian must notify the attorney. The same applies if an attorney's appointment is terminated although the power continues (2005 Act Sch.1, paras 21, 22, 25). Cases of the attorney acting in ignorance of the revocation of the power should therefore be minimalised.

2. Purported registration

(a) Lasting powers of attorney

11–03   Although an intended lasting power of attorney is registered by the Public Guardian, it may be that no lasting power was created (e.g. because the donor was under 18). In any such case, the attorney only incurs liability because of the non-existence of the power in two cases: first, if he knows that none was created or secondly, if he is aware of circumstances which would have terminated his authority had there been a valid power (2005 Act s.14(1), (2)).

(b) Enduring powers of attorney

Where a purported enduring power of attorney has been regis- **11–04** tered, and even if the registration was later cancelled, but did not in fact create a valid power, there is protection for the attorney. He only incurs liability as a result of the non-existence of the power in three cases. They are: if he knows that there was no valid power, if he knows of an event which would have revoked the power had it been valid, or if he knows that the power, had it been valid, would by then have expired (2005 Act Sch.1, para.18(1), (2))

3. Retrospective protection

When an enduring power of attorney has been registered, the **11–05** Court of Protection has jurisdiction to relieve the attorney wholly or partly of any liability he may have incurred on account of a breach of his duties as attorney (2005 Act Sch.1, para. 16(2)(f)).

4. Protection in the power

The donor of a power of attorney can expressly relieve the **11–06** attorney from liability to him in all or specific circumstances. Clearly, if the instrument contains a provision to that effect, the donor would be estopped from taking any action. However, it is doubtful whether the donor could relieve the attorney for the consequences of the attorney's acts after the donor's death (when the property would no longer be his) and it seems unlikely that the donor could effectively protect the attorney from actions by third parties.

5. Limitation period

There is no period of limitation which runs in favour of an **11–07** attorney to prevent the donor taking action against him for misuse of his authority. This is because, although the attorney is not truly a trustee, he is nevertheless in a fiduciary position (*Burdick v Garrick* (1870) L.R. 5 Ch. App. 233).

Chapter 12

Position of Third Parties

1. Subsistence of power

A third party dealing with an attorney must, in order to ensure 12–01
that any contract he negotiates with the attorney binds the donor
of the power, assure himself of two things. First, he must be
satisfied that the power is still in force. Secondly, he must ascertain
that the attorney is acting within the scope of his authority.

Statutory presumptions for the benefit of third parties and
purchasers discussed below apply to acts and transactions after
October 1, 1971. The date on which the power of attorney was
granted is immaterial (1971 Act s.5(7)).

(a) Power revoked: general

Even if a power of attorney has in fact been brought to an end 12–02
by revocation, a third party may deal with the attorney in ignorance
of the revocation. In such a case, in favour of the third party, the
transaction is as valid as if the power were still in existence (1971
Act s.5(2)). That does not excuse the third party from investigating
to make sure that the power was granted in proper form, that there
were no circumstances preventing the donor from validly granting
a power, and that the transaction falls within the scope of the
attorney's authority. The statutory protection simply amounts to
the fact that the revocation by itself makes no difference to the
position of a third party who knew nothing about it.

A third party who knows of some fact that has the effect of
revoking the power, such as the donor's death, knows of the
revocation for this purpose and therefore loses the statutory
protection (1971 Act s.5(5)).

It is suggested that this provision should be interpreted to mean
that protection extends to a third party who did not know, and
should not have known, of the revocation, for example, a third

party who did not make any enquiries that in the circumstances would have been reasonable, should be treated as knowing what those enquiries would have revealed to him.

(b) Lasting powers of attorney

12–03   If a purported lasting power of attorney has been registered even though no valid lasting power was created, a transaction between the attorney and a third party if generally as valid as if the power of attorney had been in existence. There are exceptions in two cases, where the transaction is ineffective: first, if the third party knew that a lasting power of attorney was not created, and secondly, if he was aware of circumstances which would have terminated the attorney's authority had there been a valid power (2005 Act s.14(3)).

(c) Enduring powers of attorney

12–04   A third party is protected when dealing with an attorney appointed under a purported enduring power of attorney which, although in fact not effective, has been registered, even if the registration was later cancelled. Subject to exceptions, the transaction is as valid as if the power had been in existence. The exceptions are when the third party knows that the instrument did not create a valid enduring power, or knows that an event has occurred which would have revoked the power had it been effective, or knows that the power would by then have expired (2005 Act Sch.1, para.18(3)).

(d) Power coupled with an interest

12–05   A power coupled with an interest, or, as the 1971 Act terms it, a power given by way of security, is in a special position. If the instrument creating it states that the power is to be irrevocable, a third party is entitled to assume that it can only be revoked by the donor with the attorney's consent. The only exception to this is if the third party knows that the power was not in fact given by way of security.

A third party dealing with an attorney under this form of power has the protection of one who does not know of the revocation, unless he knows that it was revoked by the donor with the attorney's consent (1971 Act s.5(3)). Knowledge of a purported unilateral revocation by the donor does not remove the third party's protection.

(e) Power in favour of trust of land beneficiaries

12–06   There is a general presumption in favour of someone who deals in good faith with an attorney to whom trustees of land have delegated functions under their power to delegate to the beneficiaries. The attorney is presumed to be someone to whom the functions could be delegated, unless at the time of the transaction the person dealing with the attorney knew that he was not (1996 Act s.9(2)).

2. Protection of purchasers

(a) Generally

Special provisions, reinforcing the presumption in favour of third **12–07** parties of the validity of powers of attorney, protect purchasers. They apply where a purchaser's interest depends on the validity of the transaction between the attorney and the third party, and where the appropriate procedure has been followed. For this purpose, "purchaser" means a purchaser in good faith for valuable consideration. It includes a lessee, mortgagee, chargee by way of legal mortgage, or other person who for valuable consideration acquires an interest in property. "Purchase" has a corresponding meaning (Law of Property Act 1925 s.205(1)(xxi); 1971 Act s.5(6); 1985 Act s.9(7)).

When a transaction which depends on the validity of the power is completed within 12 months of the power coming into operation, or within three months of completion the third party makes a statutory declaration, there is a presumption that the person dealing with the attorney did not at the material time know of the revocation of the power (1971 Act s.5(4)). The declaration must say that the third party did not, when the transaction was completed, know that the power was revoked.

Precedents for this statutory declaration, and others required in the circumstances outlined below, are included in Appendix 3, paras A3–11, A3–12.

(b) Lasting and enduring powers of attorney

A purchaser's interest may depend on the validity of an earlier **12–08** transaction with someone acting as attorney under a power which was in fact invalid. If the instrument was a purported lasting power of attorney validated by the provision dealt with in para.12–03, or a purported enduring power of attorney validated by the provision dealt with in para.12–04, the purchaser can be protected. In favour of a purchaser, the earlier transaction is conclusively presumed to be valid in either of two circumstances. It is presumed valid if the transaction to which the attorney was a party was completed within 12 months of the date on which the purported power was registered. Alternatively, the presumption also applies if, within three months of completing the purchase, the person who dealt with the attorney makes a statutory declaration that at the time of dealing with the attorney he had no reason to doubt the attorney's right to dispose of the property (2005 Act s.14(4), Sch.4, para.18(4)).

(c)   Delegation to beneficiaries of trusts of land

12–09   There are conclusive presumptions in favour of a purchaser whose interest depends on the validity of an earlier transaction with the attorney, if the person dealing with the attorney makes an appropriate statutory declaration. The presumptions are that the person dealing with the attorney did so in good faith, and did not know that he was a person to whom the trustee functions could not be delegated. The statutory declaration must be to that effect (see Appendix 3, para.A3–13) and must be made within three months after the completion of the purchase (1996 Act s.9(2)).

(d)   Trustee beneficiaries

12–10   The validity of an ordinary or enduring power of attorney granted by a trustee of land who has a beneficial interest in that land depends upon his having a beneficial interest when the attorney acts (1999 Act s.1(1)). A signed statement by the attorney that the donor had a beneficial interest at the appropriate time is conclusive evidence in favour of the purchaser that he did indeed do so. The statement may be made when the attorney acts, so it can be included in the conveyance, or at any time within the next three months (1999 Act s.2).

(e)   Stock exchange transactions

12–11   Special statutory protection is conferred in the case of the transfer of a registered security for the purpose of a stock exchange transaction. See para.19–09.

3. Scope of attorney's authority

12–12   A transaction between an attorney and a third party can only bind the donor of a power of attorney if it is within the attorney's authority. This is something that the third party has to investigate. The donor will not only be bound by an act within the attorney's actual authority, but also by one within his ostensible authority.

(a)   Actual authority

12–13   The scope of the actual authority of an attorney is dealt with in Ch.2, p.11. Normally, it will be defined by the power of attorney. It can be extended by the donor by a direct communication from him to a third party (*Reckitt v Barnett, Pembroke and Slater Ltd.* [1929] A.C. 176: the donor wrote to his bank extending the attorney's authority to draw cheques on his account). The attorney's actual authority can also be restricted by a private communication. If it is only the attorney who is notified, his authority is cut down, but third parties who know nothing of the restriction will probably not be prejudiced because the attorney's ostensible authority will be unimpaired.

A third party is also deemed to know of a limit on the attorney's power of which he was given the opportunity to learn, even though he did not avail himself of that chance (*Jacobs v Morris* [1902] 1 Ch. 816: the attorney misrepresented his power to borrow; he produced the power of attorney from which the position would have been clear, but the third party did not read it). In the case of bills of exchange, statutory force is given to this rule that a third party is deemed to know the limits of an agent's actual authority if he has notice that the ostensible authority may be circumscribed.

"A signature by procuration operates as notice that the agent has but a limited authority to sign, and the principal is only bound by such signature if the agent in so signing was acting within the actual limits of his authority"

(Bills of Exchange Act 1882 s.25).

(b) Ostensible authority

The ostensible authority of an attorney is the authority with 12–14 which the donor appears to have invested him. The extent of that authority may be judged from the wording of the power, if the third party does not know that it has been modified by some collateral instruction, from general custom or from a course of dealings between the parties in question.

If

"an agent is clothed with ostensible authority no private instructions prevent his acts within the scope of the authority from binding his principal"

(*National Bolivian Navigation Co v Wilson* (1880) 5 App. Cas. 176 at 209 *per* Lord Blackburn). A third party is entitled to rely upon the attorney's ostensible authority even though he did not know when he contracted with him that the attorney was not acting as a principal (*Watteau v Fenwick* [1893] 1 Q.B. 346).

A restriction on an attorney's authority may be conveyed directly to the third party, or it may be announced publicly to everyone likely to deal with him (*Overbrooke Estates Ltd. v Glencombe Properties Ltd.* [1974] 1 W.L.R. 1335: auction conditions declared that the auctioneers had no authority to make or give any representation or warranty about the property). The limit on the donor's authority may stem from the donor's power to effect a particular transaction, and this may be a matter of law that third parties are assumed to know if they are aware of the relevant facts. The limits on the powers of a trustee or mortgagee to lease property are examples: the ostensible authority of an attorney appointed by a trustee or mortgagee would not extend further, if it was clear to the third party in what capacity the donor was acting.

(c) Companies

12–15   Special rules apply to companies registered under the Companies Act 1985 or earlier Acts. The validity of a company's act cannot be called into question on the ground of lack of capacity because of anything in its memorandum of association. In favour of a person dealing with a company in good faith, the powers of the directors to bind the company and to authorise others to do so are deemed to be free of any limit under the company's constitution. Moreover, a third party is not bound to inquire into the company's capacity or any limitation on the directors' powers (Companies Act 1985 ss.35–35B; Companies Act 1989 s.108(1)). Accordingly, a third party dealing with a company's attorney appointed by a power executed by the company—which will naturally involve at least one director signing—will not have to investigate any question of capacity unless he has some outside indication of malpractice by any director involved (which might prevent the third party's acting in good faith).

4. Attorney without authority

12–16   A third party may be misled by an attorney into thinking that the attorney has authority. If that causes him loss—because the donor is not bound by the attorney's act—the third party may have an action against the attorney. An attorney who acts under a power that has been revoked without his knowledge does not thereby incur liability (1971 Act s.5(1)).

An attorney may mislead a third party into thinking that the circumstances exist that are necessary to make a conditional power valid. For example, when granted a power to be exercised only while the donor is abroad, the attorney may assure the third party that the donor is abroad when he is not.

The nature and extent of the attorney's liability in such cases varies according to what the attorney knows of the facts.

(a) Deceit

An attorney who knowingly represents to a third party that he **12–17** has authority to act when he has not, and thereby causes loss to the third party, is guilty of the tort of deceit (*Polhill v Walter* (1832) 3 B. & Ad. 114).

(b) Warranty of authority

An attorney who innocently acts without authority may be liable **12–18** to a third party who suffers loss for breach of warranty of authority. The attorney is not, however, liable for breach of a contract made on the donor's behalf. The donor cannot be sued if the attorney has no authority, either actual or ostensible, but neither is the attorney liable, because he contracts on behalf of a named principal (*Smout v Ilbery* (1842) 10 M. & W. 1). The third party can recover from the attorney, as part of his damages for breach of warrants of authority, any costs thrown away in suing the donor on such a contract (*Godwin v Francis* (1870) L.R. 5 C.P. 29).

The attorney's liability under the warranty has been defined in this way.

"The obligation arising in such a case is well expressed by saying that a person professing to contract as agent for another, impliedly, if not expressly, undertakes to, or promises, the person who enters into such contract upon the faith of the professed agent being duly authorised, that the authority which he professes to have does in point of fact exist. The fact of entering into the transaction with the professed agent, as such, is good consideration for the promise"

(*Collen v Wright* (1857) 8 E. & B. 647 *per* Willes J.).

The attorney's representation carries no responsibility if it is as to a matter of law, for instance, as to the correct interpretation of a document (*Rashdall v Ford* (1866) L.R. 2 Eq. 750).

Chapter 13

Trustees

1. Duty of care

Whenever a trustee delegates his functions, whatever is the **13–01** power which authorises the delegation, he is under a duty of care. This applies in particular to selecting the attorney and fixing the terms of his appointment. It means that he must exercise the care and skill which is reasonable in the circumstances. Special knowledge or experience must be taken into account if the trustee holds himself out as possessing it, or, in the case of a trustee acting in the course of a business or profession, if it is reasonable to expect it of a person so acting (2000 Act s.1, Sch.1, para.3(1)(d), (2)).

2. Restrictions on delegation by individual trustees

(a) Scope

Traditionally, a trustee was not entitled to delegate the exercise **13–02** of his powers and duties, unless the trust instrument authorised him to do so, as he had voluntarily agreed to take on that role. He is covered by the rule *delegatus non potest delegare* (an agent may not himself further delegate). If he did attempt to delegate to someone else, he remained liable for that person's defaults (*Turner v Corney* (1841) 5 Beav. 515 at 517). A power of attorney purporting to delegate a trustee's powers without statutory authority has been held invalid (*Green v Whitehead* [1930] 1 Ch. 38).

(b) Exceptions

Statute has created exceptions to the general rule, permitting **13–03** individual trustees to delegate in certain circumstances, although the rule that the trustee remains liable for the acts and defaults of his attorney remains (1925 Act s.25(7)). There are now two exceptions, although they do not apply if they are excluded when the trust is established:

(i) a general power for all trustees to delegate for a limited period;

(ii) a power for a trustee of land who also has a beneficial interest in the property to delegate functions in relation to the land.

3. Temporary delegation by any trustee

(a) Scope

13–04 Originally, the general statutory power of delegation was for trustees who were going abroad. Now, unless the trust instrument prohibits or restricts delegation (1925 Act s.69(2)), a trustee is entitled to delegate all or any of his functions as trustee for a limited period (1925 Act s.25(1)).

Formerly, a trustee was not entitled to appoint an individual who was his only co-trustee as his attorney. That restriction has been lifted in respect of powers granted after March 1, 2000, when amendments to the 1925 Act came into effect (1999 Act s.5(1)).

The Council of the Law Society expressed the opinion in 1931 that the costs of a power of attorney granted by a trustee who was about to go abroad—to which s.25 of the 1925 Act was then limited—are properly paid from the trust fund (1 *Law Society's Digest* 480).

(b) Period

13–05 A trustee may delegate his functions for up to a year, but the power may specify a shorter time (1925 Act s.25(2)). The period starts on the date the power states, or if it is silent on the date it is executed.

The 12-month limit on delegation is of little effect. There is nothing to prevent a trustee granting an unlimited number of successive powers of attorney, each lasting for a year. The 1999 Act amendments to s.25 of the 1925 Act, allowing the power to state a future date for the start of the 12–month period (1925 Act s.25(2)(a)), offer a further possibility. A number of powers can be granted at the same time, each specifying a different 12–month period, so that those periods run consecutively. The only challenge the trustee seems likely to face is the possibility of removal from office on the grounds that he has been absent from the United

Kingdom for more than 12 months, or being unfit or incapable (1925 Act s.36(1)).

(c) Notice

Before or within seven days after the power is created, the donor **13–06** has to notify his fellow trustees and anyone entitled to appoint new trustees. They must be told:

(i) the date on which the power comes into operation;

(ii) for how long it will last;

(iii) the attorney's name;

(iv) the reason for the delegation; and,

(v) if the delegation is not total, which trusts, powers and discretions are delegated.

However, failure to give this notification does not, so far as someone dealing with the attorney is concerned, invalidate anything he does (1925 Act s.25(4)).

The notice requirements also apply, with modifications, to trustees of particular types. A personal representative who grants a power of attorney must give notice to the other personal representatives, but not to an executor who has renounced; a tenant for life must give notice to the trustees of the settlement, and anyone else who jointly constitutes the tenant for life; a statutory owner must give notice to anyone else jointly constituting the statutory owner, and, in the case of a strict settlement, to the trustees (1925 Act s.25(10)).

(d) Form

The 1999 Act introduced a new statutory short form of general **13–07** trustee power of attorney (1925 Act s.25(5)). It can be used by a single trustee to delegate all his powers exercisable under one identified trust to a single attorney. As an alternative a power "to the like effect", expressed to be made under s.25(5) of the 1925 Act can be used (1925 Act s.25(5)). As in the case of the statutory short form of general power, it may not be advisable to use it where the attorney is likely to have to deal with assets abroad. People outside the country may not be familiar with the effect which statute gives to the succinct form.

(e) Administrative acts

13–08   The common law accepted that a trustee could delegate mechanical acts of administration which involved no exercise of judgment (*Att.-Gen. v Scott* (1749) 1 Ves. Sen. 413). Similarly, delegating a ministerial function which carries into effect the consequences of an earlier exercise of discretion is allowed (*Offen v Harman* (1859) 29 L.J. Ch. 307). To receive the purchase money following the sale of a trust asset falls into this category (*Re Hetling and Merton's Contract* [1893] 3 Ch. 269).

Two cases need to be distinguished. On the one hand, there is a trustee who seeks to delegate the responsibilities which he was probably asked to undertake because of his personal qualities. He is not entitled to delegate without statutory authority. On the other hand, a trustee who seeks assistance in the mechanical tasks which he has already decided need to be undertaken may delegate them.

4. Delegation by trustee/beneficiary of land

(a) Scope

13–09   There are special statutory provisions concerning land, and income from it and the capital proceeds of it, which are subject to a trust. A trustee who has a beneficial interest in the land may grant a power of attorney to delegate his functions in relation to it. His attorney may act freely so long as the trustee still has such an interest. This is an important new exception, introduced by the 1999 Act, to the restrictions on trustees granting powers of attorney. It applies generally to powers of attorney granted after March 1, 2000, but also to enduring powers of attorney granted earlier, from the date that they are no longer valid to delegate trustee functions to the attorney (1999 Act s.4(6); 2005 Act Sch.5, para.14(4)).

Where the new arrangements are not wanted, the trustee/beneficiaries do not have to be given this new authority. The provisions can be excluded by the trust instrument, or the instrument may impose conditions to which they will be subject (1999 Act s.1(5)). The instrument creating the power may nevertheless validly limit what the attorney can do (1999 Act s.1(1), (3)). "Land" is defined widely for this purpose (1925 Act s.68(6); 1999 Act s.11(1)).

(b) Form

13–10   A power of attorney granted by a trustee/beneficiary with an interest in trust land does not have to be granted as a trustee power of attorney under s.25 of the 1925 Act. A general power of attorney, including one in the short statutory form (1971 Act s.10; 1999 Act, s.3), can be used. An enduring power of attorney is also effective. Indeed, an enduring power which was granted to take advantage of the provision for delegating trustee functions Enduring Power of Attorney Act 1985 s.3(3), repealed by the 1999 Act), remains effective to the extent that it falls within the trustee/beneficiary provision (1999 Act s.4(6); 2005 Act Sch.5, para.14(4)).

(c) Period

Because s.25 of the 1925 Act does not apply, a power granted by **13–11** a trustee/beneficiary is not subject to the 12-month time limit which applies to general trustee powers. Further, the power of attorney can be granted as a lasting power, so that it remains effective even if the donor becomes incapable.

(d) Appropriate statements

Clearly, in order to establish for the benefit of third parties that **13–12** an attorney is validly exercising a power granted by a trustee under this provision, he must establish that the trustee still has the necessary beneficial interest in trust land. To avoid the need to investigate the equitable title, this can be established in favour of a purchaser ("a person who acquires an interest in or charge on property for money or money's worth": Law of Property Act 1925 s.105(1)(xxi); 1999 Act s.2(1)) by "an appropriate statement" which provides conclusive evidence (1999 Act s.2(2)). The statement is made by the attorney, and says that the trustee has a beneficial interest in the property at the time of the attorney's act. It must be made when the attorney acts or within the next three months (1999 Act s.2(2)).

Because it is the attorney, not the trustee, who has to make the appropriate statement it will not normally be possible to include it in the power of attorney. Besides, that will generally also be precluded by the fact that the statement cannot be made before the attorney acts. It will conveniently be included in the conveyance, lease, etc., which the attorney executes.

A false appropriate statement makes the attorney liable in the same way if he had made a false statutory declaration (1999 Act s.2(4)).

(e) Two-trustee rules

In many cases where a trustee/beneficiary's power of attorney is **13–13** used, a two-trustee rule will apply. Namely, disregarding the special position of trust corporations,

(i) Capital monies arising from land must be paid to, or at the direction of, at least two trustees (Law of Property Act 1925 s.27(2); Settled Land Act 1925 ss.18(1)(c), 94);

(ii) A valid receipt for such capital monies cannot be given by a sole trustee (1925 Act s.14(2));

(iii) A conveyance or deed which is to overreach any powers of interest affecting a legal estate must be made by at least two trustees (Law of Property Act 1925 s.(2)(ii)).

The 1999 Act clarified and tightened up those provisions. A person who is acting both in the capacity of trustee in his own right and as another trustee's attorney does not satisfy the requirement for two trustees. There must be two separate people acting. This means that if there are two joint owners of a property, and one grants a power of attorney to the other, the second one cannot act on his own in any of the cases affected by a two-trustee rule. If there are more than two trustees, the same restriction applies to one trustee who is also attorney for all the other trustees. These restrictions apply whether the power of attorney was granted before or after March 1, 2000, subject to the transitional provisions applying to the repeal of s.3(3) of the Enduring Power of Attorney Act 1985 (1999 Act, s.7).

To comply with a two-trustee rule, it may be necessary to appoint an additional trustee. The fact that another trustee is needed in order to complete certain transactions could be difficult if an enduring power were being used and the trustee who granted it was no longer mentally capable of making a new appointment. The 1999 Act recognises this.

An enduring power granted after March 1, 2000 which does not provide to the contrary, gives the attorney power in certain circumstances to appoint an additional trustee (1925 Act s.36(6A), (6D); 1999 Act s.8(2)). The power must have been registered, which presupposes that the trustee donor is becoming or has become mentally incapable. The attorney may appoint a new trustee if he intends to do one of two things. Either, he must intend to exercise a function as attorney of a trustee/beneficiary under section 1 of the 1999 Act. Or, he must intend to exercise a trustee function in relation to land, the income from or capital proceeds of land, delegated under s.25 of the 1925 Act or the trust instrument (1925 Act s.36(6B)).

Naturally, this power to appoint an additional trustee cannot apply if there are already four trustees: that is the maximum number of trustees who can hold land (1925 Act s.34).

5. Delegation by trustees collectively

(a) Express authority

The trust instrument may validly authorise the trustee to dele- **13–14** gate aspects of their responsibilities (see, e.g. *Williams' Trustees v Inland Revenue Commissioners* [1947] A.C. 448).

(b) Statutory power to delegate

Subject to any restrictions in the trust instrument, trustees have a **13–15** general statutory power to delegate most of their functions, whenever the trust was created. There is no requirement that the delegation be by power of attorney, but trustees who delegate their asset management functions must do so by a written agreement, or one evidenced in writing (2000 Act ss.11(1), 15(1), 26, 27).

In the case of a non-charitable trust, there are certain functions which cannot be delegated under these powers. They are: decisions about distribution, whether payments should come from income or capital, appointing new trustees and any power of delegation. Nor may trustees of a trust of land delegate functions in such a way that they cannot comply with their duty to consult beneficiaries and give effect to their wishes. For a charitable trust, only specified functions may be delegated. They are: carrying out a decision taken by the trustees, investing assets and raising funds (unless that is by the profits of a trade integral to the trust's charitable purpose) (2000 Act ss.11(2)–(4), 13(4)).

The agent appointed may be one of the trustees, but may not be a beneficiary (even if also a trustee). The terms of appointment may include remuneration. But, unless it is reasonably necessary, they cannot allow the agent to appoint a substitute, restrict his liability to the trustees or any beneficiary not to act when he may have a conflict of interest (2000 Act ss.12, 14).

If trustees exceed their statutory powers of delegation in authorising an agent to exercise their powers, the agent's authority is nevertheless valid. Presumably, the third parties may rely on the agent's authority to the extent that they may rely on an attorney's ostensible authority. A trustee who has complied with his duty of care has no liability for the act or default of an agent. But trustees who have delegated their powers are required to keep the arrangements under review (2000 Act ss.22–24).

(c) Beneficiaries of trusts of land

The trustees of a trust of land (a trust of property which consists **13–16** of or includes land: 1996 Act s.1(1)(a)) may jointly delegate any of their functions in relation to the land by power of attorney. The delegation must be to one or more beneficiaries of full age who are beneficially entitled to an interest in possession in land which is subject to the trust (1996 Act s.9(1)). Neither a lasting power of attorney nor an enduring power of attorney can be used for this purpose (1996 Act s.9(6)).

The power may specify the period for which the functions are delegated, or it may be indefinite (1996 Act s.9(5)). Any of the trustees may revoke the power, unless it is given by way of security and described as irrevocable. It is automatically revoked if someone else is appointed as a trustee, but not by the death or retirement of one of the trustees who granted it (1996 Act s.9(3)). If a beneficiary ceases to have an interest under the trust which qualifies him for delegation, the power is revoked so far as it relates to him (1996 Act s.9(4)).

Outsiders will not know whether the attorney is someone to whom the trustees are entitled to delegate. This is dealt with by statutory provisions. Someone who in good faith deals with the attorney in relation to the land may rely on a presumption that the attorney is a beneficiary to whom the functions could be delegated, unless at the time of the transaction he knew that he was not. There is a conclusive presumption to protect a later purchaser ("a person who acquires an interest in or charge on property for money or money's worth": Law of Property Act 1925 s.105(1)(xxi); 1996 Act s.23(1)), whose title depends on the validity of that transaction, that the person dealing with the attorney was in good faith and did not know that the attorney was not a qualifying beneficiary. That presumption operates if the person who dealt with the attorney made a statutory declaration before or within three months after completion of the purchase.

The protection is therefore in two stages. The person dealing directly with the attorney can rely on a presumption if he has no contrary information, but as it is only a presumption, it can be defeated by proof to the contrary. A purchaser from him is, however, protected by a conclusive presumption, which would be indefeasible, provided that the person who dealt directly with the attorney makes an appropriate declaration. It is clearly important that someone who acquires property from an attorney in these circumstances should make the declaration immediately, because were he to die before disposing of it, his successors would not be able to make a good title to it without the declaration.

Once the trustees have delegated functions under these provisions, the beneficiaries have trustees' duties and liabilities in that connection, although they are not to be regarded as trustees for other purposes. They cannot, e.g. delegate further, nor act as trustees in receiving capital money. The trustees are responsible for the acts and defaults of the beneficiaries, but only if they did not exercise reasonable care in deciding whether to delegate the functions (1996 Act s.9(7), (8)).

6. Charity trustees

(a) General

Charity trustees have the powers to delegate enjoyed by individ- **13–17** ual trustees which are explained above. However, delegation may be less important as their decisions may be taken by a majority rather than unanimously.

(b) Executing deeds

There is special legislation to take account of the fact that there **13–18** is no limit on the number of trustees of a charity, which might make it inconvenient to execute deeds and other instruments. This is an authority to delegate, although it does not have to be exercised by power of attorney. Separate provisions apply to unincorporated trustees (Charities Act 1993 s.82) and to incorporated trustees (s.60).

The power given to unincorporated trustees is subject to any modification in the trust deed. Subject to that, the trustees may give any two or more of their number the power to execute deeds, etc., on behalf of the charity and, where appropriate on behalf of the official custodian.

Trustees may be incorporated by certificate of the Charity Commission (Charities Act 1993 s.50). This is the type of incorporated body whose trustees enjoy the right to delegate the power to execute documents; it is to be distinguished from a charity incorporated under the Companies Acts. Where the incorporated body does not have a common seal, or chooses not to use it, a deed must usually be executed by being signed by a majority of the trustees. However, the trustees may confer a general or limited authority on any two or more of their number to execute deeds in the name of the charity.

In the case of both unincorporated and incorporated trustees, these points apply to the authority they can give:

(a) it may be given in writing or by a resolution of the trustees; no deed is required;

(b) it may be restricted to named trustees, any trustees of a minimum number, or in any other way; it is, however, limited to those who are trustees;

(c) it continues until revoked, notwithstanding any change of trustees; it is, nevertheless, necessarily ended if named trustees who are given the power to execute cease to be trustees.

(c) Third party protection

13–19   There is statutory protection for those dealing in good faith with trustees who have exercised their powers to delegate the execution of deeds. In favour of a purchaser, lessee, mortgagee or other person acquiring an interest in property for valuable consideration, a deed is deemed duly executed and the position is made clear on its face. It must purport to be signed by the trustees authorised to sign it on the charity's behalf (Charities Act 1993 ss.60(8), 82(4)).

The requirement of "good faith" clearly means that the third party has no protection if he knows that the statutory requirements have not been fully complied with. It is not clear how far he must initiate investigations, but it is suggested that he should make reasonable enquiries to ascertain the terms of the delegation and satisfy himself that they have been fulfilled.

7. Enduring powers of attorney

13–20   It was formerly possible for a trustee to delegate his powers by enduring power of attorney. This continues to apply in a limited number of cases. An application must have been made to register the enduring power before March 1, 2001, and the consequent registration must be continuing (Enduring Powers of Attorney Act 1985 s.3(3); 1999 Act s.4(3); 2005 Act Sch.5, para.14(4).

8. Incapable trustees

13–21   When a trustee loses mental capacity, but had previously appointed an attorney under an enduring power of attorney, there are two circumstances in which that attorney can facilitate trans-actions which might otherwise have been stymied.

(a) Sale of land

13–22   An attorney for a trustee may find himself unable to deal with land because, by virtue of the mental incapacity of the trustees or the other trustees, he cannot satisfy a two-trustee rule. In those circumstances he can exercise the statutory power to appoint a new trustee. This applies if the power of attorney, whether an ordinary power or a registered lasting or enduring power, was granted after March 1, 2000, and neither the power nor the trust instrument expresses a contrary intention (1925 Act s.36(6)–(6D)).

If a trustee of land loses mental capacity, it is normally imposs-ible to deal with the legal estate without some preliminary action.

Either, he must be replaced—which will be essential if there are only two trustees and a two-trustee rule will apply to the disposition—or he must be discharged (Law of Property Act 1925 s.22(2)). However, an attorney under a lasting power of attorney or an enduring power of attorney (whenever granted), with authority to act for the incapable trustee, may act on the trustee's behalf to effect the transaction (s.22(3); 1999 Act s.9(2)).

(b) Appointing new trustee

Obvious difficulties arise if a trustee loses mental capacity, and **13–23** either there is no-one who is entitled to appoint a new trustee in his place or there is no-one willing and able to do so. In these circumstances, there is a solution if the trust beneficiaries are of full age and capacity and, together, are absolutely entitled to the trust property.

The beneficiaries are entitled to give a written direction to an attorney appointed by the trustee under a lasting power of attorney or an enduring power of attorney, naming one or more people to be appointed trustees in place of the incapable trustee (1996 Act s.20). This necessarily depends on the trustee having granted a lasting or an enduring power, but the provision does not specify anything about the scope of that power. In particular, in appears to apply where the donor has only granted a lasting power of attorney relating to his personal welfare. However, as the attorney will not be exercising any discretion, but simply carrying out the beneficiaries' direction, the fact that the trustee might not have vested any relevant powers in him does not seem to be material.

Chapter 14

Registering Lasting Powers of Attorney

1. Introduction

A lasting power of attorney is not created unless it is registered **14–01** with the Public Guardian, and a purported power of attorney which is not registered confers no authority at all (2005 Act s.9(2)(b), (3)). Registration is therefore an essential part of granting a lasting power. An application may be made either by the donor or by the attorney(s).

It is an offence knowingly to make a false statement in a registration application. It carries a penalty on summary conviction of imprisonment for up to 12 months or a fine up to the statutory maximum (£5,000), or both, or on conviction on indictment of imprisonment for up to two years or a fine, or both (2005 Act s.4(4)).

2. Application

(a) Who applies

The registration application to the Public Guardian may be **14–02** made either by the donor or by the attorneys. Attorneys who are appointed to act jointly must all make the application, but if they are able to act jointly and severally in respect of any matter, any of them may apply (2005 Act Sch.1, para.4(2).

(b) Procedure

To apply to register a lasting power of attorney the following **14–03** must be sent to the Public Guardian, Archway Tower, 2 Junction Road, London N19 5SZ:

(i)   the prescribed application form (form LPA 002: 2007 Regs Sch.3), including any prescribed information;

(ii) the original power of attorney;

(iii) a photographic or other facsimile copy of it certified by the donor, a solicitor or a notary (2007 Regs, reg.11);

(iv) the fee (£150, but no fee for certain donors on benefit).

3. Notification

(a)   Named person

14–04   The first notification requirement must be complied with before making the application to register.

A lasting power of attorney must either name one or more people whom the donor wishes to be notified of an application to register it, or state that there is no such person. Anyone who is so identified is a "named person" (2005 Act Sch.1, para.2(1)(c), (4)). Before applying to the Public Guardian to register a lasting power of attorney, the donor or the attorneys, as the case may be, must notify the named persons. The notification must be in the prescribed form (form LPA 001: 2007 Regs Sch.2), containing any prescribed information (2005 Act Sch.1, paras 6, 9).

If the Court of Protection considers that no useful purpose would be served by giving notice, it may dispense with these notification requirements (2005 Act Sch.1, para.10).

(b)   Donor and attorneys

14–05   Once a registration application has been made, the Public Guardian must, as soon as practicable, give notification. If the donor applies, this goes to the attorney(s) (form LPA 003A: 2007 Regs reg.13(1), Sch.4, Pt 1); if an attorney applies, the donor and any attorney not joining in the application must be notified (form LPA 003B: 2007 Regs reg.13(2), Sch.4, Pt 2). A notice to an attorney who did not apply contains prescribed details of how to object to registration and the grounds (2005 Act Sch.1, paras 7, 8, 9(1)).

In addition, if the Public Guardian considers that there is good reason, he must provide the donor personally with an explanation of the notice sent to him, in a way appropriate to the donor's circumstances (e.g. simple language, visual aids, etc.) (2007 Regs reg.13(3), (4)).

4. Application considered

(a) Registration required

Subject to specified matters, the Public Guardian must register a **14–06** lasting power of attorney at the end of six weeks from the date, or the latest date, on which he gave notice the application to register (2007 Regs reg.12). The matters which may delay or prevent registration—defective instrument, deputy appointed, objections— are dealt with below.

(b) Defective instrument

If an instrument presented for registration as a lasting power of **14–07** attorney does not comply with the statutory requirements, the Public Guardian may only register it if the Court of Protection directs him to do so.

If the Public Guardian considers that the instrument contains a provision which would be ineffective as part of a lasting power of attorney, or would prevents its operating as a valid lasting power, he must apply to the Court of Protection to determine the matter. The Court has the power to sever the provision in question or to direct the Public Guardian not to register. In the case of severance, a note to that effect is attached to the registration (2005 Act s.11).

This procedure is limited to cases where something is included in the instrument which should not be in a lasting power. It would e.g. allow the severance of a provision which purported to give the attorney power to appoint a substitute or successor (precluded by the 2005 Act s.10(8)(a)). However, it would not offer a way to cure an irregularity with the execution of the instrument, as that would not be severable.

(c) Deputy appointed

If the Court of Protection has appointed a deputy for the donor, **14–08** and the deputy's powers would conflict with those of the attorney were the power to be registered, the Public Guardian may only register the instrument if the Court directs him to do so (2005 Act Sch.1, para.12).

A receiver appointed before October 1, 2007, under the Mental Health Act 1983 s.99, is treated as a deputy (2005 Act Sch.5, para.1).

(d) Objection by donor

The donor may object to a registration application by the **14–09** attorney by giving notice to the Public Guardian within five weeks of the date on which he was given notice of the application. The

notice of objection must be in writing. As well as stating the
ground for the objection, it must give the name and address of the
donor objector and the attorney(s) (if known) (2007 Regs
reg.14(2), (3)).

The registration only proceeds if the Court of Protection so
directs. It is for the attorney to apply to the Court, which must be
satisfied that the donor lacks capacity to object to the registration
(2005 Act Sch.1, para.14). So, a donor who still has capacity can
exercise a veto against registration.

(e) Objection by named person or attorney

14–10   After the Public Guardian has notified them of a registration
application, a named person or an attorney can raise an objection.
An objection must be made within five weeks from the date that
the objector was given notice of the application (2007 Regs regs
14(2), 15(3)).

An objector has two alternative courses of action. Either, he may
object to the Public Guardian. The notice of objection must be in
writing. As well as stating the ground for the objection, it must give
the name and address of the objector, the donor and the
attorney(s) (if known) (2007 Regs reg.14(3)). The possible grounds
are:

(i) in the case of a power relating to the donor's property and
affairs, that the donor has become bankrupt;

(ii) that the attorney has disclaimed the appointment;

(iii) that the attorney is dead or (except so far as the power is to
relate to the donor's personal welfare) bankrupt, or if a trust
corporation has been wound-up or dissolved;

(iv) the dissolution or annulment of a marriage or civil partnership between the donor and the attorney, unless the
instrument provides that this is not to revoke it;

(v) the attorney lacks capacity.

The Public Guardian may ask the objector for further information and must give notice to say whether or not he is satisfied that
the ground for objection is established (2007 Regs reg.14(4), (5)).
If satisfied, he must register the instrument, otherwise he must only
register if the Court so directs (2005 Act Sch.1, para.13).

The objector's alternative course is to apply to the Court of
Protection, and notify the Public Guardian in writing. This type of
objection may be on any of the following grounds (2007 Regs
reg.15(1)):

(i) that one or more of the requirements for a lasting power of attorney have not been met;

(ii) that the power has been revoked or otherwise ended. This ground does not apply in the following circumstances: the donor's bankruptcy or the dissolution of his marriage or civil partnership with the attorney; the attorney's death, bankruptcy, dissolution, lack of capacity or disclaimer;

(iii) that, in granting the lasting power, the donor was subjected to fraud or undue pressure;

(iv) that any attorney has behaved in a way that contravenes his authority or which is not in the donor's best interests, or that he proposes to do so.

The donor of a power may object to an application to register made by an attorney. He must do so, within five weeks of receiving notice, by writing to the Public Guardian giving his name and address, those of the attorney(s) if known and the grounds of his objection (2007 Regs reg.14A).

(f) Application rejected

Where the application for registration fails on certain grounds, **14–11** the Public Guardian gives notice to the applicant. They are: the power was not made as required, a deputy had been appointed, an attorney or named person objected on grounds of bankruptcy, disclaimer, death etc., the donor objected, the power or a certified copy was not sent with the application (2007 Regs reg.16).

5. Registration

(a) Notification and evidence

Once the Public Guardian has registered an instrument as a **14–12** lasting power of attorney, he returns the original power or the certified copy to the applicant and retains a copy. He must give the donor and each attorney notice on form LPA 004 (2005 Act Sch.1, para.15; 2007 Regs Sch.5).

The contents of a lasting power of attorney and the fact that it has been registered may be established by the evidence of an office copy issued by the Public Guardian. (2005 Act Sch.1, para.16(1)).

(b) Alterations

In the following cases, the Public Guardian attaches an appropri- **14–13** ate note to a registered lasting power of attorney (2005 Act Sch.1, paras 21–25):

(i) if it suspended or revoked in relation to the donor's property and affairs, but not other matters;

(ii) if an attorney's appointment has been terminated, without the power being revoked;

(iii) if the attorney has been replaced under the terms of the instrument;

(iv) if the Court of Protection notifies the Public Guardian that it has severed a provision of the instrument.

In any such case, the Public Guardian gives notice to the attorney, or the other attorneys, requiring them to return the original registered power, together with any office copy or certified copy. If any has been lost or destroyed, they must notify the Public Guardian in writing of the date and circumstances, or, if not known, a statement of when the document was last in the possession of the person required to return it. The Public Guardian returns documents which are sent in with the required note attached (2007 Regs regs 18, 19).

(c) Cancellation of registration

14–14   The Public Guardian must cancel the registration of a lasting power of attorney and notify the donor and every attorney if he is satisfied that any of the following applies (2005 Act Sch.1, para.17):

(i) in the case of a power relating to the donor's property and affairs, that the donor has become bankrupt;

(ii) that the attorney has disclaimed the appointment;

(iii) that the attorney is dead or, except so far as the power is to relate to the donor's personal welfare, bankrupt (but not merely because of an interim bankruptcy restrictions order), or if a trust corporation has been wound-up or dissolved;

(iv) the dissolution or annulment of a marriage or civil partnership between the donor and the attorney, unless the instrument provides that this is not to revoke it;

(v) the attorney lacks capacity.

There are cases in which the Court of Protection must direct the Public Guardian to cancel the registration of a lasting power of attorney (2005 Act Sch.1, paras 18, 19):

(i) when it determines that a requirement for creating a lasting power was not met, that the power has been revoked or otherwise ended;

(ii) when it revokes the power because of fraud or undue pressure on the donor;

(iii) when a lasting power contains an ineffective provision and the Court decides not to sever it.

When the registration of a lasting power of attorney is cancelled, the instrument and any office copies must be delivered up to the Public Guardian for cancellation (2005 Act Sch.1, para.20).

Chapter 15

Enduring Powers of Attorney

1. Introduction

Enduring powers of attorney were the first powers which were **15–01** not revoked by the donor's loss of mental capacity, the forerunners of lasting powers of attorney. Enduring powers were introduced by the Enduring Powers of Attorney Act 1985, which was repealed with effect from October 1, 2007 (2005 Act s.66(1)(b)). No new enduring power can now be created (2005 Act s.66(2)). But the repeal of the 1985 Act did not invalidate powers granted earlier, for which provision was made in the 2005 Act.

An enduring power had to be granted while the donor still had mental capacity. Depending on its terms, it could take effect immediately, or its effect could be delayed until the donor lost capacity. In either case, the power had to be registered after the donor lost capacity. Pending registration, the attorney's authority severely limited. An enduring power, which can take full effect before registration if the donor retains mental capacity, therefore differs from a lasting power of attorney, which is not finally created until it is registered (2005 Act s.9(2)(b)).

2. Form of power

An enduring power of attorney must be in the prescribed form, **15–02** incorporating the lengthy prescribed explanatory information, although it may differ in an immaterial respect (2005 Act Sch.4, para.2(1)–(4)). Over the period that enduring powers could be granted, different forms were prescribed by statutory instrument. The one valid at the date the power was granted had to be used. The different versions of the prescribed form are reproduced in Appendix 6.

The different regulations were in force as follows (the dates overlapped to provide transitional periods):

March 10, 1986—June 30, 1988	Enduring Powers of Attorney (Prescribed Form) Regulations 1986
November 1, 1987—July 30, 1991	Enduring Powers of Attorney (Prescribed Form) Regulations 1987
July 31, 1990—September 30, 2007	Enduring Powers of Attorney (Prescribed Form) Regulations 1990
December 5, 2005—September 30, 2007	Enduring Powers of Attorney (Prescribed Form) (Amendment) Regulations 2005

In addition a Welsh language version was prescribed:

| March 1, 2000—September 30, 2007 | Enduring Powers of Attorney (Welsh Language Prescribed Form) Regulations 2000 |
| December 5, 2005—September 30, 2007 | Enduring Powers of Attorney (Welsh Language Prescribed Form) Regulations 2005 |

An enduring power of attorney must be executed by both the donor and the attorney. When the attorney executes, which may be after the power is granted, he must be at least 18 and not bankrupt, or a trust corporation (2005 Act Sch.4, para.2(5).

3. Scope of attorney's authority

(a) General

15–03   An enduring power of attorney may give the attorney authority to do, on the donor's behalf, anything which an attorney could lawfully be authorised to do when the power was granted. In effect, this extends to the management of the donor's property and affairs, but not to personal welfare. In an individual case, the power may restrict the donor's authority or impose conditions on it (2005 Act Sch.4, para.3(1)). An enduring power cannot authorise the attorney to appoint a substitute or successor (2005 Act Sch.4, para.2(6)).

When the donor loses mental capacity, the attorney's authority is suspended pending registration, with minor exceptions. He may only take action to maintain the donor, to prevent loss to his estate and, so far as it is permitted under the power, to maintain himself and others (2005 Act Sch.4, para.1).

(b) Gifts

15–04   Subject to any terms in the power, the attorney has authority to use the donor's assets for purposes which do not directly benefit the donor. He may provide for his own or a third party's needs if the donor might be expected to do so, and may make reasonably sized gifts to charity, or on seasonal or other occasions (e.g. birthdays, Christmas, weddings) (2005 Act Sch.4, para.3(2),(3)). If an attorney disposes of the donor's property in breach of this authority and the recipient knows of the circumstances, the transaction can be set aside (*Vale v Armstrong* [2004] EWHC 1160 (Ch.)).

Whether or not a person falls into the category of those for whom the donor might be expected to provide is judged subjectively, taking account of the actual views of the donor. Equivalent words in the Mental Health Act 1959 s.102(1)(c), referring to a will making power, were interpreted by Megarry V.C. in *Re D(J)* [1982] Ch. 237 at 43:

> "Before losing testamentary capacity the patient may have been a person of strong antipathies or deep affection for particular persons or causes, or with vigorous religious or political views . . . I think the court must take the patient as he or she was before losing testamentary capacity. No doubt allowance must be made for the passage of years . . . for sometimes strong feelings mellow into indifference, and even family feuds evaporate. . . . I do not think the court should give effect to antipathies or affections of the patient which are beyond reason. But subject to all due allowances, I think the court must seek to make a will which the actual patient, acting reasonably, would have made if notionally restored to full mental capacity, memory and foresight."

The Court of Protection also has power to authorise further acts benefiting the donor or others, subject to any conditions or restriction in the power of attorney (2005 Act Sch.4, para.16(2)(e)). Gifts made as part of inheritance tax planning should be authorised in this way (*Re W* [2000] 1 All E.R. 175).

(c) Remuneration

There is some doubt about the ability of an attorney appointed **15–05** under an enduring power of attorney to charge for his services. Although, subject to restrictions in the power and imposed by statute, the attorney may do on the donor's behalf anything which the donor could lawfully do by an attorney, there are strict limits on his benefiting himself. He is restricted to what the donor might be expected to do to meet his needs (2005 Act Sch.4, para.3(1), (2)). That does not seem appropriate to cover the payment of professional fees. However, the notes which are part of the prescribed form of enduring power say,

"If your attorney(s) are professional people, for example solicitors or accountant, they may be able to charge for their professional services as well [as recovering out-of-pocket expenses]".

In the light of this ambiguity, the Law Society recommended that, where a professional attorney was appointed, a charging clause be inserted in the power. It would be possible for an attorney to apply to the Court of Protection for authority to pay fees for his own benefit (2005 Act Sch.4, para.16(2)(e)).

4. Registration

15–06   As soon as the attorney has reason to believe that the donor is, or is becoming, mentally incapable, he has a duty to register an enduring power of attorney with the Public Guardian (formerly with the Court of Protection) (2005 Act Sch.4, para.4(1), (2)). The registration procedure falls into two parts. First, the attorney must give a series of notices—to relatives, to the donor and to other attorneys—and secondly, he must make the application to register. Notices sent by post are treated as given when posted (2005 Act Sch.4, para.12). The registration fee is £120, which is waived for certain donors on benefit.

(a)   Notice to relatives

15–07   The attorney has to give notice of his intention to apply for registration to all the specified relatives of the donor. There is a prescribed form (form EP1PG: 2007 Regs, Sch.7) stating that the attorney proposes to apply to the Public Guardian for registration and informing the recipient of the right to object, and summarising the grounds (2005 Act Sch.4, para 9). Notice must go to up to three relatives, taken from the following list in this order of preference. But if one person in any category is entitled to receive notice, then notice must go to every person in that category even though that means that more than three people receive notice (2005 Act Sch.4, para.6(1), (2), (4)). The relatives entitled are:

   (i)   spouse or civil partner,

   (ii)   children,

   (iii)   parents,

   (iv)   siblings, of the whole or the half blood,

   (v)   widow, widower or surviving civil partner, of a child

(vi) grandchildren,

(vii) children of siblings of the whole blood,

(ix) children of siblings of the half blood,

(x) uncles and aunts of the whole blood,

(xi) children of uncles and aunts of the whole blood.

Accordingly, if the donor has a spouse and three adult children, all of them must receive notice—although that means giving notice to four relatives—but no relative in any remoter class is entitled to notice.

To this, there are exceptions. The attorney need not give notice to: anyone whom the attorney has reason to believe is under 18 or is mentally incapable; anyone whose name and address the attorney does not know, and cannot reasonably ascertain; another attorney who is jointly applying to register; the attorney himself. The attorney may also apply to the court to dispense with giving notice to someone if it would be undesirable or impracticable or it would serve no useful purpose (2005 Act Sch.4, paras 6(2), 7).

(b) Notice to donor

The attorney must give the donor notice of an application to **15–08** register, unless the court dispenses with notice on the ground that it would be undesirable or impracticable or it would serve no useful purpose. There is a prescribed form stating that the attorney proposes to apply to the Public Guardian for registration and telling the donor that after registration the power can only be revoked with the court's confirmation (2005 Act Sch.4, paras 8, 10). In addition to the notice, the attorney must provide the donor personally with an explanation of the notice, in a way which is appropriate to his circumstances (2007 Regs reg.23).

(c) Notice to other attorneys

An attorney who intends to apply to register a joint and several **15–09** power must give notice of his intention to any other attorney who is not joining in the application. The notice is on form EP1PG (2007 Regs Sch.7) and states that the attorney proposes to apply to the Public Guardian for registration. It tells the recipient of his right to object, and sets out the possible grounds. This does not apply if the attorney who is applying does not know the other attorney's address and cannot reasonably ascertain it, if the applying attorney believes that the other is under 18 or is mentally incapable or if the court dispenses with the notice on the ground that notice would be undesirable, impracticable or would serve no useful purpose (2005 Act Sch.4, para.11).

(d) Application to register

15–10 An application to register an enduring power of attorney is made in the prescribed form (form EP2PG: 2007 Regs Sch.8) to the Public Guardian. It must be accompanied by the original power or a copy of it, certified as required to prove its contents (para.8–05; 1971 Act s.3; 2007 Regs, reg.24). Registration is automatic, except in the following cases (2005 Act, Sch.4, paras 4(4), 13(1)–(8)):

(i) if the court has appointed a deputy for the donor, to make decisions on his behalf in relation to specified matters (2005 Act s.16), the Public Guardian may only register in accordance with the court's directions;

(ii) on the attorney's application, the court may order registration even though notice of the application was not given to a particular person, if to do so would be undesirable, impracticable or would serve no useful purpose;

(iii) if a person entitled to receive notice of the application gives the Public Guardian a valid notice of objection within five weeks from the date, or the last date, on which the attorney gave notice, the Public Guardian must only register in accordance with the court's directions. If any ground is established to the court's satisfaction, it must direct the Public Guardian not to register, otherwise it must direct registration;

(iv) if the application states that no notice of the application has been given or the Public Guardian has reason to believe that appropriate enquiries might bring to light evidence of one of the grounds of objection, he must undertake enquiries. If he is satisfied that one of the grounds for objection has been established, he must only register the power in accordance with the court's directions;

(v) if neither the original power nor a certified copy accompanied the application to register, the Public Guardian may only register it if the court directs him to do so.

(e) Objections to registration

15–11 Notice of an object to registration must be given in writing to the Public Guardian. It must set out the names and addresses of the objector, the donor (if different) and the attorney(s) (if known). It must also state the ground for making the objection (2007 Regs reg.25).

There are five grounds for objection to registration (2005 Act Sch.4, para.13(9)):

(i) That the instrument did not create a valid power of attorney. The burden of proof that there was no valid power rests on the objector (*Re W* [2001] Ch. 609);

(ii) That the power is no longer subsisting;

(iii) That the application is premature, because the donor is not yet becoming mentally incapable;

(iv) That the donor was induced to grant the power by fraud or undue pressure;

(v) That the attorney is unsuitable to be the donor's attorney, having regard to all the circumstances and in particular the attorney's relationship to or connection with the donor. If the attorney is a competent person, the hostility of a sibling, without evidence that continuing hostility will impede the proper administration of the estate, does not establish this ground of objection (*Re F, The Times*, April 29, 2004).

Where a power appoints more than one attorney to act jointly and severally, an objection may sustained in respect of some but not others. In that event, it may be registered in relation only to the attorneys about whom there was not a valid objection. An appropriate entry is then made in the register and the power is endorsed (2007 Regs reg.28).

(f) Finalising registration application

If the Public Guardian cannot register an enduring power on **15–12** certain grounds, he notifies the applicant(s). The grounds are: deputy already appointed, valid objection, further enquiries to be made, no deed or copy supplied (2007 Regs reg.26).

When registration has been effected, the Public Guardian keeps a copy of the enduring power of attorney, and returns the original or the certified copy to the applicant(s) (2007 Regs reg.27).

5. Duration of enduring power

(a) Bankruptcy

An enduring power of attorney is revoked if the donor or any **15–13** attorney becomes bankrupt, although if this is merely because an interim bankruptcy restrictions order has been made the power is simply suspended. The bankruptcy of an attorney appointed by a joint power terminates the authority of every other attorney, but in the case of a joint and several attorney the authority of other attorneys is not affected (2005 Act Sch.4, paras 2(7), (8), 21(2), 22(1), (2)).

(b) Appointment of deputy

15–14   If the court exercises its powers to make decisions about the donor's personal welfare or to appoint a deputy (2005 Act ss.16–20) and directs that the enduring power be revoked, the power is revoked (2005 Act Sch.4, para.2(9).

(c) Disclaimer

15–15   An attorney who wishes to disclaim an enduring power must give written notice of the disclaimer to the donor before it can take effect. However, once the attorney has reason to believe that the donor is or is becoming mentally incapable, so that he is under a duty to register the enduring power of attorney, the notice of disclaimer must be given to the Public Guardian. The same applies, necessarily, after the power has been registered (2005 Act Sch.4, paras 2(10), 4(6), 15(1)).

(d) Objection to registration

15–16   If the court directs the Public Guardian not to register a power either on the ground that the donor was induced to grant it by fraud or undue influence, or on the ground that the attorney is unsuitable, it must order that the power be revoked (2005 Act Sch.4, para 13(11)).

(e) Revocation

15–17   After an enduring power of attorney has been registered, the donor can only revoke it after confirmation by the court. The court must be satisfied that the donor has done what was necessary in law to effect an express revocation and that he was mentally capable of revoking a power when he did so (2005 Act Sch.4, paras 15(1)(a), 16(3)).

6. Cancelling registration

15–18   In certain cases, the court must direct the Public Guardian to cancel the registration of an enduring power of attorney. They are (2005 Act Sch.4, para.16):

(i) when the power has expired, been revoked, or the court directs that it is to be;

(ii) when the donor is and is likely to remain mentally capable;

(iii) if the power was not valid and subsisting when registered;

(iv) if fraud or undue pressure induced the donor to create the power;

(v) on being satisfied that the attorney is unsuitable to be the donor's attorney.

The original power of attorney must be delivered up to the Public Guardian to be cancelled if the court directs that the registration be cancelled, except where the reason is that the donor is not incapable (2005 Act Sch.4, para.16(6)). If the document has been lost or destroyed, the person who should have delivered it up must give the Public Guardian a written statement of the date and circumstances, but if they are not known must say when the document was last in his possession (2007 Regs reg.29).

7. Transitional provisions

The repeal of the Enduring Powers of Attorney Act 1985 does **15–19** not prejudice the effect of actions under that Act. Specifically (2005 Act Sch.5, paras 11, 12):

(i) an enduring power of attorney registered under it by the Court of Protection is treated as having been registered by the Public Guardian. A pending application to register is treated as an application to the Public Guardian;

(ii) an order or determination made under the 1985 Act continues to have effect;

(iii) a pending application, or object to registration, is treated as the equivalent under the 2005 Act.

Chapter 16

Filed Powers

Note: In this chapter, references to section 25 of the Trustee Act 1925 are references to it as originally enacted.

1. Introduction

Before October 1, 1971 certain powers of attorney had to be **16–01** filed at the Central Office of the Supreme Court or at the Land Registry. In addition, other powers could be filed at the court voluntarily. The object of filing was to create a permanent record and to facilitate proof of the contents of the power. Office copies of filed powers could be obtained that were equally admissible with the original.

The possibility of filing powers of attorney was withdrawn on October 1, 1971 (1971 Act s.2(1); repealed, Supreme Court Act 1981 Sch.7). From that date, the revised system of providing the contents of a power by a certified photostat copy superseded proof by production of an office copy.

The former rules about filing powers remain of importance in assessing the validity of powers pursuant to which documents were executed or acts undertaken prior to October 1, 1971, for example, in examining the title to land. Notwithstanding the withdrawal of filing facilities, it is still possible to obtain office copies of some filed powers.

2. Compulsory filing

In certain cases a power of attorney had to be filed if it was to be **16–02** valid.

(a) Land

A power authorising the attorney to dispose of or deal with any **16–03** interest in or charge on land had to be filed. As an alternative, a certified copy of all the relevant portions of it had to be filed (Law of Property Act 1925 s.125(1)). To this, there were three exceptions:

(i) if the power related to a single transaction and the original was handed over on completion;

(ii) if the power related only to registered land or a registered charge and, as an alternative, was filed at HM Land Registry;

(iii) if the power of attorney was executed before January 1, 1926 (Law of Property Act 1925 s.125(3)).

A power granted by a trustee who was going to be absent from the United Kingdom might give power to deal with registered land. In that case, the power had first to be filed at the court, and then an office copy had to be filed at HM Land Registry (1925 Act s.25(6)).

(b) Trustees

16–04 A power of attorney executed by a trustee who intended to remain out of the United Kingdom for over a month, and which delegated any of the trustee's trusts, powers and discretions, had to be filed at the court within ten days after its execution. When filed, it had to be accompanied by a statutory declaration by the donor that he intended to remain abroad for more than a month from the date of the declaration or from a date stated in it (1925 Act s.25(4)). For this purpose, the term "trustee" included a tenant for life and a statutory owner (s.25(11)).

(c) Servicemen

16–05 Powers of attorney executed between June 12, 1940 and July 31, 1953 by members of the armed forces outside the United Kingdom, and those executed by British subjects in enemy occupied territory, had to be filed (Evidence and Powers of Attorney Act 1940 s.3).

3. Proof of filed powers

(a) Central Office

16–06 Office copies of powers of attorney filed in the Central Office of the Supreme Court after 1967 may still be obtained from the Central Office. Those filed between 1942 and 1967 have been destroyed. Older ones were transferred to the Public Record Office (see below). An office copy is proof of the contents of the power and of the fact that it has been filed, and is admissible in evidence (Supreme Court Act 1981 s.134).

Anyone may search the alphabetical index of donors' names in Room 81 in the Royal Courts of Justice, Strand, London WC2A 2LL, and may inspect any filed instrument or copy. Office copies may be obtained.

(b) National Archives

Powers of attorney which were filed at the Central Office of the **16–07** Supreme Court before 1942 are now housed at the National Archives, Ruskin Avenue, Surrey TW9 4DN (*http:// www.nationalarchives.gov.uk*). Advance notice should be given before inspecting. A certified copy under the seal of the Public Record Office is admissible in evidence (Public Records Act 1958 s.9).

(c) Land Registry

A power of attorney, of which the original or a copy is filed at **16–08** H.M. Land Registry, will normally be referred to on the register. An official copy may be requested, and can often be obtained in electronic form. An official copy is admissible in evidence to the same extent as the original (Land Registration Act 2002 s.67(1)).

4. Filing deeds of revocation

A deed revoking a power of attorney could also be filed at the **16–09** Central Office of the Supreme Court. If the power had been filed, it was marked "revoked". It was not, of course, possible to ensure that office copies issued earlier were so endorsed.

It is still possible to file a deed of revocation.

Chapter 17

Land

1. Registered land procedure

(a) Confirming attorney's authority

When any document executed by an attorney is delivered to the **17–01** land registry, the authenticity of the execution must be established. This is done by producing one of the following (Land Registration Rules 2003 r.61):

   (i) the original power of attorney;

  (ii) a copy which meets the statutory requirements for proving the contents of the power (para.8–05);

 (iii) an office copy of a lasting power of attorney (2005 Act Sch.1, para.16), of an enduring power of attorney (Enduring Powers of Attorney Act 1985 s.7(3) or 2005 Act Sch.4, para.15(3)) or of a power executed by a member of the armed services overseas (Evidence and Powers of Attorney Act 1940 s.4);

 (iv) a certificate signed by a solicitor, licensed conveyancer or fellow of the Institute of Legal Executives. This is in a prescribed form (Land Registration Rules 2003 Sch.3, Form 1). It gives the date of the power, confirms that it is in existence and has been registered if required, that he is satisfied that it is valid and authorises the use made of it and that he holds the original or a copy in one of the categories above.

In addition, any order made by the Court of Protection relating to the power or to the donor (Enduring Powers of Attorney Act 1985 s.8 ss.22, 26; 2005 Act Sch.4, para.16), must be produced.

(b) Proof of non-revocation

17–02   When more than 12 months have elapsed between when the power of attorney came into operation and the completion of the transaction to the registered, the Registrar may—but will not usually—require proof that the power of attorney has not been revoked. If the completion was within the year, it is irrelevant that the registration application is later.

The evidence may consist of or include a statutory declaration by the person dealing with the attorney or a conveyancer's certificate (Land Registration Rules 2003 r.62). The certificate—to be given by a solicitor, a licensed conveyancer, a fellow of the Institute of Legal Executives or a certificated notary public—or the statutory declaration is in a prescribed form (Land Registration Rules 2003 Sch.3, Form 2).

In all cases the statutory declaration or certificate confirms no knowledge of:

   (i)   the revocation of the power,

   (ii)   the donor's death, bankruptcy, winding up or dissolution,

   (iii)   or, unless the power is a valid lasting or enduring power, any incapacity of the donor.

In the case of a power of attorney which is not an ordinary power, further matters must be added.

LASTING POWER OF ATTORNEY
The statutory declaration or certificate also confirms no knowledge of:

   (i)   the fact that a lasting power was not created,

   (ii)   circumstances which, had a lasting power been created, would have ended the attorney's authority.

ENDURING POWER OF ATTORNEY
The statutory declaration or certificate also confirms no knowledge of:

   (i)   the fact that the power is not a valid enduring power,

   (ii)   an order of the Court of Protection revoking the power, or

   (iii)   the bankruptcy of the attorney.

IRREVOCABLE POWER OF ATTORNEY
The statutory declaration or certificate also confirms no knowledge of:

   (i) that the power was not in fact given by way of security,

  (ii) any revocation of the power with the attorney's consent, or

 (iii) any other event which would revoke the power.

DELEGATION TO BENEFICIARIES OF TRUST OF LAND
The statutory declaration or certificate also confirms no knowledge of:

   (i) an appointment of another trustee,

  (ii) any other event which would revoke the power,

 (iii) any lack of good faith on the part of those who dealt with the attorney, or

 (iv) the attorney being someone to whom the trustees could not delegate their functions.

In this case, there may also be an additional requirement consisting of evidence relating to the person who dealt with the attorney. The evidence may consist of or include a statutory declaration by that person or a conveyancer's certificate (Land Registration Rules 2003 r.63). The certificate—to be given by a solicitor, a licensed conveyancer, a fellow of the Institute of Legal Executives or a certificated notary public—or the statutory declaration is in a prescribed form (Land Registration Rules 2003, Sch.3, Form 3). It confirms no knowledge of:

   (i) a lack of good faith on the part of the person dealing with the attorney, of

  (ii) the attorney being a person to whom the trustees could not delegate their functions.

The forms of statutory declaration or certificate are reproduced in Appendix 2.

(c) Joint proprietors

If a joint proprietor of registered land takes advantage of the **17–03** ability to grant an ordinary, a lasting or an enduring power of attorney to deal with his beneficial share in the property (which is, necessarily, trust property), the attorney needs to give a written statement within three months that the donor had a beneficial interest in the property.

The Land Registry suggests that this may most conveniently be done in the disposition itself (*Practice Guide 9*). This could be:

(i) a statement in the body of the document, "[The attorney] confirms that [the donor] has a beneficial interest in the property at the date of this [transfer/charge/lease]";

(ii) by adapting the attestation clause, "Signed as a deed by [the donor], who has a beneficial interest in the property, at the date of this [transfer/charge/lease], acting by [the attorney] his attorney in the presence of";

(iii) adding to the signature, "[The donor] by his attorney [the attorney] who confirms that [the donor] has a beneficial interest in the property at this date".

2. Unregistered land

(a) Title

17–04   A power of attorney forms part of the title to unregistered land when any abstracted document was executed by an attorney. In order to be sure that the document had the effect claimed for it, the validity of the power at the date it was used must be established. The title to land is defective if one of the deeds which goes to make it up was executed under a power of attorney invalid for the purpose (*Walia v Michael Naughton Ltd.* [1985] 1 W.L.R. 1115).

The power must therefore be abstracted. This applies even if the power was granted before the execution of the root of title, which will necessarily be the case if the document constituting the root of title was itself executed by an attorney (Law of Property Act 1925 s.45(1)). It also applies even if that instrument is the root of title as it is more than 15 years old (*Re Copelin's Contract* [1937] 4 All E.R. 447). If the power was one that should have been filed at the Central Office of the Supreme Court the abstract should provide evidence that it was indeed filed. A statement in a power granted during the period from June 12, 1940 to July 31, 1953 to the effect that the Evidence and Powers of Attorney Act 1940 did not apply can be relied upon by a purchaser (s.3(3)).

A purchaser of any interest in or charge upon land is entitled to have any power of attorney executed after January 1, 1926 and affecting his title, or a copy of all or the material portions of it, delivered to him free of expense (Law of Property Act 1925 s.125(2)). This right applies equally to a lessee or mortgagee (s.205(1)(xxi)). It cannot be excluded by any contract to the contrary, nor can a contract be rescinded merely because of the enforcement of this right to a copy (s.125(3)).

(b) Pre-1971 Act irrevocable powers

17–05   Before the 1971 Act came into force on October 1, 1971, there were other statutory provisions for creating irrevocable powers of attorney after December 31, 1882, on which it may be necessary to rely in making title to unregistered land. There were two categories of irrevocable powers.

First, a power of attorney given for valuable consideration could be expressed to be irrevocable (Law of Property Act 1925 s.126). Secondly, a power could be expressed to be irrevocable for a fixed term of up to one year (s.127).

In either case, this had three effects, either permanently in the case of powers in the first category, or, for those in the second category, during the period for which it was expressed to be irrevocable. In favour of a bona fide purchaser for value, lessee or mortgagee:

(i) the power was not revoked by the death, disability or bankruptcy of the donor, or by any act of the donor without the attorney's concurrence;

(ii) any act of the attorney was as valid as it would have been ignoring any of those events in (i) which did not revoke the power; and

(iii) neither the attorney, nor the purchaser, lessee or mortgagee, was prejudiced by notice of any of the events in (i) declared not to revoke the power.

Questions arose as to the extent to which these powers could be relied upon. It was suggested, for example, that an attorney could not continue to act under the authority conferred by the power after he knew of the donor's death. Also, it was not clear how far a conveyance by the attorney could be effective where the death of the donor had vested the legal estate in his personal representatives.

Nevertheless, it was not the practice to query the execution of an instrument during the period for which a power was expressed to be irrevocable, in the absence of unusual circumstances putting the purchaser on enquiry. Considering the period that must now necessarily have elapsed since a power of attorney was exercised in reliance on these provisions, it is suggested that the grounds for reversing the presumption *omnia praesumuntur solemniter ac rite esse acta* would have to be all the stronger.

Once a period of irrevocability expired, the power did not become void. It continued as a revocable one. In that case, or if there had been no period of irrevocability, the attorney could make a statutory declaration that he had not received any notice or information of the revocation of the power by death or otherwise. A declaration made immediately before or within three months after an act performed under the power was conclusive proof of non-revocation at the time the act was done (Law of Property Act 1925 s.124(2)).

(c) Waiver of defect

17–06   If a seller of land knows of a defect in title relating to a power of attorney, he can by contract oblige the buyer to accept the title as it is, except that he cannot exclude the buyer's right to the delivery of any relevant power of attorney (Law of Property Act 1925 s.125(2)). In the case of a power that is irretrievably lost, the solution appears to be to formulate a contract condition that the seller will make title without reliance upon the instrument executed under the power, even if that means offering a purely possessory title.

In other cases, the buyer can be required to accept a title that is less than perfect as long as he is not misled. Appropriate special conditions might read:

PERIOD OF IRREVOCABILITY EXPIRED
A conveyance of the property   dated to which the parties were   was executed on behalf of   , who then sold the property, by an attorney appointed by a power of attorney dated   which was expressed to be irrevocable for one year from the date that it was executed. That conveyance was executed more than one year after the power of attorney was granted. The Seller has no evidence that the power of attorney had then been revoked. The Buyer shall assume without requisition or objection that the power of attorney was and remained valid and had not been revoked when the conveyance was executed.

VALIDITY OF CONDITIONAL POWER OF ATTORNEY
A conveyance of the property dated   to which the parties were   was executed on behalf of   ("the donor"), who then sold the property, by an attorney appointed by a power of attorney dated   which was expressed to be valid during such time as the donor was out of the United Kingdom. The conveyance contains a recital stating that at that date the donor was out of the United Kingdom. The Seller has not reason to doubt the accuracy of that recital. The Buyer shall assume it to be a fact and shall not be entitled to raise any requisition or object in relation to it.

3. Interpretation

17–07   When any power granted after March 1, 2000, authorises the attorney to do an act in relation to land, that authority extends to every interest which the donor has in the land at the date the act is done unless the power provides otherwise (1999 Act, s.10). So, power "to sell my house Blackacre" applies to a sale of the legal estate and/or any equitable interest which the donor has. This is particularly important in relation to jointly beneficially owned property. The donor will be both joint owner of the legal estate as trustee and, as beneficiary, owner of an equitable interest, but the way that powers are worded often ignores this technicality.

4. Examples of use

(a) Mortgage of flat and company share

Many schemes for developing flats , and occasionally other types **17–08** of property, include provision for each leaseholder of a flat to hold one share in a company which provides services for the block. Sometimes the company owns the freehold reversion. The intention is that the leases and the shares shall always belong to the same people. The leases and the articles of association of the company restrict ownership of the one to the person who owns the other.

Difficulties arise when a leaseholder wants to mortgage his lease. The mortgagee must ensure that if he has to exercise his power of sale, not only can he vest the lease in the purchaser, but also the share in the service company. The share itself has little or no intrinsic value, but its ownership is essential to comply with the tenant's covenants in the lease. The necessary power can be conferred by a clause in the mortgage granting a power of attorney.

Precedent

> The Borrower irrevocably[1] appoints the Lender to be his attorney to execute a transfer of the ordinary share of £1 in
>   Limited registered in the name of the Borrower to any person to whom the Lender sells the property[2]

(b) Sale of block of flats

When the landlord of a block of flats wants to dispose of his **17–09** interest he will often have to offer the tenants of the individual flats a statutory right of first refusal (Landlord and Tenant Act

---

[1] Although expressed to be irrevocable to obtain the advantage of s.5(3) of the 1971 Act, the power will necessarily come to an end on the redemption of the mortgage. Section 6 will not apply, as this share will not be in a quoted company.

[2] It would be more reassuring to the borrower to limit the power by adding the words "in exercise of the statutory power of sale", but that would involve the company in investigating the nature of the sale of the lease before registering the share transfer. As the sale of the share must necessarily be ancillary to the sale of the flat, this extra safeguard hardly seems necessary.

1987, Pt 1). If they pay the same price as the landlord would have obtained elsewhere, which is the intention, it may be thought that he is not prejudiced. But there may be some months of uncertainty before it is clear whether or not the tenants will exercise their rights.

Nothing in the Act precludes a landlord persuading his tenants to contract with him not to exercise their rights. There is a statutory procedure excluding the right of first refusal if a sufficient proportion of tenants notify a prospective purchaser that they will not avail themselves of it (s.18). This does not appear to be available to the landlord in advance of his finding a buyer, but it is suggested that he can legitimately contract to become attorney for the tenants to waive their rights when a prospective buyer serves notices with a view to obtaining waivers.

Precedent

The Tenant irrevocably[3] appoints the Landlord to be his attorney until [date] to receive and respond to any notice served under section 18 of the Landlord and Tenant Act 1987 relating to the sale of [property] for no less than £[4]

(c) Letting commonhold unit

17–10   One of the fundamental features of a commonhold development is that the owners of the commonhold units, the unitholders, are members of the commonhold association which owns the common parts and is responsible for the provision of services. That is how they participate in the communal management. If a commonhold unit is let, the tenant does not have that right of participation. Where the tenant has paid a premium, so that the letting is on terms which transfers the major economic interest in the premises to the tenant—which is mainly likely to affect commercial properties, as the terms on which residential units can be let are restricted—the landlord can cede his role in the management of the development by granting a power of attorney in the lease.

Precedent

As a member of the Commonhold Association Limited ("Association"), the Landlord irrevocably appoints the Tenant for the

---

[3] Although expressed to be irrevocable, the power necessarily express when the stated period ends.
[4] Even though the power is given as part of a contract for which the Landlord pays a consideration to the Tenant, it must be a deed to make the power of attorney valid.

time being to be his attorney for the duration of the term of the lease, to act on the Landlord's behalf to receive all notices from the Association, to attend and to speak at general meetings of the Association and to vote on resolutions proposed.

Chapter 18

Grants of Representation

1. Grants to attorney

(a) Capable donor

An executor or a person entitled to be appointed administrator **18–01** may, if he has mental capacity, appoint an attorney to apply for letters of administration on his use and behalf. The grant is limited until further representation is granted, or in any other way the registrar directs (Non Contentious Probate Rules 1987 r.31(1)). If the donor is an executor, notice of the application must be given to every other executor, unless the registrar disposes with it (r.31(2)).

An executor who has renounced can apply for a grant as someone else's attorney, but a person who has renounced administration can only do so if a registrar directs (r.37(1),(2)). An attorney's substitute may take a grant if the power gives authority to appoint a substitute (*Palliser v Ord* (1724) Bunb. 166). Similarly, an attorney's attorney can apply, where the form of delegation is allowed by the law of the deceased's domicile (*In the Goods of Abdul Hamid Bey* (1898) 67 L.J.P. 59).

(b) Donor lacking mental capacity

An attorney under a lasting power of attorney or under an **18–02** enduring power of attorney may apply for a grant of representation on behalf of a donor who lacks mental capacity and different rules apply (Non-Contentious Probate Rules 1987, r.31(3)). Two conditions must be met.

First, all those entitled to a grant in the same degree as the donor must be cleared off, unless a registrar otherwise directs. Secondly, there must be no-one authorised to apply by the Court of Protection (r.35(1),(2)).

Notice of an application must be given to the Court of Protection (r.35(5)). The grant is to the attorney for the use and benefit of the donor. It is limited until further representation is granted or in such other way as the registrar directs.

2. Power of attorney

(a) Scope

18–03   It must be clear from the power of attorney that it grants authority to the attorney to apply for a grant of administration, normally naming the deceased. A general power is acceptable, particularly in the 1971 Act general form, and may even have been granted before the deceased died (*In the Goods of Barker* [1891] P. 251). A power of attorney which only gives authority to administer particular parts of a deceased's estate will not normally be accepted for the purposes of a grant. The authority of a donor and of the attorney should be coextensive.

There is no need for the power to contain any special provisions to enable the attorney to apply for a grant in another estate, to which his position as personal representative in the first one entitles him.

For a precedent of a power of attorney granted by an executor and of a power of attorney granted by a person entitled to letters of administration, see Appendix 3, paras A3–21, A3–220.

(b) Form

18–04   Execution of a power of attorney which complies with the 1971 Act satisfies the requirements for appointing an attorney to apply for a grant. The execution should be attested by a disinterested witness. If the donor executes the power in England or Wales before going abroad it should show that he was about to leave. The attorney must swear in his oath that the donor is then residing outside the jurisdiction if that is the case.

Where one attorney is appointed to act on behalf of more than one executor, and the executors live in different countries, there need not be a joint appointment by a single power, although that is acceptable. The alternative is a series of powers in similar terms each making the same appointment on behalf of one of the executors.

Special attention must be paid to the form of the power if it is granted in a country which is not English speaking. When it is written in English it is acceptable if the witness to the donor's signature is a notary or a British consul. In the absence of that attestation, there must be a sufficient indication that the donor understood English. The extracting solicitor can provide a certificate to that effect. If the power is not in English, a translation certified by a competent authority is required. In cases of doubt whether a country is regarded as English speaking, the question should be referred to a registrar.

(c) Filing

The normal practice is for the power of attorney to be perma- **18–05** nently filed in the registry. A general power which is required for other purposes can be issued out again. A copy is lodged with the power and a request for its return. It is then issued with the grant. This arrangement cannot apply to a power that is limited to obtaining the grant.

The power of attorney may have been deposited with a notary or court of law abroad. In such a case, a notarial copy may be filed. It must be accompanied by an affidavit of law that the copy is as valid as the original and would be accepted instead by the court of domicile.

(d) Donor's incapacity

The authority of an attorney under an ordinary power of **18–06** attorney will come to an end if the grantor becomes mentally incapable before the administration of the deceased's estate has been finished. However, if the donor has appointed the same attorney under an enduring power of attorney with sufficiently wide authority, and that power has been registered with the Court of Protection, the attorney will be able to continue with the administration of the estate.

(e) Donor's death

The donor's death revokes the power of attorney, and therefore **18–07** the attorney's authority to act in the administration (*Suwerkrop v Day* (1838) 8 A. & E. 624). An attorney who continues to act in ignorance of the donor's death has the general statutory protection. If the administration of the estate is interrupted by the death of the donor, a further grant *de bonis non* is required.

3. Attorney

(a) Capacity

As the grant of administration will be made to the attorney in his **18–08** own name, albeit for the use and benefit of the donor, the attorney must have the capacity to take a grant. A minor does not qualify

(Non Contentious Probate Rules 1987, r.32). A power of attorney for this purpose may be granted in favour of a member for the time being of a named firm. The attorney's oath must then show that he is a member of the firm.

(b) Responsibilities

18–09 An attorney to whom letters of administration are granted is personally fully liable as administrator (*Re Rendell, Wood v Rendell* [1901] 1 Ch. 230). That liability entitles the attorney to retain the assets while there are outstanding claims against the part of the estate within the jurisdiction, but he must account to his principal for any ascertained surplus. A receipt for that from his principal is a good discharge to the attorney (*Eames v Hacon* (1881) 18 Ch. D. 347).

(c) Death

18–10 The death of the attorney necessarily brings to an end his power to administer the estate. If the administration is not complete, a cessate grant is needed. The donor may appoint another attorney or may apply for a direct grant.

4. Joint executors

(a) Form of power

18–11 Joint executors can all execute one power of attorney appointing a single attorney, or joint attorneys on behalf of them all; or they can execute separate powers, either appointing the same or different attorneys.

If there are more than four executors, and they all execute the same power, it must limit the term of the attorney's appointment. The limitation must be "until any of us, not exceeding four in number, shall apply . . . ". A power not including that numerical limitation is not acceptable.

(b) Limit on grant

18–12 The limit placed on the grant of administration depends on the circumstances.

(1) *Attorney for all executors* The grant is limited until all the executors apply for and obtain probate. If, later, some only of the executors apply, a grant will be made to them if the others have not intermeddled, even through their attorney. If one of the executors dies, the position is uncertain. The grant may cease to be effective. The survivor can revoke the power of attorney, whereupon the court can revoke the grant and issue a fresh one to another attorney appointed under another power (*In the Estate of Dinshaw* [1930] P. 180).

(2) *Executors' separate attorneys* The grant ceases on the death of either executor or either attorney. An application for a grant of probate by either executor also brings the attorney grant to an end.

5. Delegation by personal representatives

The power of a personal representative to delegate his function **18–13** as such after obtaining a grant of representation in his own name is the same as the delegation power of a trustee under the Trustee Act (1925 Act s.25(10)).

6. Consuls

A consul of a country named by Order in Council may apply for **18–14** a grant of representation in place of a foreign national not resident in England, who is named as an executor, where no attorney applies on his behalf (Consular Conventions Act 1949 s.1(1)). Such a consul also has the power to receive money and property in England, which is due to a foreign national not resident in England on behalf of a deceased's estate. He can give a valid discharge as if he were appointed by a power of attorney (s.1(2)).

Chapter 19

Companies

1. Shareholder's proxy

(a) Right to grant

A proxy is a person appointed by a shareholder of a company to **19–01** attend and vote at a meeting of the company. Confusingly, the word is also applied to the document granting that authority. The proxy's authority may be general or limited. In the sphere to which his authority relates, a proxy is in effect the shareholder's attorney. He need not himself be a member of the company.

A member of a private company is only entitled to appoint one proxy for any one occasion, unless the articles of the company provide otherwise (Companies Act 1985 s.372(1),(2)).

The right to appoint a proxy applies to members of all companies formed or registered under the Companies Act 1985 and companies existing when that Act was passed (s.735(1)(a)), other than companies without a share capital. In that case, the company's articles can allow the appointment of proxies (s.372(1),(2)).

The appointment of a proxy may be revoked at any time before it is acted upon.

A corporate shareholder has an additional right. It can appoint, by a resolution of the directors or other governing body, a person to attend meetings of any company of which it is a member (s.375(1)). That representative is not a proxy. A proxy's power may be limited, but a corporation's representative is entitled to exercise all the powers that the corporation would have had if it had been an individual shareholder (s.375(2)). He is accordingly counted as one of a quorum (*Re Kelantan Coconut Estates (Ltd. and Reduced)* (1920) 64 S.J. 700).

The Companies Act 2006 will allow the articles of association of a company to authorise a member to nominate someone else to exercise rights which they specify. Among those rights can be the right to appoint a proxy (Companies Act 2006 s.145).

(b) Exercising right to appoint

19–02   A notice calling a meeting of the members of a company with a share capital must contain a statement, given reasonable prominence, about members' rights to appoint proxies. It must say that a member entitled to attend and vote is entitled to appoint a proxy—or, if allowed, more than one proxy—to attend and vote instead of him. It must add that the proxy need not be a member of the company. If the statement is not included, the officers of the company are guilty of an offence (Companies Act 1985 s.372(3),(4)).

The articles of a company normally require that an instrument appointing a proxy shall be deposited at the registered office of the company, or with its registrar or secretary, prior to the meeting (e.g. Companies Act 1948, Table A, art.69; Companies (Tables A to F) Regulations 1985, Table A, art.62). If lodged too late, an appointment is not valid (*Shaw v Tari Concessions Ltd.* [1913] 1 Ch. 292). Any provision requiring an instrument to be lodged more than forty-eight hours before the meeting is void (Companies Act 1985, s.372(5)).

Companies frequently distribute forms for appointing proxies to their members. To do so to only some of the members entitled to be sent notice of a meeting, unless at the written request of a member, is an offence on the part of the officers knowingly and wilfully authorising or permitting it (s.372(6)). Companies whose shares are listed on the Stock Exchange have to undertake to send with a notice convening a meeting two way proxy appointments—i.e. forms enabling the shareholder to direct the proxy whom he appoints to vote either for or against, instead of leaving it to the proxy's discretion—for voting on all resolutions intended to be proposed.

(c) Form

19–03   A proxy may be appointed generally or for a particular meeting. When appointed in respect of one meeting, the appointment may instruct the proxy how to vote on all or any of the resolutions to be proposed.

The articles of association of a company may prescribe a form of appointment of a proxy (e.g. Companies Act 1929, Sch.1, Table A, art.61; Companies Act 1948, Table A, arts 70, 71; Companies (Tables A to F) Regulations 1985, Table A, arts 60, 61). The Stock Exchange requires that any provision in the articles of a listed company shall not preclude the use of a two way form, and that the articles allow a duly authorised officer of a corporate shareholder to execute a form of proxy under hand.

For examples of instruments appointing a proxy and a resolution appointing a representative, see Appendix 3, paras A3–23—A3–26.

(d) Powers of proxy

A proxy only has an automatic right to speak at a company **19–04** meeting that he is appointed to attend if the company is a private company (Companies Act 1985, s.372(1)). Only if the articles of the company allow can a proxy vote on a show of hands (*Bombay-Burmah Trading Corporation v Dorabji Cursetji Shroff* [1905] A.C. 213). A proxy is entitled to demand or join in demanding a poll, by virtue of his authority to vote (s.373(2)).

The proxy's basic right is to vote on a poll. However, if the shareholder who appointed the proxy attends the meeting and votes himself, the proxy's votes will be rejected (*Cousins v International Brick Co.* [1931] 2 Ch. 90). A proxy may be instructed to cast some of the shareholder's votes in one way and some in another. If he casts some of the votes as directed, but withholds the remainder, the votes that he casts are valid (*Oliver v Dalgleish* [1963] 1 W.L.R. 1274).

(e) Companies Act 2006

The relevant sections of the Companies Act 2006 have not yet **19–05** been brought into force, but, as they are likely to become effective during the currency of this edition of this book, it will be convenient to summarise their provisions.

A member of a company is entitled to appoint a proxy to exercise all his rights to attend, to speak and to vote (which includes demanding a poll: s.329) at a meeting of the company. If the company has a share capital, a member may appoint more than one proxy, each to exercise the rights attached to different shares (s.324). A company's articles may confer more extensive rights (s.331). The new statutory rights contrast with those under the Companies Act 1985, which only speak of a member appointing a single proxy and only allow a proxy to speak in the case of private companies,

Every notice convening a company meeting must state, with reasonable prominence, a member's statutory rights to appoint proxies and any more extensive rights conferred by the articles (s.325).

2. Winding up

(a) Proxies

A creditor or contributory may appoint a proxy to attend, speak **19–06** and vote for him at meetings in the course of a winding up. Some general rules apply to all cases. At any one meeting, only one proxy may actually represent a person entitled to attend, although alternative proxies may be appointed. The chairman of the meeting or the official receiver may be appointed. A proxy must be an adult (Insolvency Rules 1986, r.8.1).

Where the official receiver is appointed, the proxy may be exercised by his deputy, another official receiver or an officer of the Department whom he authorises. A proxy given for a particular meeting extends to adjournments of it (r.8.3).

A proxy may only vote in favour of a resolution which will directly or indirectly result in him, or an associate, receiving remuneration from the insolvent estate if he is specifically directed to do so (r.8.6).

(b) Forms

19–07 A series of proxy forms are prescribed by the Insolvency Rules 1986 for use in different cases:

Form 8.1: company or individual voluntary arrangements.

Form 8.2: administration.

Form 8.3: administrative receivership.

Form 8.4: winding up by the court or bankruptcy.

Form 8.5: members' or creditors' voluntary winding up.

When notice is given of a meeting to be held in insolvency proceedings, forms of proxy are sent out with it and no one may be named on it. That form, or one in substantially similar form must be used. It must be signed by the principal, or someone authorised by him stating the nature of his authority (r.8.2).

3. Directors

19–08 A director cannot appoint a proxy to act or vote on his behalf as a member of the board. His appointment is personal. The articles of the company may, however, entitle him to appoint an alternate. They should make precise provisions as to the appointment, status and tenure of office of an alternate.

Normally, an alternate is appointed by the director for whom he is a substitute, with the consent of the other directors. The period for which an appointment is made is often limited. While the appointment continues, the alternate exercises the powers, and therefore has the responsibilities, of a director in his own right. His appointment can generally be revoked or suspended by the appointor resuming his duties.

4. Stock exchange transfers

The 1971 Act confers special protection on a person taking a **19–09** transfer of a registered security when the transfer is executed by an attorney for the purposes of a stock exchange transaction. If the attorney makes a statutory declaration on or within three months of the date of the transfer that the power had not been revoked on that date, there is a conclusive presumption in the transferee's favour that it is so (1971 Act, s.6(1)). This protection is in addition to that provided by s.5, so no declaration is needed when the transfer is made within twelve months of the power coming into operation.

"Registered securities" are transferable securities (shares, stock, debentures, debenture stock, loan stock, bonds, unit trust units, or other securities) whose holders are entered in a register wherever it is maintained. A "stock exchange transaction" is a sale and purchase of securities in which each party is a member of a stock exchange acting in the ordinary course of his business as such, or is acting through the agency of such a member (Stock Transfer Act 1963 s.4(1); 1971 Act s.6(2)).

5. Example of use: share pre-emption

The articles of association of a private company frequently **19–10** provide that a shareholder who wishes to sell his shares must first offer them to other members of the company. This is a way for a family to retain control of a family business, or to restrict the participation of antipathetic people. To ensure that the pre-emption provisions are promptly complied with, even where the selling shareholder is reluctant, the articles may give the directors power of attorney to execute a transfer of shares. It is not lawful to register a transfer of shares unless a proper instrument of transfer is delivered to the company (Companies Act 1985 s.183(1)). Granting a power of attorney avoids the impasse that could be created if the selling shareholder will not execute a transfer.

Articles of association are not executed as a deed, and indeed may not even have been signed by any of the current members of the company. It is, however, considered that the appointment of an attorney by the articles would comply with the requirements of section 1 of the 1971 Act that "an instrument creating a power of attorney shall be executed as a deed by . . . the donor". Nevertheless there is a new doubt. Section 14 of the Companies Act 1985, reads

". . . the memorandum and articles, when registered, bind the company and its members to the same extent as if they respectively had been signed and sealed by each member . . .", and, until 1990, this was assumed to be sufficient. However, that provision has not been amended to accord with the new method for individuals to execute deeds (Law of Property (Miscellaneous Provisions) Act 1989, s.1). The general provision adapting earlier statutory requirements (s.1(7)) does not seem appropriately to cover the position. This doubt remains to be allayed.

Precedent

(a) A member ("transferor") wishing to transfer any shares [otherwise than to another member][1] shall give written notice ("transfer notice"), stating the number of shares and the price of each, to the Secretary and shall lodge with him the certificate relating to such shares.[2] The Secretary shall thereupon notify the other members of the contents of the transfer notice and the date of its service

(b) Any member ("purchaser") wishing to buy all or any of the shares referred to in the transfer notice shall give notice ("purchase notice") to the Secretary within twenty-eight days of the service of the transfer notice, stating how many such shares he wishes to buy

(c) The transferor shall sell to each purchaser who shall buy the number of shares stated in his purchase notice. If the total number of shares stated in all the purchase notices exceeds the number stated in the transfer notice, the number sold to each purchaser shall be abated rateably

(d) The price for the sale of the shares shall be as stated in the transfer notice unless the purchaser within forty-two days of the service of the transfer notice requests the auditors acting as experts to determine the price, in which event the price shall be as so determined

(e) The sale and purchase of the shares under the terms of this article shall be completed within forty-two days of the service of the transfer notice or (if later) within fourteen days of the determination of the price by the auditors

(f) In default the directors shall have the power at the request of the purchaser to appoint, by a deed executed by two of them, an attorney to execute a transfer of the shares into the

---

[1] Members may be left free to transfer shares to existing members, but if the shareholders wish to be able to maintain their proportional shareholdings, the preemption article should apply to all transfers.

[2] If the share certificate is lodged, difficulties arising from registering a transfer without cancelling the former certificate will be avoided.

name of the purchaser upon receipt of the price which the attorney shall pay to the company to hold on trust for the transferor

(g) If no purchase notice is served within twenty-eight days of the service of the transfer notice, or to the extent that the total number of shares stated in all the purchase notices falls short of the number stated in the transfer notice, the transferor shall be free to transfer those shares or the balance of them free from the provisions of this article.

APPENDIX 1

RELEVANT ACTS

Trustee Act 1925 ss.25 and 36

(15 & 16 GEO. 5. C. 19)

Delegation of trustee's function by power of attorney

[**25.**—(1) Notwithstanding any rule of law or equity to the **A1–01** contrary, a trustee may, by power of attorney, delegate the execution or exercise of all or any of the trusts, powers and discretions vested in him as trustee either alone or jointly with any other person or persons.

(2) A delegation under this section—

(a) commences as provided by the instrument creating the power or, if the instrument makes no provision as to the commencement of the delegation, with the date of the execution of the instrument by the donor; and

(b) continues for a period of twelve months or any shorter period provided by the instrument creating the power.

(3) The persons who may be donees of a power of attorney under this section include a trust corporation.

(4) Before or within seven days after giving a power of attorney under this section the donor shall give written notice of it (specifying the date on which the power comes into operation and its duration, the donee of the power, the reasons why the power is given and, where some only are delegated, the trusts, powers and discretions delegated) to—

(a) each person (other than himself), if any, who under any instrument creating the trust has power (whether alone or jointly) to appoint a new trustee; and

(b) each of the other trustees, if any;

but failure to comply with this subsection shall not, in favour of a person dealing with the donee of the power, invalidate any act done or instrument executed by the donee.

(5) A power of attorney given under this section by a single donor—

(a) in the form set out in subsection (6) of this section; or
(b) in a form to the like effect but expressed to be made under this subsection,

shall operate to delegate to the person identified in the form as the single donee of the power the execution and exercise of all the trusts, powers and discretions vested in the donor as trustee (either alone or jointly with any other person or persons) under the single trust so identified.

(6) [*This form is reproduced in Appendix 3, Forms of Document p.277.*]

(7) The donor of a power of attorney given under this section shall be liable for the acts or defaults of the donee in the same manner as if they were the acts or defaults of the donor.

(8) For the purpose of executing or exercising the trusts or powers delegated to him, the donee may exercise any of the powers conferred on the donor as trustee by statute or by the instrument creating the trust, including power, for the purpose of the transfer of any inscribed stock, himself to delegate to an attorney power to transfer, but not including the power of delegation conferred by this section.

(9) The fact that it appears from any power of attorney given under this section, or from any evidence required for the purposes of any such power of attorney or otherwise, that in dealing with any stock the donee of the power is acting in the execution of a trust shall not be deemed for any purpose to affect any person in whose books the stock is inscribed or registered with any notice of the trust.

(10) This section applies to a personal representative, tenant for life and statutory owner as it applies to a trustee except that subsection (4) shall apply as if it required the notice there mentioned to be given—

(a) in the case of a personal representative, to each of the other personal representatives, if any, except any executor who has renounced probate;
(b) in the case of a tenant for life, to the trustees of the settlement and to each person, if any, who together with the person giving the notice constitutes the tenant for life; and
(c) in the case of a statutory owner, to each of the persons, if any, who together with the person giving the notice constitute the statutory owner and, in the case of a statutory owner by virtue of section 23(1)(a) of the Settled Land Act 1925, to the trustees of the settlement.]

[*Section 25 was substituted by the Trustee Delegation Act 1999 s.5(1).*]

Power of appointing new or additional trustees

36.—(1) Where a trustee, either original or substituted, and **A1–02** whether appointed by a court of otherwise, is dead, or remains out of the United Kingdom for more than twelve months, or desires to be discharged from all or any of the trusts or powers reposed in or conferred on him, or refuses or is unfit to act therein, or is incapable of acting therein, or is an infant, then, subject to the restrictions imposed by this Act on the number of trustees,—

    (a) the person or persons nominated for the purpose of appointing new trustees by the instrument, if any, creating the trust; or

    (b) if there is no such person, or no such person able and willing to act, then the surviving or continuing trustees or trustee for the time being, or the personal representatives of the last surviving or continuing trustee;

may, by writing, appoint one or more other persons (whether or not being the persons exercising the power) to be a trustee or trustees in the place of the trustee so deceased remaining out of the United Kingdom, desiring to be discharged, refusing, or being unfit or being incapable, or being an infant, as aforesaid.

(2) Where a trustee has been removed under a power contained in the instrument creating the trust, a new trustee or new trustees may be appointed in the place of the trustee who is removed, as if he were dead, or, in the case of a corporation, as if the corporation desired to be discharged from the trust, and the provisions of this section shall apply accordingly, but subject to the restrictions imposed by this Act on the number of trustees.

(3) Where a corporation being a trustee is or has been dissolved, either before or after the commencement of this Act, then, for the purposes of this section and of any enactment replaced thereby, the corporation shall be deemed to be and to have been from the date of the dissolution incapable of acting in the trusts or powers reposed in or conferred on the corporation.

(4) The power of appointment given by subsection (1) of this section or any similar previous enactment to the personal representatives of a last surviving or continuing trustee shall be and shall be deemed always to have been exercisable by the executors for the time being (whether original or by representation) of such surviving or continuing trustee who have proved the will of their testator or by the administrators for the time being of such trustee without the concurrence of any executor who has renounced or has not proved.

(5) But a sole or last surviving executor intending to renounce, or all the executors where they all intend to renounce, shall have and shall be deemed always to have had power, at any time before renouncing probate, to exercise the power of appointment given by this section, or by any similar previous enactment, if willing to act

for that purpose and without thereby accepting the office of executor.

(6) where, in the case of any trust, there are not more than three trustees—

(a) the person or persons nominated for the purpose of appointing new trustees by the instrument, if any, creating the trust: or

(b) if there is no such person, or no such person able and willing to act, then the trustee or trustees for the time being;

may, be writing appointment another person or other persons to be an additional trustee or additional trustees, but it shall not be obligatory to appoint any additional trustee, unless the instrument, if any, creating the trust, or any statutory enactment provides to the contrary, not shall the number of trustees be increased beyond four by virtue of any such appointment.

[(6A)A person who is either—

(a) both a trustee and attorney for the other trustee (if one other), or for both of the other trustees (if two others), under a registered power; or

(b) attorney under a registered power for the trustee (if one) or for both or each of the trustees (if two or three),

may, if subsection (6B) of this section is satisfied in relation to him, make an appointment under subsection (6)(b) of this section on behalf of the trustee or trustees.

(6B) This subsection is satisfied in relation to an attorney under a registered power for one or more trustees if (as attorney under the power)—

(a) he intends to exercise any function of the trustee or trustees by virtue of section 1(1) of the Trustee Delegation Act 1999; or

(b) he intends to exercise any function of the trustee or trustees in relation to any land, capital proceeds of a conveyance of land or income from land by virtue of its delegation to him under section 25 of this Act or the instruments (if any) creating the trust.

(6C) In subsections (6A) and (6B) of this section "registered power" means [an enduring power of attorney or lasting power of attorney registered under the Mental Capacity Act 2005.

(6D) Subsection (6A) of this section—

(a) applies only if and so far as a contrary intention is not expressed in the instrument creating the power of attorney (or, where more than one, any of them) or the instrument (if any) creating the trust: and

(b) has effect subject to the terms of those instruments.]

(7) Every new trustee appointed under this section as well before as after all the trust property becomes by law, or by assurance, or otherwise, vested in him, shall have the same powers, authorities, and discretions, and may in all respects act as if he had

been originally appointed a trustee by the instrument, if any, creating the trust.

(8) The provisions of this section relating to a trustee who is dead include the case of a person nominated trustee in a will but dying before the testator, and those relative to a continuing trustee include a refusing or retiring trustee, if willing to act in the execution of the provisions of this section.

(9) Where a trustee [lacks capacity to exercise] his functions as trustee and is also entitled in possession to some beneficial interest in the trust property, no appointment of a new trustee in his place shall be made by virtue of paragraph (b) of subsection (1) of this section unless leave to make the appointment has been given by [the Court of Protection]

[*Subsections (6A)–(6D) were added by the Trustee Delegation Act 1999 s.8(1).*]

[*Words in square brackets in subs.(6C) substituted by the Mental Capacity Act 2005 Sch.6, para.3.*]

[*Words in square brackets in subs.(9) substituted by the Mental Capacity Act 2005 Sch.6, para.3.*]

Law of Property Act 1925, s.22

(15 & 16 GEO, 5, C.20)

Conveyances on behalf of persons suffering from mental disorder and as to land held by them in trust

22.—(1) Where a legal estate in land (whether settled or not) is **A1–03** vested [, either solely or jointly with any other person or persons, in a person lacking capacity (within the meaning of the Mental Capacity Act 2005) to convey or create a legal estate, a deputy appointed for him by the Court of Protection or (if no deputy is appointed] for him) any person authorised in that behalf shall, under an order of [the court of Protection], or of the court, or under any statutory power, make or concur in making all requisite dispositions for conveying or creating a legal estate in his name and on his behalf.

(2) If land subject to a trust of land is vested, either solely or jointly with any other persons, in a person who [lacks capacity (within the meaning of that Act) to exercise] his function as trustee, a new trustee shall be appointed in the place of that person, or he shall be otherwise discharged from the trust, before the legal estate is dealt with by the trustees.

[(3) Subsection (2) of this section does not prevent a legal estate being dealt with without the appointment of a new trustee, or the discharge of the incapable trustee, at a time when the donee of [an enduring power of attorney or lasting power of attorney (within the meaning of the 2005 Act) is entitled to act for the trustee who lacks capacity in relation to the dealing.]]

[*Words in square brackets in section 22 substituted by the Mental Capacity Act 2005 Sch.6, para.4.*]

[*Subsection (3) added by Trustee Delegation Act 1999 s.9(1).*]

Powers of Attorney Act 1971

(c.27)

An Act to make new provision in relation to powers of attorney and the delegation by trustees of their trusts, powers and discretions.

[May 12, 1971]

Execution of powers of attorney

A1–04   **1.**—(1) An instrument creating a power of attorney shall be [executed as a deed by] the donor of the power.

(2) [*Repealed by Law of Property (Miscellaneous Provisions) Act 1989 ss.1(8)(9)(11), 4, Sch.1, para.6(b), Sch.2*]

(3) This section is without prejudice to any requirement in, or having effect under, any other Act as to the witnessing of instruments creating powers of attorney and does not affect the rules relating to the execution of instruments by bodies corporate.

[*The words in square brackers in subs.(1) substituted by Law of Property (Miscellaneous Provisions) Act 1989 s.1(8)(9)(11), Sch.1, para.6(a).*]

[*Section 2 repealed by Supreme Court Act 1981 s.152(4), Sch.7.*]

Proof of instruments creating powers of attorney

A1–05   **3.**—(1) The contents of an instrument creating a power of attorney may be proved by means of a copy which—

(a) is a reproduction of the original made with a photographic or other device for reproducing documents in facsimile; and

(b) contains the following certificate or certificates signed by the donor of the power or by a solicitor [duly certificated notary public] or stockbroker, that is to say—

(i) a certificate at the end of the effect that the copy is a true and complete copy of the original; and

(ii) if the original consists of two or more pages, a certificate at the end of each page of the copy to the effect that it is a true and complete copy of the corresponding page of the original.

(2) Where a copy of an instrument creating a power of attorney has been made which complies with subsection (1) of this section, the contents of the instrument may also be proved by means of a copy of that copy if the further copy itself complies with that subsection, taking reference in it to the original as references to the copy from which the further copy is made.

(3) In this section ['duly certificated notary public' has the same meaning as it has in the Solicitors Act 1974 by virtue of section 87(1) of that Act and] "stockbroker" means a member of any stock exchange within the meaning of Stock Transfer Act 1963 or the Stock Transfer Act (Northern Ireland) 1963.

(4) This section is without prejudice to section 4 of the Evidence and Powers of Attorney Act 1940 (proof of deposited instruments by office copy) and to any other method of proof authorised by law.

(5) For the avoidance of doubt, in relation to an instrument made in Scotland the references to a power of attorney in this section and in section 4 of the Evidence and Powers of Attorney Act 1940 include references to a factory and commission.

[The Words in square brackets in subss.(1), (3) were inserted by the Courts and Legal Services Act 1990 s.125(2), Sch.17, para.4(a).]

Powers of attorney given as security

4.—(1) Where a power of attorney is expressed to be irrevocable **A1–06** and is given to secure—

(a) a proprietary interest of the donee of the power; or

(b) the performance of an obligation owed to the donee, then, so long as the donee has that interest or the obligation remains undischarged, the power shall not be revoked—

   (i) by the donor without the consent of the donee; or

   (ii) by the death, incapacity or bankruptcy of the donor or, if the donor is a body corporate, by its winding up or dissolution.

(2) A power of attorney given to secure a proprietary interest may be given to the person entitled to the interest and persons deriving title under him to that interest, and those persons shall be duly constituted donees of the power for all purposes of the power but without prejudice to any right to appoint substitutes given by the power.

(3) This section applies to powers of attorney wherever created.

Protection of donee and third persons where power of attorney is revoked

5.—(1) A donee of a power of attorney who acts in pursuance of **A1–07** the power at a time when it has been revoked shall not, by reason of the revocation, incur any liability (either to the donor or to any other person) if at that time he did not know that the power had been revoked.

(2) Where a power of attorney has been revoked and a person, without knowledge of the revocation, deals with the donee of the power, the transaction between them shall, in favour of that person, be as valid as if the power had then been in existence.

(3) Where the power is expressed in the instrument creating it to be irrevocable and to be given by way of security then, unless the person dealing with the donee knows that it was not in fact given by way of security, he shall be entitled to assume that the power is incapable of revocation except by the donor acting with the consent of the donee and shall accordingly be treated for the purposes of subsection (2) of this section as having knowledge of the revocation only if he knows that it has been revoked in that manner.

(4) Where the interest of a purchaser depends on whether a transaction between the donee of a power of attorney and another person was valid by virtue of subsection (2) of this section, it shall be conclusively presumed in favour of the purchaser that that person did not at the material time know of the revocation of the power if—

(a) the transaction between that person and the donee was completed within twelve months of the date on which the power came into operation; or

(b) that person makes a statutory declaration, before or within three months after the completion of that purchase, that he did not at the material time know of the revocation of the power.

(5) Without prejudice to subsection (3) of this section, for the purposes of this section knowledge of the revocation of a power of attorney includes knowledge of the occurrence of any event (such as the death of the donor) which has the effect of revoking the power.

(6) In this section "purchaser" and "purchase" have the meanings specified in section 205(1) of the Law of Property Act 1925.

(7) This section applies whenever the power of attorney was created but only to acts and transactions after the commencement of this Act.

[*Section 5 modified by Enduring Powers of Attorney Act 1985 ss.1(1)(c), 9(5).*]

Additional protection for transferees under stock exchange transactions

A1–08   **6.**—(1) Without prejudice to section 5 of this Act, where—

(a) the donee of a power of attorney executes, as transferor, an instrument transferring registered securities; and

(b) the instrument is executed for the purposes of a stock exchange transaction.

it shall be conclusively presumed in favour of the transferee that the power had not been revoked at the date of the instrument if a statutory declaration to that effect is made by the donee of the power on or within three months after that date.

(2) In this section "registered securities" and "stock exchange transaction" have the same meanings as in the Stock Transfer Act 1963.

Execution of instruments etc. by donee of power of attorney

7.—(1) If the donee of a power of attorney is an individual, he **A1–09** may, if he thinks fit—

(a) execute any instrument with his own signature, and

(b) do any other thing in his own name.

by the authority of the donor of the power; and any instrument executed or thing done in that manner shall, subject to subsection (1A) of this section, be as effective as if executed by the donee in any manner which would constitute due execution of that instrument by donor or, as the case may be, as if done by the donee in the name of the donor.

(1A) Where an instrument is executed by the donee as a deed, it shall be as effective as if executed by the donee in a manner which would constitute due execution of it as a deed by the donor if it is executed in accordance with section 1(3)(a) of the Law of Property (Miscellaneous Provisions) Act 1989.

(2) For the avoidance of doubt it is hereby declared that an instrument to which subsection (3) of section 74 of the Law of Property Act 1925 applies may be executed either as provided in that subsection or as provided in this section.

(3) *[Repealed by SI 2005/1906 (Regulatory Reform (Execution of Deeds and Documents) Order), Sch.2, para.1.]*

(4) This section applies whenever the power of attorney was created.

[Section 8 was repealed by the Law of Property Act 1925 s.129.]

[Section 9 was repealed by the Trustee Delegation Act 1999 Sch.1, para.1.]

Effect of general power of attorney in specified form

10.—(1) Subject to subsection (2) of this section, a general **A1–10** power of attorney in the form set out in Schedule 1 to this Act, or in a form to the like effect but expressed to be made under this Act, shall operate to confer—

(a) on the donee of the power; or

(b) if there is more than one donee, on the donees acting jointly or acting jointly or severally, as the case may be,

authority to do on behalf of the donor anything which he can lawfully do by an attorney.

(2) [Subject to section 1 of the Trustee Delegation Act 1999, this section] does not apply to functions which the donor has as a trustee or personal representative or as a tenant for life or statutory owner within the meaning of the Settled Land Act 1925.

[*The Words in square bracket in subs.(2) substituted by Trustee Delegation Act 1999 s.3*]

Short title, repeals, consequential amendments, commencement and extent

A1–11   **11.**—(1) This Act may be cited as the Powers of Attorney Act 1971.

(2–4)[*Repealed by Statute Law (Repeals) Act 2004 Sch.1 (17)(11), para.1.*]

(5) Section 3 of this Act extends to Scotland and Northern Ireland but, save as aforesaid, this Act extends to England and Wales only.

SCHEDULES

SCHEDULE 1 Section 10

FORM OF GENERAL POWER OF ATTORNEY FOR PURPOSES OF SECTION 10

A1–12   [*This form is reproduced in Appendix 3, Forms of Document, p.271.*]

Trusts of Land and Appointment of Trustees Act 1996 s.9

(c 47)

Delegation by trustees.

A1–13   **9.**—(1) The trustees of land may, by power of attorney, delegate to any beneficiary or beneficiaries of full age and beneficially entitled to an interest in possession in land subject to the trust any of their functions as trustees which relate to the land.

(2) Where trustees purport to delegate to a person by a power of attorney under subsection (1) functions relating to any land and another person in good faith deals with him in relation to the land, he shall be presumed in favour of that other person to have been a

person to whom the functions could be delegated unless that other person has knowledge at the time of the transaction that he was not such a person.

And it shall be conclusively presumed in favour of any purchaser whose interest depends on the validity of that transaction that other person dealt in good faith and did not have such knowledge if that other person makes a statutory declaration to that effect before or within three months after the completion of the purchase.

(3) A power of attorney under subsection (1) shall be given by all the trustees jointly and (unless expressed to be irrevocable and to be given by way of security) may be revoked by any one or more of them; and such a power is revoked by the appointment as a trustee of a person other than those by whom it is given (though not by any of those person dying or otherwise ceasing to be a trustee).

(4) Where a beneficiary to whom functions are delegated by a power of attorney under subsection (1) ceases to be a person beneficially entitled to an interest in possession in land subject to the trust—

(a) if the functions are delegated to him alone, the power is revoked,

(b) if the functions are delegated to him and to other beneficiaries to be exercised by them jointly (but not separately), the power is revoked if each of the other beneficiaries ceases to be so entitled (but otherwise function exercisable in accordance with the power are so exercisable by the remaining beneficiary or beneficiaries), and

(c) if the functions are delegated to him and to other beneficiaries to be exercised by them separately (or either separately or jointly), the power is revoked in so far as it relates to him.

(5) A delegation under subsection (1) may be for any period or indefinite.

(6) A power of attorney under subsection (1) cannot be [an enduring power of attorney or lasting power of attorney within the meaning of the Mental Capacity Act 2005].

(7) Beneficiaries to whom functions have been delegated under subsection (1) are, in relation to the exercise of the functions, in the same position as trustees (with the same duties and liabilities); but such beneficiaries shall not be regarded as trustees for any other purposes (including, in particular, the purposes of any enactment permitting the delegation of functions by trustees or imposing requirements relating to the payment of capital money).

(8) [*Repealed by Trustee Act 2000 Sch.4(11), para.1.*]

(9) Neither this section nor the repeal by this Act of section 29 of the Law of Property Act 1925 (which is superseded by this section) affects the operation after the commencement of this Act of any delegation effected before that commencement.

[The words in square brackets in section 6 were substituted by the Mental Capacity Act 2005 Sch.6, para.42.]

Trustee Delegation Act 1999

(c.15)

An Act to amend the law relating to the delegation of trustee functions by power of attorney and the exercise of such functions by the donee of a power of attorney; and to make provision about the authority of the donee of a power of attorney to act in relation to land.

[July 15, 1999]

Exercise of trustee functions by attorney

A1–14 1.—(1) The donee of a power of attorney is not prevented from doing an act in relation to—
  (a) land,
  (b) capital proceeds of a conveyance of land, or
  (c) income from land,
by reason only that the act involves the exercise of a trustee function of the donor if, at the time when the act is done, the donor has a beneficial interest in the land, proceeds or income.
  (2) In this section—
  (a) "conveyance" has the same meaning as the Law of Property Act 1925, and
  (b) references to a trustee function of the donor are to a function which the donor has as trustee (either alone or jointly with any other person or persons).
  (3) Subsection (1) above—
  (a) applies only if and so far as a contrary intention is not expressed in the instrument creating the power of attorney, and
  (b) has effect subject to the terms of that instrument.
  (4) The donor of the power of attorney—
  (a) is liable for the acts or defaults of the donee in exercising any function by virtue of subsection (1) above in the same manner as if they were acts or defaults of the donor, but
  (b) is not liable by reason only that a function is exercised by the donee by virtue of that subsection.
  (5) Subsections (1) and (4) above—
  (a) apply only if and so far as a contrary intention is not expressed in the instrument (if any) creating the trust, and
  (b) have effect subject to the terms of such an instrument.

(6) The fact that it appears that, in dealing with any shares or stock, the donee of the power of attorney is exercising a function by virtue of subsection (1) above does not affect with any notice of any trust a person in whose books the shares are, or stock is, registered or inscribed.

(7) In any case where (by way of exception to section 3(1) of the Trusts of Land and Appointment of Trustees Act 1996) the doctrine of conversion continues to operate, any person who, by reason of the continuing operation of that doctrine, has a beneficial interest in the proceeds of sale of land shall be treated for the purposes of this section and section 2 below as having a beneficial interest in the land.

(8) The donee of a power of attorney is not to be regarded as exercising a trustee function by virtue of subsection (1) above if he is acting under a trustee delegation power; and for this purpose a trustee delegation power is a power of attorney given under—

(a) a statutory provision, or

(b) a provision of the instrument (if any) creating a trust,

under which the donor of the power is expressly authorised to delegate the exercise of all or any of his trustee functions by power of attorney.

(9) Subject to section 4(6) below, this section applies only to powers of attorney created after the commencement of this Act.

Evidence of beneficial interest

2.—(1) This section applies where the interest of a purchaser **A1–15** depends on the donee of a power of attorney having power to do an act in relation to any property by virtue of section 1(1) above. In this subsection "purchaser" has the same meaning as in Part 1 of the Law of Property Act 1925.

(2) Where this section applies an appropriate statement is, in favour of the purchaser, conclusive evidence of the donor of the power having a beneficial interest in the property at the time of the doing of the act.

(3) In this section "an appropriate statement" means a signed statement made by the donee—

(a) when doing the act in question, or

(b) at any other time within the period of three months beginning with the day on which the act is done,

that the donor has a beneficial interest in the property at the time of the donee doing the act.

(4) If an appropriate statement is false, the donee is liable in the same way as he would be if the statement were contained in a statutory declaration.

General powers in specified form

3. In section 10(2) of the Powers of Attorney Act 1971 (which **A1–16** provides that a general power of attorney in the form set out in Schedule 1 to that Act, or a similar form, does not confer on the donee of the power any authority to exercise functions of the donor as trustee etc.), for the words "This section" substitute "Subject to section 1 of the Trustee Delegation Act 1999, this section".

[Enduring powers

A1–17   **4.**—(1) Section 3(3) of the Enduring Powers of Attorney Act 1985 (which entitles the donee of an enduring power to exercise any of the donor's functions as trustee and to give receipt for capital money etc.) does not apply to enduring powers created after the commencement of this Act.

(2) Section 3(3) of the Enduring Powers of Attorney Act 1985 ceases to apply to enduring powers created before the commencement of this Act—

    (a) where subsection (3) below applies, in accordance with that subsection, and

    (b) otherwise, at the end of the period of one year from that commencement.

(3) Where an application for the registration of the instrument creating such an enduring power is made before the commencement of this Act, or during the period of one year from that commencement, section 3(3) of the Enduring Powers of Attorney Act 1985 ceases to apply to the power—

    (a) if the instrument is registered pursuant to the application (whether before commencement or during or after that period), when the registration of the instrument is cancelled, and

    (b) if the application is finally refused during or after that period, when the application is finally refused.

(4) In subsection (3) above—

    (a) "registration" and "registered" means registration and registered under section 6 of the Enduring Powers of Attorney Act 1985, and

    (b) "cancelled" means cancelled under section 8(4) of that Act.

(5) For the purposes of subsection (3)(b) above an application is finally refused—

    (a) if the application is withdrawn or any appeal is abandoned, when the application is withdrawn or the appeal is abandoned, and

    (b) otherwise, when proceedings on the application (including any proceedings on, or in consequence of, an appeal) have been determined and any time for appealing or further appealing has expired.

(6) Section 1 above applies to an enduring power created before the commencement of this Act from the time when (in accordance with subsections (2) to (5) above) section 3(3) of the Enduring Powers of Attorney Act 1985 ceases to apply to it.

Delegation under section 25 of the Trustee Act 1925

5.—(1) [*Section 5(1) amends s.25 of the Trustee Act 1925 which is* **A1–18**
reproduced on pp.151–152.]

(2) Subsection (1) above has effect in relation to powers of
attorney created after the commencement of this Act.

(3) In section 34(2)(b) of the Pensions Act 1995 (delegation by
trustees of trustee scheme under section 25 of the Trustee Act
1925), for "during absence abroad" substitute "for period not
exceeding twelve months".

Section 25 powers as enduring powers

6. Section 2(8) of the Enduring Powers of Attorney Act 1985 **A1–19**
(which prevents a power of attorney under section 25 of the
Trustee Act 1925 from being an enduring power) does not apply to
powers of attorney created after the commencement of this Act.

Two-trustee rules

7.—(1) A requirement imposed by an enactment—   **A1–20**
  (a) that capital money be paid to, or dealt with as directed by, at
      least two trustees or that a valid receipt for capital money be
      given otherwise than by a sole trustee, or
  (b) that in order for an interest or power to be overreached, a
      conveyance or deed be executed by at least two trustees,
is not satisfied by money being paid to or dealt with as directed by,
or a receipt for money being given by, a relevant attorney or by a
conveyance or deed being executed by such an attorney.

(2) In this section "relevant attorney" means a person (other
than a trust corporation within the meaning of the Trustee Act
1925) who is acting either—
  (a) both as a trustee and as attorney for one or more other
      trustees, or
  (b) as attorney for two or more trustees,
and who is not acting together with any other person or persons.

(3) This section applies whether a relevant attorney is acting
under a power created before or after the commencement of this
Act (but in the case of such an attorney acting under an enduring
power created before that commencement is without prejudice to
any continuing application of section 3(3) of the Enduring Powers
of Attorney Act 1985 to the enduring power after that commencement in accordance with section 4 above).

Appointment of additional trustee by attorney

8.—(1) [*Section 8(1) inserts new subss.(6A)–(6D) in s.36 of the* **A1–21**
Trustee Act 1925 which is reproduced on pp.153–155.]

(2) The amendment made by subsection (1) above has effect
only where the power, or (where more than one) each of them, is
created after the commencement of this Act.

Attorney acting for incapable trustee

A1–22   **9.**—(1) [*Section 9(1) inserts a new subs(3) under subs.(2) of s.22 of the Law of Property Act 1925, which is reproduced on pp.155–156.*]

(2) The amendment made by subsection (1) above has effect whether the enduring power was created before or after the commencement of this Act.

Extent of attorney's authority to act in relation to land

A1–23   **10.**—(1) Where the donee of a power of attorney is authorised by the power to an act of any description in relation to any land, his authority to do an act of that description at any time includes authority to do it with respect to any estate or interest in the land which is held at that time by the donor (whether alone or jointly with any other person or persons).

(2) Subsection (1) (above)—

(a) applies only if and so far as a contrary intention is not expressed in the instrument creating the power of attorney, and

(b) has effect subject to the terms of that instrument.

(3) This section applies only to powers of attorney created after the commencement of this Act.

Interpretation

A1–24   **11.**—(1) In this Act—

"land" has the same meaning as in the Trustee Act 1925, and

"enduring power" has the same meaning as in the Enduring Powers of Attorney Act 1985.

(2) References in this Act to the creation of a power of attorney are to the execution by the donor of the instrument creating it.

Repeals

A1–25   **12.** The enactments specified in the Schedule to this Act are repealed to the extent specified in the third column, but subject to the note at the end.

Commencement, extent and short title

A1–26   **13.**—(1) The preceding provisions of this Act shall come into force on such day as the Lord Chancellor may by order made by statutory instrument appoint.

(2) This Act extends to England and Wales only.

(3) This Act may be cited as the Trustee Delegation Act 1999.

Trustee Act 2000

(c.29)

The duty of care

1.—(1) Whenever the duty under this subsection applies to a **A1–27** trustee, he must exercise such care and skill as is reasonable in the circumstances, having regard in particular—

(a) to any special knowledge or experience that he has or holds himself out as having, and

(b) if he acts as trustee in the course of a business or profession, to any special knowledge or experience that it is reasonable to expect of a person acting in the course of that kind of business or profession.

(2) In this Act the duty under subsection (1) is called "the duty of care".

Power to employ agents

11.—(1) Subject to the provisions of this Part, the trustees of a **A1–28** trust may authorise any person to exercise any or all of their delegable functions as their agent.

(2) In the case of a trust other than a charitable trust, the trustees' delegable functions consist of any function other than—

(a) any function relating to whether or in what way any assets of the trust should be distributed,

(b) any power to decide whether any fees or other payment due to be made out of the trust funds should be made out of income or capital,

(c) any power to appoint a person to be a trustee of the trust, or

(d) any power conferred by any other enactment or the trust instrument which permits the trustees to delegate any of their functions or to appoint a person to act as a nominee or custodian.

(3) In the case of a charitable trust, the trustees' delegable functions are—

(a) any function consisting of carrying out a decision that the trustees have taken;

(b) any function relating to the investment of assets subject to the trust (including, in the case of land held as an investment, managing the land and creating or disposing of an interest in the land);

(c) any function relating to the raising of funds for the trust otherwise than by means of profits of a trade which is an integral part of carrying out the trust's charitable purpose;

(d) any other function prescribed by an order made by the Secretary of State.

(4) For the purposes of subsection (3)(c) a trade is an integral part of carrying out a trust's charitable purpose if, whether carried on in the United Kingdom or elsewhere, the profits are applied solely to the purposes of the trust and either—

(a) the trade is exercised in the course of the actual carrying out of a primary purpose of the trust, or

(b) the work in connection with the trade is mainly carried out by beneficiaries of the trust.

(5) The power to make an order under subsection (3)(d) is exercisable by statutory instrument which shall be subject to annulment in pursuance of a resolution of either House of Parliament.

Persons who may act as agents

A1–29   **12.**—(1) Subject to subsection (2), the persons whom the trustees may under section 11 authorise to exercise functions as their agent include one or more of their number.

(2) The trustees may not authorise two (or more) persons to exercise the same function unless they are to exercise the function jointly.

(3) The trustees may not under section 11 authorise a beneficiary to exercise any function as their agent (even if the beneficiary is also a trustee).

(4) The trustees may under section 11 authorise a person to exercise functions as their agent even though he is also appointed to act as their nominee or custodian (whether under section 16, 17 or 18 or any other power).

Review of agents, nominees and custodians etc.

A1–30   **22.**—(1) While the agent, nominee or custodian continues to act for the trust, the trustees—

(a) must keep under review the arrangements under which the agent, nominee or custodian acts and how those arrangements are being put into effect,

(b) if circumstances make it appropriate to do so, must consider whether there is a need to exercise any power of intervention that they have, and

(c) if they consider that there is a need to exercise such a power, must do so.

(2) If the agent has been authorised to exercise asset management functions, the duty under subsection (1) includes, in particular—

(a) a duty to consider whether there is any need to revise or replace the policy statement made for the purposes of section 15,

(b) if they consider that there is a need to revise or replace the policy statement, a duty to do so, and

(c) a duty to assess whether the policy statement (as it has effect for the time being) is being complied with.

(3) Subsections (3) and (4) of section 15 apply to the revision or replacement of a policy statement under this section as they apply to the making of a policy statement under that section.

(4) "Power of intervention" includes—

(a) a power to give directions to the agent, nominee or custodian;

(b) a power to revoke the authorisation or appointment.

Liability for agents, nominees and custodians etc.

23.—(1) A trustee is not liable for any act or default of the agent, nominee or custodian unless he has failed to comply with the duty of care applicable to him, under paragraph 3 of Schedule 1— **A1–31**

(a) when entering into the arrangements under which the person acts as agent, nominee or custodian, or

(b) when carrying out his duties under section 22.

(2) If a trustee has agreed a term under which the agent, nominee or custodian is permitted to appoint a substitute, the trustee is not liable for any act or default of the substitute unless he has failed to comply with the duty of care applicable to him, under paragraph 3 of Schedule 1—

(a) when agreeing that term, or

(b) when carrying out his duties under section 22 in so far as they relate to the use of the substitute.

Effect of trustees exceeding their powers

24. A failure by the trustees to act within the limits of the powers conferred by this Part— **A1–32**

(a) in authorising a person to exercise a function of theirs as an agent, or

(b) in appointing a person to act as a nominee or custodian, does not invalidate the authorisation or appointment.

Sole trustees

25.—(1) Subject to subsection (2), this Part applies in relation to a trust having a sole trustee as it applies in relation to other trusts (and references in this Part to trustees—except in sections 12(1) and (3) and 19(5)—are to be read accordingly). **A1–33**

(2) Section 18 does not impose a duty on a sole trustee if that trustee is a trust corporation.

Restriction or exclusion of this Part etc.

26. The powers conferred by this Part are— **A1–34**

(a) in addition to powers conferred on trustees otherwise than by this Act, but
(b) subject to any restriction or exclusion imposed by the trust instrument or by any enactment or any provision of subordinate legislation.

Existing trusts

A1–35   27. This Part applies in relation to trusts whether created before or after its commencement.

SCHEDULE 1

APPLICATION OF DUTY OF CARE

Agents, nominees and custodians

A1–36   3.—(1) The duty of care applies to a trustee—
(a) when entering into arrangements under which a person is authorised under section 11 to exercise functions as an agent;

. . .

(d) when entering into arrangements under which, under any other power, however conferred, a person is authorised to exercise functions as an agent or is appointed to act as a nominee or custodian;
(e) when carrying out his duties under section 22 (review of agent, nominee or custodian, etc.).

. . .

Mental Capacity Act 2005

(c.9)

PART 1

PERSONS WHO LACK CAPACITY

The principles

The principles

A1–37   1.—(1) The following principles apply for the purposes of this Act.

(2) A person must be assumed to have capacity unless it is established that he lacks capacity.

(3) A person is not to be treated as unable to make a decision unless all practicable steps to help him to do so have been taken without success.

(4) A person is not to be treated as unable to make a decision merely because he makes an unwise decision.

(5) An act done, or decision made, under this Act for or on behalf of a person who lacks capacity must be done, or made, in his best interests.

(6) Before the act is done, or the decision is made, regard must be had to whether the purpose for which it is needed can be as effectively achieved in a way that is less restrictive of the person's rights and freedom of action.

Preliminary

People who lack capacity

2.—(1) For the purposes of this Act, a person lacks capacity in **A1–38** relation to a matter if at the material time he is unable to make a decision for himself in relation to the matter because of an impairment of, or a disturbance in the functioning of, the mind or brain.

(2) It does not matter whether the impairment or disturbance is permanent or temporary.

(3) A lack of capacity cannot be established merely by reference to—

(a) a person's age or appearance, or

(b) a condition of his, or an aspect of his behaviour, which might lead others to make unjustified assumptions about his capacity.

(4) In proceedings under this Act or any other enactment, any question whether a person lacks capacity within the meaning of this Act must be decided on the balance of probabilities.

(5) No power which a person ("D") may exercise under this Act—

(a) in relation to a person who lacks capacity, or

(b) where D reasonably thinks that a person lacks capacity,

is exercisable in relation to a person under 16.

(6) Subsection (5) is subject to section 18(3).

Inability to make decisions

3.—(1) For the purposes of section 2, a person is unable to **A1–39** make a decision for himself if he is unable—

(a) to understand the information relevant to the decision,

    (b) to retain that information,

    (c) to use or weigh that information as part of the process of making the decision, or

    (d) to communicate his decision (whether by talking, using sign language or any other means).

(2) A person is not to be regarded as unable to understand the information relevant to a decision if he is able to understand an explanation of it given to him in a way that is appropriate to his circumstances (using simple language, visual aids or any other means).

(3) The fact that a person is able to retain the information relevant to a decision for a short period only does not prevent him from being regarded as able to make the decision.

(4) The information relevant to a decision includes information about the reasonably foreseeable consequences of—

    (a) deciding one way or another, or

    (b) failing to make the decision.

Best interests

A1–40   **4.**—(1) In determining for the purposes of this Act what is in a person's best interests, the person making the determination must not make it merely on the basis of—

    (a) the person's age or appearance, or

    (b) a condition of his, or an aspect of his behaviour, which might lead others to make unjustified assumptions about what might be in his best interests.

(2) The person making the determination must consider all the relevant circumstances and, in particular, take the following steps.

(3) He must consider—

    (a) whether it is likely that the person will at some time have capacity in relation to the matter in question, and

    (b) if it appears likely that he will, when that is likely to be.

(4) He must, so far as reasonably practicable, permit and encourage the person to participate, or to improve his ability to participate, as fully as possible in any act done for him and any decision affecting him.

(5) Where the determination relates to life—sustaining treatment he must not, in considering whether the treatment is in the best interests of the person concerned, be motivated by a desire to bring about his death.

(6) He must consider, so far as is reasonably ascertainable—

    (a) the person's past and present wishes and feelings (and, in particular, any relevant written statement made by him when he had capacity),

    (b) the beliefs and values that would be likely to influence his decision if he had capacity, and

    (c) the other factors that he would be likely to consider if he were able to do so.

(7) He must take into account, if it is practicable and appropriate to consult them, the views of—

(a) anyone named by the person as someone to be consulted on the matter in question or on matters of that kind,

(b) anyone engaged in caring for the person or interested in his welfare,

(c) any donee of a lasting power of attorney granted by the person, and

(d) any deputy appointed for the person by the court,

as to what would be in the person's best interests and, in particular, as to the matters mentioned in subsection (6).

(8) The duties imposed by subsections (1) to (7) also apply in relation to the exercise of any powers which—

(a) are exercisable under a lasting power of attorney, or

(b) are exercisable by a person under this Act where he reasonably believes that another person lacks capacity.

(9) In the case of an act done, or a decision made, by a person other than the court, there is sufficient compliance with this section if (having complied with the requirements of subsections (1) to (7)) he reasonably believes that what he does or decides is in the best interests of the person concerned.

(10) "Life—sustaining treatment" means treatment which in the view of a person providing health care for the person concerned is necessary to sustain life.

(11) "Relevant circumstances" are those—

(a) of which the person making the determination is aware, and

(b) which it would be reasonable to regard as relevant.

Lasting powers of attorney

Lasting powers of attorney

9.—(1) A lasting power of attorney is a power of attorney under **A1–41** which the donor ("P") confers on the donee (or donees) authority to make decisions about all or any of the following—

(a) P's personal welfare or specified matters concerning P's personal welfare, and

(b) P's property and affairs or specified matters concerning P's property and affairs,

and which includes authority to make such decisions in circumstances where P no longer has capacity.

(2) A lasting power of attorney is not created unless—

(a) section 10 is complied with,

(b) an instrument conferring authority of the kind mentioned in subsection (1) is made and registered in accordance with Schedule 1, and

    (c) at the time when P executes the instrument, P has reached 18 and has capacity to execute it.

(3) An instrument which—

    (a) purports to create a lasting power of attorney, but

    (b) does not comply with this section, section 10 or Schedule 1, confers no authority.

(4) The authority conferred by a lasting power of attorney is subject to—

    (a) the provisions of this Act and, in particular, sections 1 (the principles) and 4 (best interests), and

    (b) any conditions or restrictions specified in the instrument.

Appointment of donees

A1–42   **10.**—(1) A donee of a lasting power of attorney must be—

    (a) an individual who has reached 18, or

    (b) if the power relates only to P's property and affairs, either such an individual or a trust corporation.

(2) An individual who is bankrupt may not be appointed as donee of a lasting power of attorney in relation to P's property and affairs.

(3) Subsections (4) to (7) apply in relation to an instrument under which two or more persons are to act as donees of a lasting power of attorney.

(4) The instrument may appoint them to act—

    (a) jointly,

    (b) jointly and severally, or

    (c) jointly in respect of some matters and jointly and severally in respect of others.

(5) To the extent to which it does not specify whether they are to act jointly or jointly and severally, the instrument is to be assumed to appoint them to act jointly.

(6) If they are to act jointly, a failure, as respects one of them, to comply with the requirements of subsection (1) or (2) or Part 1 or 2 of Schedule 1 prevents a lasting power of attorney from being created.

(7) If they are to act jointly and severally, a failure, as respects one of them, to comply with the requirements of subsection (1) or (2) or Part 1 or 2 of Schedule 1—

    (a) prevents the appointment taking effect in his case, but

    (b) does not prevent a lasting power of attorney from being created in the case of the other or others.

(8) An instrument used to create a lasting power of attorney—

    (a) cannot give the donee (or, if more than one, any of them) power to appoint a substitute or successor, but

    (b) may itself appoint a person to replace the donee (or, if more than one, any of them) on the occurrence of an event mentioned in section 13(6)(a) to (d) which has the effect of terminating the donee's appointment.

Lasting powers of attorney: restrictions

11.—(1) A lasting power of attorney does not authorise the **A1–43** donee (or, if more than one, any of them) to do an act that is intended to restrain P, unless three conditions are satisfied.

(2) The first condition is that P lacks, or the donee reasonably believes that P lacks, capacity in relation to the matter in question.

(3) The second is that the donee reasonably believes that it is necessary to do the act in order to prevent harm to P.

(4) The third is that the act is a proportionate response to—

(a) the likelihood of P's suffering harm, and

(b) the seriousness of that harm.

(5) For the purposes of this section, the donee restrains P if he—

(a) uses, or threatens to use, force to secure the doing of an act which P resists, or

(b) restricts P's liberty of movement, whether or not P resists, or if he authorises another person to do any of those things.

(6) But the donee does more than merely restrain P if he deprives P of his liberty within the meaning of Article 5(1) of the Human Rights Convention.

(7) Where a lasting power of attorney authorises the donee (or, if more than one, any of them) to make decisions about P's personal welfare, the authority—

(a) does not extend to making such decisions in circumstances other than those where P lacks, or the donee reasonably believes that P lacks, capacity,

(b) is subject to sections 24 to 26 (advance decisions to refuse treatment), and

(c) extends to giving or refusing consent to the carrying out or continuation of a treatment by a person providing health care for P.

(8) But subsection (7)(c)—

(a) does not authorise the giving or refusing of consent to the carrying out or continuation of life—sustaining treatment, unless the instrument contains express provision to that effect, and

(b) is subject to any conditions or restrictions in the instrument.

Scope of lasting powers of attorney: gifts

12.—(1) Where a lasting power of attorney confers authority to **A1–44** make decisions about P's property and affairs, it does not authorise a donee (or, if more than one, any of them) to dispose of the donor's property by making gifts except to the extent permitted by subsection (2).

(2) The donee may make gifts—

(a) on customary occasions to persons (including himself) who are related to or connected with the donor, or

   (b) to any charity to whom the donor made or might have been
       expected to make gifts,
if the value of each such gift is not unreasonable having regard
to all the circumstances and, in particular, the size of the donor's
estate.

   (3) "Customary occasion" means—
   (a) the occasion or anniversary of a birth, a marriage or the
       formation of a civil partnership, or
   (b) any other occasion on which presents are customarily given
       within families or among friends or associates.

   (4) Subsection (2) is subject to any conditions or restrictions in
the instrument.

Revocation of lasting powers of attorney etc.

A1–45   **13.**—(1) This section applies if—
   (a) P has executed an instrument with a view to creating a
       lasting power of attorney, or
   (b) a lasting power of attorney is registered as having been
       conferred by P,
and in this section references to revoking the power include
revoking the instrument.

   (2) P may, at any time when he has capacity to do so, revoke the
power.

   (3) P's bankruptcy revokes the power so far as it relates to P's
property and affairs.

   (4) But where P is bankrupt merely because an interim bankruptcy restrictions order has effect in respect of him, the power is
suspended, so far as it relates to P's property and affairs, for so
long as the order has effect.

   (5) The occurrence in relation to a donee of an event mentioned
in subsection (6)—
   (a) terminates his appointment, and
   (b) except in the cases given in subsection (7), revokes the
       power.

   (6) The events are—
   (a) the disclaimer of the appointment by the donee in accord-
       ance with such requirements as may be prescribed for the
       purposes of this section in regulations made by the Lord
       Chancellor,
   (b) subject to subsections (8) and (9), the death or bankruptcy
       of the donee or, if the donee is a trust corporation, its
       winding—up or dissolution,
   (c) subject to subsection (11), the dissolution or annulment of a
       marriage or civil partnership between the donor and the
       donee,
   (d) the lack of capacity of the donee.

   (7) The cases are—

(a) the donee is replaced under the terms of the instrument,

(b) he is one of two or more persons appointed to act as donees jointly and severally in respect of any matter and, after the event, there is at least one remaining donee.

(8) The bankruptcy of a donee does not terminate his appointment, or revoke the power, in so far as his authority relates to P's personal welfare.

(9) Where the donee is bankrupt merely because an interim bankruptcy restrictions order has effect in respect of him, his appointment and the power are suspended, so far as they relate to P's property and affairs, for so long as the order has effect.

(10) Where the donee is one of two or more appointed to act jointly and severally under the power in respect of any matter, the reference in subsection (9) to the suspension of the power is to its suspension in so far as it relates to that donee.

(11) The dissolution or annulment of a marriage or civil partnership does not terminate the appointment of a donee, or revoke the power, if the instrument provided that it was not to do so.

Protection of donee and others if no power created or power revoked

14.—(1) Subsections (2) and (3) apply if—   A1–46

(a) an instrument has been registered under Schedule 1 as a lasting power of attorney, but

(b) a lasting power of attorney was not created,

whether or not the registration has been cancelled at the time of the act or transaction in question.

(2) A donee who acts in purported exercise of the power does not incur any liability (to P or any other person) because of the non—existence of the power unless at the time of acting he—

(a) knows that a lasting power of attorney was not created, or

(b) is aware of circumstances which, if a lasting power of attorney had been created, would have terminated his authority to act as a donee.

(3) Any transaction between the donee and another person is, in favour of that person, as valid as if the power had been in existence, unless at the time of the transaction that person has knowledge of a matter referred to in subsection (2).

(4) If the interest of a purchaser depends on whether a transaction between the donee and the other person was valid by virtue of subsection (3), it is conclusively presumed in favour of the purchaser that the transaction was valid if—

(a) the transaction was completed within 12 months of the date on which the instrument was registered, or

(b) the other person makes a statutory declaration, before or within 3 months after the completion of the purchase, that he had no reason at the time of the transaction to doubt that the donee had authority to dispose of the property which was the subject of the transaction.

(5) In its application to a lasting power of attorney which relates to matters in addition to P's property and affairs, section 5 of the Powers of Attorney Act 1971 (c. 27) (protection where power is revoked) has effect as if references to revocation included the cessation of the power in relation to P's property and affairs.

(6) Where two or more donees are appointed under a lasting power of attorney, this section applies as if references to the donee were to all or any of them.

SCHEDULE 1

LASTING POWERS OF ATTORNEY: FORMALITIES

PART 1

MAKING INSTRUMENTS

General requirements as to making instruments

A1–47   **1.** (1) An instrument is not made in accordance with this Schedule unless—
  (a) it is in the prescribed form,
  (b) it complies with paragraph 2, and
  (c) any prescribed requirements in connection with its execution are satisfied.

(2) Regulations may make different provision according to whether—
  (a) the instrument relates to personal welfare or to property and affairs (or to both);
  (b) only one or more than one donee is to be appointed (and if more than one, whether jointly or jointly and severally).

(3) In this Schedule—
  (a) "prescribed" means prescribed by regulations, and
  (b) "regulations" means regulations made for the purposes of this Schedule by the Lord Chancellor.

Requirements as to content of instruments

A1–48   **2.** (1) The instrument must include—
  (a) the prescribed information about the purpose of the instrument and the effect of a lasting power of attorney,
  (b) a statement by the donor to the effect that he—
    (i) has read the prescribed information or a prescribed part of it (or has had it read to him), and
    (ii) intends the authority conferred under the instrument to include authority to make decisions on his behalf in circumstances where he no longer has capacity,

(c) a statement by the donor—
    (i) naming a person or persons whom the donor wishes to be notified of any application for the registration of the instrument, or
    (ii) stating that there are no persons whom he wishes to be notified of any such application,
(d) a statement by the donee (or, if more than one, each of them) to the effect that he—
    (i) has read the prescribed information or a prescribed part of it (or has had it read to him), and
    (ii) understands the duties imposed on a donee of a lasting power of attorney under sections 1 (the principles) and 4 (best interests), and
(e) a certificate by a person of a prescribed description that, in his opinion, at the time when the donor executes the instrument—
    (i) the donor understands the purpose of the instrument and the scope of the authority conferred under it,
    (ii) no fraud or undue pressure is being used to induce the donor to create a lasting power of attorney, and
    (iii) there is nothing else which would prevent a lasting power of attorney from being created by the instrument.
(2) Regulations may—
(a) prescribe a maximum number of named persons;
(b) provide that, where the instrument includes a statement under sub-paragraph (1)(c)(ii), two persons of a prescribed description must each give a certificate under sub-paragraph (1)(e).
(3) The persons who may be named persons do not include a person who is appointed as donee under the instrument.
(4) In this Schedule, "named person" means a person named under sub-paragraph (1)(c).
(5) A certificate under sub-paragraph (1)(e)—
(a) must be made in the prescribed form, and
(b) must include any prescribed information.
(6) The certificate may not be given by a person appointed as donee under the instrument.

Failure to comply with prescribed form

3. (1) If an instrument differs in an immaterial respect in form **A1–49** or mode of expression from the prescribed form, it is to be treated by the Public Guardian as sufficient in point of form and expression.
(2) The court may declare that an instrument which is not in the prescribed form is to be treated as if it were, if it is satisfied that the persons executing the instrument intended it to create a lasting power of attorney.

PART 2

REGISTRATION

Applications and procedure for registration

A1–50 **4.** (1) An application to the Public Guardian for the registration of an instrument intended to create a lasting power of attorney—

(a) must be made in the prescribed form, and

(b) must include any prescribed information.

(2) The application may be made—

(a) by the donor,

(b) by the donee or donees, or

(c) if the instrument appoints two or more donees to act jointly and severally in respect of any matter, by any of the donees.

(3) The application must be accompanied by—

(a) the instrument, and

(b) any fee provided for under section 58(4)(b).

(4) A person who, in an application for registration, makes a statement which he knows to be false in a material particular is guilty of an offence and is liable—

(a) on summary conviction, to imprisonment for a term not exceeding 12 months or a fine not exceeding the statutory maximum or both;

(b) on conviction on indictment, to imprisonment for a term not exceeding 2 years or a fine or both.

5. Subject to paragraphs 11 to 14, the Public Guardian must register the instrument as a lasting power of attorney at the end of the prescribed period.

Notification requirements

A1–51 **6.** (1) A donor about to make an application under paragraph 4(2)(a) must notify any named persons that he is about to do so.

(2) The donee (or donees) about to make an application under paragraph 4(2)(b) or (c) must notify any named persons that he is (or they are) about to do so.

7. As soon as is practicable after receiving an application by the donor under paragraph 4(2)(a), the Public Guardian must notify the donee (or donees) that the application has been received.

8. (1) As soon as is practicable after receiving an application by a donee (or donees) under paragraph 4(2)(b), the Public Guardian must notify the donor that the application has been received.

(2) As soon as is practicable after receiving an application by a donee under paragraph 4(2)(c), the Public Guardian must notify—

(a) the donor, and

(b) the donee or donees who did not join in making the application, that the application has been received.

9. (1) A notice under paragraph 6 must be made in the prescribed form.

(2) A notice under paragraph 6, 7 or 8 must include such information, if any, as may be prescribed.

Power to dispense with notification requirements

10. The court may—   A1–52

(a) on the application of the donor, dispense with the requirement to notify under paragraph 6(1), or

(b) on the application of the donee or donees concerned, dispense with the requirement to notify under paragraph 6(2),

if satisfied that no useful purpose would be served by giving the notice.

Instrument not made properly or containing ineffective provision

11. (1) If it appears to the Public Guardian that an instrument A1–53 accompanying an application under paragraph 4 is not made in accordance with this Schedule, he must not register the instrument unless the court directs him to do so.

(2) Sub-paragraph (3) applies if it appears to the Public Guardian that the instrument contains a provision which—

(a) would be ineffective as part of a lasting power of attorney, or

(b) would prevent the instrument from operating as a valid lasting power of attorney.

(3) The Public Guardian—

(a) must apply to the court for it to determine the matter under section 23(1), and

(b) pending the determination by the court, must not register the instrument.

(4) Sub-paragraph (5) applies if the court determines under section 23(1) (whether or not on an application by the Public Guardian) that the instrument contains a provision which—

(a) would be ineffective as part of a lasting power of attorney, or

(b) would prevent the instrument from operating as a valid lasting power of attorney.

(5) The court must—

(a) notify the Public Guardian that it has severed the provision, or

(b) direct him not to register the instrument.

(6) Where the court notifies the Public Guardian that it has severed a provision, he must register the instrument with a note to that effect attached to it.

Deputy already appointed

A1–54　**12.** (1) Sub-paragraph (2) applies if it appears to the Public Guardian that—
  (a) there is a deputy appointed by the court for the donor, and
  (b) the powers conferred on the deputy would, if the instrument were registered, to any extent conflict with the powers conferred on the attorney.
(2) The Public Guardian must not register the instrument unless the court directs him to do so.

Objection by donee or named person

A1–55　**13.** (1) Sub-paragraph (2) applies if a donee or a named person—
  (a) receives a notice under paragraph 6, 7 or 8 of an application for the registration of an instrument, and
  (b) before the end of the prescribed period, gives notice to the Public Guardian of an objection to the registration on the ground that an event mentioned in section 13(3) or (6)(a) to (d) has occurred which has revoked the instrument.
(2) If the Public Guardian is satisfied that the ground for making the objection is established, he must not register the instrument unless the court, on the application of the person applying for the registration—
  (a) is satisfied that the ground is not established, and
  (b) directs the Public Guardian to register the instrument.
(3) Sub-paragraph (4) applies if a donee or a named person—
  (a) receives a notice under paragraph 6, 7 or 8 of an application for the registration of an instrument, and
  (b) before the end of the prescribed period—
    (i) makes an application to the court objecting to the registration on a prescribed ground, and
    (ii) notifies the Public Guardian of the application.
(4) The Public Guardian must not register the instrument unless the court directs him to do so.

Objection by donor

A1–56　**14.** (1) This paragraph applies if the donor—
  (a) receives a notice under paragraph 8 of an application for the registration of an instrument, and
  (b) before the end of the prescribed period, gives notice to the Public Guardian of an objection to the registration.
(2) The Public Guardian must not register the instrument unless the court, on the application of the donee or, if more than one, any of them—

   (a) is satisfied that the donor lacks capacity to object to the
registration, and

   (b) directs the Public Guardian to register the instrument.

Notification of registration

15. Where an instrument is registered under this Schedule, the **A1–57**
Public Guardian must give notice of the fact in the prescribed form
to—

   (a) the donor, and

   (b) the donee or, if more than one, each of them.

Evidence of registration

16. (1) A document purporting to be an office copy of an **A1–58**
instrument registered under this Schedule is, in any part of the
United Kingdom, evidence of—

   (a) the contents of the instrument, and

   (b) the fact that it has been registered.

   (2) Sub-paragraph (1) is without prejudice to—

   (a) section 3 of the Powers of Attorney Act 1971 (c. 27) (proof
by certified copy), and

   (b) any other method of proof authorised by law.

PART 3

CANCELLATION OF REGISTRATION AND NOTIFICATION OF SEVERANCE

17. (1) The Public Guardian must cancel the registration of an **A1–59**
instrument as a lasting power of attorney on being satisfied that the
power has been revoked—

   (a) as a result of the donor's bankruptcy, or

   (b) on the occurrence of an event mentioned in section 13(6)(a)
to (d).

   (2) If the Public Guardian cancels the registration of an instrument he must notify—

   (a) the donor, and

   (b) the donee or, if more than one, each of them.

18. The court must direct the Public Guardian to cancel the
registration of an instrument as a lasting power of attorney if it—

   (a) determines under section 22(2)(a) that a requirement for
creating the power was not met,

   (b) determines under section 22(2)(b) that the power has been
revoked or has otherwise come to an end, or

   (c) revokes the power under section 22(4)(b) (fraud etc.).

19. (1) Sub-paragraph (2) applies if the court determines under
section 23(1) that a lasting power of attorney contains a provision
which—

(a) is ineffective as part of a lasting power of attorney, or

(b) prevents the instrument from operating as a valid lasting power of attorney.

(2) The court must—

(a) notify the Public Guardian that it has severed the provision, or

(b) direct him to cancel the registration of the instrument as a lasting power of attorney.

20. On the cancellation of the registration of an instrument, the instrument and any office copies of it must be delivered up to the Public Guardian to be cancelled.

Part 4

Records of Alterations in Registered Powers

Partial revocation or suspension of power as a result of bankruptcy

A1–60   **21.** If in the case of a registered instrument it appears to the Public Guardian that under section 13 a lasting power of attorney is revoked, or suspended, in relation to the donor's property and affairs (but not in relation to other matters), the Public Guardian must attach to the instrument a note to that effect.

Termination of appointment of donee which does not revoke power

A1–61   **22.** If in the case of a registered instrument it appears to the Public Guardian that an event has occurred—

(a) which has terminated the appointment of the donee, but

(b) which has not revoked the instrument,

the Public Guardian must attach to the instrument a note to that effect.

Replacement of donee

A1–62   **23.** If in the case of a registered instrument it appears to the Public Guardian that the donee has been replaced under the terms of the instrument the Public Guardian must attach to the instrument a note to that effect.

Severance of ineffective provisions

A1–63   **24.** If in the case of a registered instrument the court notifies the Public Guardian under paragraph 19(2)(a) that it has severed a provision of the instrument, the Public Guardian must attach to it a note to that effect.

Notification of alterations

25. If the Public Guardian attaches a note to an instrument **A1–64** under paragraph 21, 22, 23 or 24 he must give notice of the note to the donee or donees of the power (or, as the case may be, to the other donee or donees of the power).

SCHEDULE 4

PROVISIONS APPLYING TO EXISTING ENDURING POWERS OF ATTORNEY

PART 1

ENDURING POWERS OF ATTORNEY

Enduring power of attorney to survive mental incapacity of donor

1. (1) Where an individual has created a power of attorney **A1–65** which is an enduring power within the meaning of this Schedule—

(a) the power is not revoked by any subsequent mental incapacity of his,

(b) upon such incapacity supervening, the donee of the power may not do anything under the authority of the power except as provided by sub-paragraph (2) unless or until the instrument creating the power is registered under paragraph 13, and

(c) if and so long as paragraph (b) operates to suspend the donee's authority to act under the power, section 5 of the Powers of Attorney Act 1971 (c. 27) (protection of donee and third persons), so far as applicable, applies as if the power had been revoked by the donor's mental incapacity,

and, accordingly, section 1 of this Act does not apply.

(2) Despite sub-paragraph (1)(b), where the attorney has made an application for registration of the instrument then, until it is registered, the attorney may take action under the power—

(a) to maintain the donor or prevent loss to his estate, or

(b) to maintain himself or other persons in so far as paragraph 3(2) permits him to do so.

(3) Where the attorney purports to act as provided by sub-paragraph (2) then, in favour of a person who deals with him without knowledge that the attorney is acting otherwise than in accordance with sub-paragraph (2)(a) or (b), the transaction between them is as valid as if the attorney were acting in accordance with sub-paragraph (2)(a) or (b).

Characteristics of an enduring power of attorney

A1–66   **2.** (1) Subject to sub-paragraphs (5) and (6) and paragraph 20, a power of attorney is an enduring power within the meaning of this Schedule if the instrument which creates the power—

   (a) is in the prescribed form,
   (b) was executed in the prescribed manner by the donor and the attorney, and
   (c) incorporated at the time of execution by the donor the prescribed explanatory information.

   (2) In this paragraph, "prescribed" means prescribed by such of the following regulations as applied when the instrument was executed—

   (a) the Enduring Powers of Attorney (Prescribed Form) Regulations 1986 (S.I. 1986/126),
   (b) the Enduring Powers of Attorney (Prescribed Form) Regulations 1987 (S.I. 1987/1612),
   (c) the Enduring Powers of Attorney (Prescribed Form) Regulations 1990 (S.I. 1990/1376),
   (d) the Enduring Powers of Attorney (Welsh Language Prescribed Form) Regulations 2000 (S.I. 2000/289).

   (3) An instrument in the prescribed form purporting to have been executed in the prescribed manner is to be taken, in the absence of evidence to the contrary, to be a document which incorporated at the time of execution by the donor the prescribed explanatory information.

   (4) If an instrument differs in an immaterial respect in form or mode of expression from the prescribed form it is to be treated as sufficient in point of form and expression.

   (5) A power of attorney cannot be an enduring power unless, when he executes the instrument creating it, the attorney is—

   (a) an individual who has reached 18 and is not bankrupt, or
   (b) a trust corporation.

   (6) A power of attorney which gives the attorney a right to appoint a substitute or successor cannot be an enduring power.

   (7) An enduring power is revoked by the bankruptcy of the donor or attorney.

   (8) But where the donor or attorney is bankrupt merely because an interim bankruptcy restrictions order has effect in respect of him, the power is suspended for so long as the order has effect.

   (9) An enduring power is revoked if the court—

   (a) exercises a power under sections 16 to 20 in relation to the donor, and
   (b) directs that the enduring power is to be revoked.

   (10) No disclaimer of an enduring power, whether by deed or otherwise, is valid unless and until the attorney gives notice of it to the donor or, where paragraph 4(6) or 15(1) applies, to the Public Guardian.

Scope of authority etc. of attorney under enduring power

3.—(1) If the instrument which creates an enduring power of **A1–67** attorney is expressed to confer general authority on the attorney, the instrument operates to confer, subject to—

(a) the restriction imposed by sub-paragraph (3), and

(b) any conditions or restrictions contained in the instrument,

authority to do on behalf of the donor anything which the donor could lawfully do by an attorney at the time when the donor executed the instrument.

(2) Subject to any conditions or restrictions contained in the instrument, an attorney under an enduring power, whether general or limited, may (without obtaining any consent) act under the power so as to benefit himself or other persons than the donor to the following extent but no further—

(a) he may so act in relation to himself or in relation to any other person if the donor might be expected to provide for his or that person's needs respectively, and

(b) he may do whatever the donor might be expected to do to meet those needs.

(3) Without prejudice to sub-paragraph (2) but subject to any conditions or restrictions contained in the instrument, an attorney under an enduring power, whether general or limited, may (without obtaining any consent) dispose of the property of the donor by way of gift to the following extent but no further—

(a) he may make gifts of a seasonal nature or at a time, or on an anniversary, of a birth, a marriage or the formation of a civil partnership, to persons (including himself) who are related to or connected with the donor, and

(b) he may make gifts to any charity to whom the donor made or might be expected to make gifts,

provided that the value of each such gift is not unreasonable having regard to all the circumstances and in particular the size of the donor's estate.

PART 2

ACTION ON ACTUAL OR IMPENDING INCAPACITY OF DONOR

Duties of attorney in event of actual or impending incapacity of donor

4.—(1) Sub-paragraphs (2) to (6) apply if the attorney under an **A1–68** enduring power has reason to believe that the donor is or is becoming mentally incapable.

(2) The attorney must, as soon as practicable, make an application to the Public Guardian for the registration of the instrument creating the power.

(3) Before making an application for registration the attorney must comply with the provisions as to notice set out in Part 3 of this Schedule.

(4) An application for registration—

(a) must be made in the prescribed form, and

(b) must contain such statements as may be prescribed.

(5) The attorney—

(a) may, before making an application for the registration of the instrument, refer to the court for its determination any question as to the validity of the power, and

(b) must comply with any direction given to him by the court on that determination.

(6) No disclaimer of the power is valid unless and until the attorney gives notice of it to the Public Guardian; and the Public Guardian must notify the donor if he receives a notice under this sub-paragraph.

(7) A person who, in an application for registration, makes a statement which he knows to be false in a material particular is guilty of an offence and is liable—

(a) on summary conviction, to imprisonment for a term not exceeding 12 months or a fine not exceeding the statutory maximum or both;

(b) on conviction on indictment, to imprisonment for a term not exceeding 2 years or a fine or both.

(8) In this paragraph, "prescribed" means prescribed by regulations made for the purposes of this Schedule by the Lord Chancellor.

PART 3

NOTIFICATION PRIOR TO REGISTRATION DUTY TO GIVE NOTICE TO RELATIVES

A1–69   **5.** Subject to paragraph 7, before making an application for registration the attorney must give notice of his intention to do so to all those persons (if any) who are entitled to receive notice by virtue of paragraph 6.

6. (1) Subject to sub-paragraphs (2) to (4), persons of the following classes ("relatives") are entitled to receive notice under paragraph 5—

(a) the donor's spouse or civil partner,

(b) the donor's children,

(c) the donor's parents,

(d) the donor's brothers and sisters, whether of the whole or half blood,

(e) the widow, widower or surviving civil partner of a child of the donor,

(f) the donor's grandchildren,

(g) the children of the donor's brothers and sisters of the whole blood,

(h) the children of the donor's brothers and sisters of the half blood,

(i) the donor's uncles and aunts of the whole blood,

(j) the children of the donor's uncles and aunts of the whole blood.

(2) A person is not entitled to receive notice under paragraph 5 if—

(a) his name or address is not known to the attorney and cannot be reasonably ascertained by him, or

(b) the attorney has reason to believe that he has not reached 18 or is mentally incapable.

(3) Except where sub-paragraph (4) applies—

(a) no more than 3 persons are entitled to receive notice under paragraph 5, and

(b) in determining the persons who are so entitled, persons falling within the class in sub-paragraph (1)(a) are to be preferred to persons falling within the class in sub-paragraph (1)(b), those falling within the class in sub-paragraph (1)(b) are to be preferred to those falling within the class in sub-paragraph (1)(c), and so on.

(4) Despite the limit of 3 specified in sub-paragraph (3), where—

(a) there is more than one person falling within any of classes (a) to (j) of sub-paragraph (1), and

(b) at least one of those persons would be entitled to receive notice under paragraph 5,

then, subject to sub-paragraph (2), all the persons falling within that class are entitled to receive notice under paragraph 5.

7. (1) An attorney is not required to give notice under paragraph 5—

(a) to himself, or

(b) to any other attorney under the power who is joining in making the application,

even though he or, as the case may be, the other attorney is entitled to receive notice by virtue of paragraph 6.

(2) In the case of any person who is entitled to receive notice by virtue of paragraph 6, the attorney, before applying for registration, may make an application to the court to be dispensed from the requirement to give him notice; and the court must grant the application if it is satisfied—

(a) that it would be undesirable or impracticable for the attorney to give him notice, or

(b) that no useful purpose is likely to be served by giving him notice.

Duty to give notice to donor

A1–70   **8.** (1) Subject to sub-paragraph (2), before making an application for registration the attorney must give notice of his intention to do so to the donor.

(2) Paragraph 7(2) applies in relation to the donor as it applies in relation to a person who is entitled to receive notice under paragraph 5.

Contents of notices

A1–71   **9.** A notice to relatives under this Part of this Schedule must—
(a) be in the prescribed form,
(b) state that the attorney proposes to make an application to the Public Guardian for the registration of the instrument creating the enduring power in question,
(c) inform the person to whom it is given of his right to object to the registration under paragraph 13(4), and
(d) specify, as the grounds on which an objection to registration may be made, the grounds set out in paragraph 13(9).

10. A notice to the donor under this Part of this Schedule—
(a) must be in the prescribed form,
(b) must contain the statement mentioned in paragraph 9(b), and
(c) must inform the donor that, while the instrument remains registered, any revocation of the power by him will be ineffective unless and until the revocation is confirmed by the court.

Duty to give notice to other attorneys

A1–72   **11.** (1) Subject to sub-paragraph (2), before making an application for registration an attorney under a joint and several power must give notice of his intention to do so to any other attorney under the power who is not joining in making the application; and paragraphs 7(2) and 9 apply in relation to attorneys entitled to receive notice by virtue of this paragraph as they apply in relation to persons entitled to receive notice by virtue of paragraph 6.

(2) An attorney is not entitled to receive notice by virtue of this paragraph if—
(a) his address is not known to the applying attorney and cannot reasonably be ascertained by him, or
(b) the applying attorney has reason to believe that he has not reached 18 or is mentally incapable.

Supplementary

A1–73   **12.** Despite section 7 of the Interpretation Act 1978 (c. 30) (construction of references to service by post), for the purposes of this Part of this Schedule a notice given by post is to be regarded as given on the date on which it was posted.

PART 4

REGISTRATION

Registration of instrument creating power

13. (1) If an application is made in accordance with paragraph **A1–74**
4(3) and (4) the Public Guardian must, subject to the provisions of
this paragraph, register the instrument to which the application
relates.

(2) If it appears to the Public Guardian that—

(a) there is a deputy appointed for the donor of the power
   created by the instrument, and

(b) the powers conferred on the deputy would, if the instrument
   were registered, to any extent conflict with the powers
   conferred on the attorney,

the Public Guardian must not register the instrument except in
accordance with the court's directions.

(3) The court may, on the application of the attorney, direct the
Public Guardian to register an instrument even though notice has
not been given as required by paragraph 4(3) and Part 3 of this
Schedule to a person entitled to receive it, if the court is satisfied—

(a) that it was undesirable or impracticable for the attorney to
   give notice to that person, or

(b) that no useful purpose is likely to be served by giving him
   notice.

(4) Sub-paragraph (5) applies if, before the end of the period of
5 weeks beginning with the date (or the latest date) on which the
attorney gave notice under paragraph 5 of an application for
registration, the Public Guardian receives a valid notice of objection to the registration from a person entitled to notice of the
application.

(5) The Public Guardian must not register the instrument except
in accordance with the court's directions.

(6) Sub-paragraph (7) applies if, in the case of an application for
registration—

(a) it appears from the application that there is no one to whom
   notice has been given under paragraph 5, or

(b) the Public Guardian has reason to believe that appropriate
   inquiries might bring to light evidence on which he could be
   satisfied that one of the grounds of objection set out in sub-
   paragraph (9) was established.

(7) The Public Guardian—

(a) must not register the instrument, and

(b) must undertake such inquiries as he thinks appropriate in all
   the circumstances.

(8) If, having complied with sub-paragraph (7)(b), the Public
Guardian is satisfied that one of the grounds of objection set out in
sub-paragraph (9) is established—

(a) the attorney may apply to the court for directions, and
(b) the Public Guardian must not register the instrument except
     in accordance with the court's directions.

(9) A notice of objection under this paragraph is valid if made
on one or more of the following grounds—

(a) that the power purported to have been created by the
     instrument was not valid as an enduring power of attorney,
(b) that the power created by the instrument no longer subsists,
(c) that the application is premature because the donor is not
     yet becoming mentally incapable,
(d) that fraud or undue pressure was used to induce the donor
     to create the power,
(e) that, having regard to all the circumstances and in particular
     the attorney's relationship to or connection with the donor,
     the attorney is unsuitable to be the donor's attorney.

(10) If any of those grounds is established to the satisfaction of
the court it must direct the Public Guardian not to register the
instrument, but if not so satisfied it must direct its registration.

(11) If the court directs the Public Guardian not to register an
instrument because it is satisfied that the ground in sub-paragraph
(9)(d) or (e) is established, it must by order revoke the power
created by the instrument.

(12) If the court directs the Public Guardian not to register an
instrument because it is satisfied that any ground in sub-paragraph
(9) except that in paragraph (c) is established, the instrument must
be delivered up to be cancelled unless the court otherwise directs.

Register of enduring powers

A1–75   **14.** The Public Guardian has the function of establishing and
maintaining a register of enduring powers for the purposes of this
Schedule.

PART 5

LEGAL POSITION AFTER REGISTRATION

Effect and proof of registration

A1–76   **15.** (1) The effect of the registration of an instrument under
paragraph 13 is that—

(a) no revocation of the power by the donor is valid unless and
     until the court confirms the revocation under paragraph
     16(3);
(b) no disclaimer of the power is valid unless and until the
     attorney gives notice of it to the Public Guardian;

(c) the donor may not extend or restrict the scope of the authority conferred by the instrument and no instruction or consent given by him after registration, in the case of a consent, confers any right and, in the case of an instruction, imposes or confers any obligation or right on or creates any liability of the attorney or other persons having notice of the instruction or consent.

(2) Sub-paragraph (1) applies for so long as the instrument is registered under paragraph 13 whether or not the donor is for the time being mentally incapable.

(3) A document purporting to be an office copy of an instrument registered under this Schedule is, in any part of the United Kingdom, evidence of—

(a) the contents of the instrument, and

(b) the fact that it has been so registered.

(4) Sub-paragraph (3) is without prejudice to section 3 of the Powers of Attorney Act 1971 (c. 27) (proof by certified copies) and to any other method of proof authorised by law.

Functions of court with regard to registered power

16. (1) Where an instrument has been registered under paragraph 13, the court has the following functions with respect to the power and the donor of and the attorney appointed to act under the power. **A1–77**

(2) The court may—

(a) determine any question as to the meaning or effect of the instrument;

(b) give directions with respect to—

    (i) the management or disposal by the attorney of the property and affairs of the donor;

    (ii) the rendering of accounts by the attorney and the production of the records kept by him for the purpose;

    (iii) the remuneration or expenses of the attorney whether or not in default of or in accordance with any provision made by the instrument, including directions for the repayment of excessive or the payment of additional remuneration;

(c) require the attorney to supply information or produce documents or things in his possession as attorney;

(d) give any consent or authorisation to act which the attorney would have to obtain from a mentally capable donor;

(e) authorise the attorney to act so as to benefit himself or other persons than the donor otherwise than in accordance with paragraph 3(2) and (3) (but subject to any conditions or restrictions contained in the instrument);

(f) relieve the attorney wholly or partly from any liability which he has or may have incurred on account of a breach of his duties as attorney.

(3) On application made for the purpose by or on behalf of the donor, the court must confirm the revocation of the power if satisfied that the donor—

   (a) has done whatever is necessary in law to effect an express revocation of the power, and

   (b) was mentally capable of revoking a power of attorney when he did so (whether or not he is so when the court considers the application).

(4) The court must direct the Public Guardian to cancel the registration of an instrument registered under paragraph 13 in any of the following circumstances—

   (a) on confirming the revocation of the power under sub-paragraph (3),

   (b) on directing under paragraph 2(9)(b) that the power is to be revoked,

   (c) on being satisfied that the donor is and is likely to remain mentally capable,

   (d) on being satisfied that the power has expired or has been revoked by the mental incapacity of the attorney,

   (e) on being satisfied that the power was not a valid and subsisting enduring power when registration was effected,

   (f) on being satisfied that fraud or undue pressure was used to induce the donor to create the power,

   (g) on being satisfied that, having regard to all the circumstances and in particular the attorney's relationship to or connection with the donor, the attorney is unsuitable to be the donor's attorney.

(5) If the court directs the Public Guardian to cancel the registration of an instrument on being satisfied of the matters specified in sub-paragraph (4)(f) or (g) it must by order revoke the power created by the instrument.

(6) If the court directs the cancellation of the registration of an instrument under sub-paragraph (4) except paragraph (c) the instrument must be delivered up to the Public Guardian to be cancelled, unless the court otherwise directs.

Cancellation of registration by Public Guardian

A1–78   **17.** The Public Guardian must cancel the registration of an instrument creating an enduring power of attorney—

   (a) on receipt of a disclaimer signed by the attorney;

   (b) if satisfied that the power has been revoked by the death or bankruptcy of the donor or attorney or, if the attorney is a body corporate, by its winding up or dissolution;

   (c) on receipt of notification from the court that the court has revoked the power;

   (d) on confirmation from the court that the donor has revoked the power.

Part 6

PROTECTION OF ATTORNEY AND THIRD PARTIES

Protection of attorney and third persons where power is invalid or revoked

18. (1) Sub-paragraphs (2) and (3) apply where an instrument **A1–79** which did not create a valid power of attorney has been registered under paragraph 13 (whether or not the registration has been cancelled at the time of the act or transaction in question).

(2) An attorney who acts in pursuance of the power does not incur any liability (either to the donor or to any other person) because of the non—existence of the power unless at the time of acting he knows—

(a) that the instrument did not create a valid enduring power,

(b) that an event has occurred which, if the instrument had created a valid enduring power, would have had the effect of revoking the power, or

(c) that, if the instrument had created a valid enduring power, the power would have expired before that time.

(3) Any transaction between the attorney and another person is, in favour of that person, as valid as if the power had then been in existence, unless at the time of the transaction that person has knowledge of any of the matters mentioned in sub-paragraph (2).

(4) If the interest of a purchaser depends on whether a transaction between the attorney and another person was valid by virtue of sub-paragraph (3), it is conclusively presumed in favour of the purchaser that the transaction was valid if—

(a) the transaction between that person and the attorney was completed within 12 months of the date on which the instrument was registered, or

(b) that person makes a statutory declaration, before or within 3 months after the completion of the purchase, that he had no reason at the time of the transaction to doubt that the attorney had authority to dispose of the property which was the subject of the transaction.

(5) For the purposes of section 5 of the Powers of Attorney Act 1971 (c.27) (protection where power is revoked) in its application to an enduring power the revocation of which by the donor is by virtue of paragraph 15 invalid unless and until confirmed by the court under paragraph 16—

(a) knowledge of the confirmation of the revocation is knowledge of the revocation of the power, but

(b) knowledge of the unconfirmed revocation is not.

Further protection of attorney and third persons

A1–80   **19.** (1) If—

(a) an instrument framed in a form prescribed as mentioned in paragraph 2(2) creates a power which is not a valid enduring power, and

(b) the power is revoked by the mental incapacity of the donor,

sub-paragraphs (2) and (3) apply, whether or not the instrument has been registered.

(2) An attorney who acts in pursuance of the power does not, by reason of the revocation, incur any liability (either to the donor or to any other person) unless at the time of acting he knows—

(a) that the instrument did not create a valid enduring power, and

(b) that the donor has become mentally incapable.

(3) Any transaction between the attorney and another person is, in favour of that person, as valid as if the power had then been in existence, unless at the time of the transaction that person knows—

(a) that the instrument did not create a valid enduring power, and

(b) that the donor has become mentally incapable.

(4) Paragraph 18(4) applies for the purpose of determining whether a transaction was valid by virtue of sub-paragraph (3) as it applies for the purpose or determining whether a transaction was valid by virtue of paragraph 18(3).

PART 7

JOINT AND JOINT AND SEVERAL ATTORNEYS

Application to joint and joint and several attorneys

A1–81   **20.** (1) An instrument which appoints more than one person to be an attorney cannot create an enduring power unless the attorneys are appointed to act—

(a) jointly, or

(b) jointly and severally.

(2) This Schedule, in its application to joint attorneys, applies to them collectively as it applies to a single attorney but subject to the modifications specified in paragraph 21.

(3) This Schedule, in its application to joint and several attorneys, applies with the modifications specified in sub-paragraphs (4) to (7) and in paragraph 22.

(4) A failure, as respects any one attorney, to comply with the requirements for the creation of enduring powers—

(a) prevents the instrument from creating such a power in his case, but

(b) does not affect its efficacy for that purpose as respects the other or others or its efficacy in his case for the purpose of creating a power of attorney which is not an enduring power.

(5) If one or more but not both or all the attorneys makes or joins in making an application for registration of the instrument—

(a) an attorney who is not an applicant as well as one who is may act pending the registration of the instrument as provided in paragraph 1(2),

(b) notice of the application must also be given under Part 3 of this Schedule to the other attorney or attorneys, and

(c) objection may validly be taken to the registration on a ground relating to an attorney or to the power of an attorney who is not an applicant as well as to one or the power of one who is an applicant.

(6) The Public Guardian is not precluded by paragraph 13(5) or (8) from registering an instrument and the court must not direct him not to do so under paragraph 13(10) if an enduring power subsists as respects some attorney who is not affected by the ground or grounds of the objection in question; and where the Public Guardian registers an instrument in that case, he must make against the registration an entry in the prescribed form.

(7) Sub-paragraph (6) does not preclude the court from revoking a power in so far as it confers a power on any other attorney in respect of whom the ground in paragraph 13(9)(d) or (e) is established; and where any ground in paragraph 13(9) affecting any other attorney is established the court must direct the Public Guardian to make against the registration an entry in the prescribed form.

(8) In sub-paragraph (4), "the requirements for the creation of enduring powers" means the provisions of—

(a) paragraph 2 other than sub-paragraphs (8) and (9), and

(b) the regulations mentioned in paragraph 2.

Joint attorneys

21. (1) In paragraph 2(5), the reference to the time when the **A1–82** attorney executes the instrument is to be read as a reference to the time when the second or last attorney executes the instrument.

(2) In paragraph 2(6) to (8), the reference to the attorney is to be read as a reference to any attorney under the power.

(3) Paragraph 13 has effect as if the ground of objection to the registration of the instrument specified in sub-paragraph (9)(e) applied to any attorney under the power.

(4) In paragraph 16(2), references to the attorney are to be read as including references to any attorney under the power.

(5) In paragraph 16(4), references to the attorney are to be read as including references to any attorney under the power.

(6) In paragraph 17, references to the attorney are to be read as including references to any attorney under the power.

Joint and several attorneys

A1–83 **22.** (1) In paragraph 2(7), the reference to the bankruptcy of the attorney is to be read as a reference to the bankruptcy of the last remaining attorney under the power; and the bankruptcy of any other attorney under the power causes that person to cease to be an attorney under the power.

(2) In paragraph 2(8), the reference to the suspension of the power is to be read as a reference to its suspension in so far as it relates to the attorney in respect of whom the interim bankruptcy restrictions order has effect.

(3) The restriction upon disclaimer imposed by paragraph 4(6) applies only to those attorneys who have reason to believe that the donor is or is becoming mentally incapable.

PART 8

INTERPRETATION

A1–84 **23.** (1) In this Schedule—
"enduring power" is to be construed in accordance with paragraph 2,
"mentally incapable" or "mental incapacity", except where it refers to revocation at common law, means in relation to any person, that he is incapable by reason of mental disorder (within the meaning of the Mental Health Act) of managing and administering his property and affairs and "mentally capable" and "mental capacity" are to be construed accordingly,
"notice" means notice in writing, and
"prescribed", except for the purposes of paragraph 2, means prescribed by regulations made for the purposes of this Schedule by the Lord Chancellor.

(2) Any question arising under or for the purposes of this Schedule as to what the donor of the power might at any time be expected to do is to be determined by assuming that he had full mental capacity at the time but otherwise by reference to the circumstances existing at that time.

SCHEDULE 5

TRANSITIONAL PROVISIONS AND SAVINGS

PART 2

REPEAL OF THE ENDURING POWERS OF ATTORNEY ACT 1985

Orders, determinations, etc.

11. (1) Any order or determination made, or other thing done, **A1–85** under the 1985 Act which has effect immediately before the commencement day continues to have effect despite the repeal of that Act.

(2) In so far as any such order, determination or thing could have been made or done under Schedule 4 if it had then been in force—

(a) it is to be treated as made or done under that Schedule, and

(b) the powers of variation and discharge exercisable by the court apply accordingly.

(3) Any instrument registered under the 1985 Act is to be treated as having been registered by the Public Guardian under Schedule 4.

(4) This paragraph is without prejudice to section 16 of the Interpretation Act 1978 (c.30) (general savings on repeal).

Pending proceedings

12. (1) An application for the exercise of a power under the **A1–86** 1985 Act which is pending immediately before the commencement day is to be treated, in so far as a corresponding power is exercisable under Schedule 4, as an application for the exercise of that power.

(2) For the purposes of sub-paragraph (1)—

(a) a pending application under section 4(2) of the 1985 Act for the registration of an instrument is to be treated as an application to the Public Guardian under paragraph 4 of Schedule 4 and any notice given in connection with that application under Schedule 1 to the 1985 Act is to be treated as given under Part 3 of Schedule 4,

(b) a notice of objection to the registration of an instrument is to be treated as a notice of objection under paragraph 13 of Schedule 4, and

(c) pending proceedings under section 5 of the 1985 Act are to be treated as proceedings on an application for the exercise by the court of a power which would become exercisable in relation to an instrument under paragraph 16(2) of Schedule 4 on its registration.

Appeals

A1–87   **13.** (1) The 1985 Act and, so far as relevant, the provisions of Part 7 of the Mental Health Act and the rules made under it as applied by section 10 of the 1985 Act are to continue to have effect in relation to any appeal brought by virtue of section 10(1)(c) of the 1985 Act which has not been determined before the commencement day.

(2) If, in the case of an appeal brought by virtue of section 105(1) of the Mental Health Act as applied by section 10(1)(c) of the 1985 Act (appeal to nominated judge), the judge nominated under section 93 of the Mental Health Act has begun to hear the appeal, he is to continue to do so but otherwise the appeal is to be heard by a puisne judge of the High Court nominated under section 46.

Exercise of powers of donor as trustee

A1–88   **14.** (1) Section 2(8) of the 1985 Act (which prevents a power of attorney under section 25 of the Trustee Act 1925 (c. 19) as enacted from being an enduring power) is to continue to apply to any enduring power—

(a) created before 1st March 2000, and

(b) having effect immediately before the commencement day.

(2) Section 3(3) of the 1985 Act (which entitles the donee of an enduring power to exercise the donor's powers as trustee) is to continue to apply to any enduring power to which, as a result of the provision mentioned in sub-paragraph (3), it applies immediately before the commencement day.

(3) The provision is section 4(3)(a) of the Trustee Delegation Act 1999 (c. 15) (which provides for section 3(3) of the 1985 Act to cease to apply to an enduring power when its registration is cancelled, if it was registered in response to an application made before 1st March 2001).

(4) Even though section 4 of the 1999 Act is repealed by this Act, that section is to continue to apply in relation to an enduring power—

(a) to which section 3(3) of the 1985 Act applies as a result of sub-paragraph (2), or

(b) to which, immediately before the repeal of section 4 of the 1999 Act, section 1 of that Act applies as a result of section 4 of it.

(5) The reference in section 1(9) of the 1999 Act to section 4(6) of that Act is to be read with sub-paragraphs (2) to (4).

Interpretation

15. In this Part of this Schedule, "the commencement day" **A1–89** means the day on which section 66(1)(b) (repeal of the 1985 Act) comes into force.

Companies Act 2006

(c.46)

[Note: On publication of this book these sections are not in force]

Rights to appoint proxies

324.—(1) A member of a company is entitled to appoint **A1–90** another person as his proxy to exercise all or any of his rights to attend and to speak and vote at a meeting of the company.

(2) In the case of a company having a share capital, a member may appoint more than one proxy in relation to a meeting, provided that each proxy is appointed to exercise the rights attached to a different share or shares held by him, or (as the case may be) to a different £10, or multiple of £10, of stock held by him.

Notice of meeting to contain statement of rights

325.—(1) In every notice calling a meeting of a company there **A1–91** must appear, with reasonable prominence, a statement informing the member of—

(a) his rights under section 324, and
(b) any more extensive rights conferred by the company's articles to appoint more than one proxy.

(2) Failure to comply with this section does not affect the validity of the meeting or of anything done at the meeting.

(3) If this section is not complied with as respects any meeting, an offence is committed by every officer of the company who is in default.

(4) A person guilty of an offence under this section is liable on summary conviction to a fine not exceeding level 3 on the standard scale.

Right of proxy to demand a poll

329.—(1) The appointment of a proxy to vote on a matter at a **A1–92** meeting of a company authorises the proxy to demand, or join in demanding, a poll on that matter.

(2) In applying the provisions of section 321(2) (requirements for effective demand), a demand by a proxy counts—

    (a) for the purposes of paragraph (a), as a demand by the member;

    (b) for the purposes of paragraph (b), as a demand by a member representing the voting rights that the proxy is authorised to exercise;

    (c) for the purposes of paragraph (c), as a demand by a member holding the shares to which those rights are attached.

Notice required of termination of proxy's authority

A1–93   **330.**—(1) This section applies to notice that the authority of a person to act as proxy is terminated ("notice of termination").

(2) The termination of the authority of a person to act as proxy does not affect—

    (a) whether he counts in deciding whether there is a quorum at a meeting,

    (b) the validity of anything he does as chairman of a meeting, or

    (c) the validity of a poll demanded by him at a meeting,

unless the company receives notice of the termination before the commencement of the meeting.

(3) The termination of the authority of a person to act as proxy does not affect the validity of a vote given by that person unless the company receives notice of the termination-

    (a) before the commencement of the meeting or adjourned meeting at which the vote is given, or

    (b) in the case of a poll taken more than 48 hours after it is demanded, before the time appointed for taking the poll.

(4) If the company's articles require or permit members to give notice of termination to a person other than the company, the references above to the company receiving notice have effect as if they were or (as the case may be) included a reference to that person.

(5) Subsections (2) and (3) have effect subject to any provision of the company's articles which has the effect of requiring notice of termination to be received by the company or another person at a time earlier than that specified in those subsections.

This is subject to subsection (6).

(6) Any provision of the company's articles is void in so far as it would have the effect of requiring notice of termination to be received by the company or another person earlier than the following time-

    (a) in the case of a meeting or adjourned meeting, 48 hours before the time for holding the meeting or adjourned meeting;

    (b) in the case of a poll taken more than 48 hours after it was demanded, 24 hours before the time appointed for the taking of the poll;

(c) in the case of a poll taken not more than 48 hours after it was demanded, the time at which it was demanded.

(7) In calculating the periods mentioned in subsections (3)(b) and (6) no account shall be taken of any part of a day that is not a working day.

Saving for more extensive rights conferred by articles

331. Nothing in sections 324 to 330 (proxies) prevents a com- **A1–94** pany's articles from conferring more extensive rights on members or proxies than are conferred by those sections.

APPENDIX 2

RELEVANT STATUTORY INSTRUMENTS

Insolvency Rules 1986, Part 8 and Forms 8.1–8.5

(SI 1986/1925)

PART 8

PROXIES AND COMPANY REPRESENTATION

Definition of "proxy"

A2–01   **8.1**—(1) For the purposes of the Rules, a proxy is an authority given by a person ("the principal") to another person ("the proxy-holder") to attend a meeting and vote as his representative.

(2) Proxies are for use at creditors', company or contributories' meetings summoned or called under the Act or the Rules.

(3) Only one proxy may be given by a person for any one meeting at which he desires to be represented; and it may only be given to one person, being an individual aged 18 or over. But the principal may specify one or more other such individuals to be proxy-holder in the alternative, in the order in which they are named in the proxy.

(4) Without prejudice to the generality of paragraph (3), a proxy for a particular meeting may be given to whoever is to be the chairman of the meeting; and for a meeting held as part of the proceedings in a winding up by the court, or in a bankruptcy, it may be given to the official receiver.

[(5) A person given a proxy under paragraph (4) cannot decline to be the proxy-holder in relation to that proxy.

(6) A proxy requires the holder to give the principal's vote on matters arising for determination at the meeting, or to abstain, or to propose, in the principal's name, a resolution to be voted on by the meeting either as directed or in accordance with the holder's own discretion.]

[Rules 8.1(5) and (6) substituted for rule 8.1(5) by SI 1987/1919 (Insolvency (Amendment) Rules) Sch.1(1)(9), para.134(2).]

Issue and use of forms

8.2—(1) When notice is given of a meeting to be held in **A2–02** insolvency proceedings, and forms of proxy are sent out with the notice, no form so sent out shall have inserted in it the name or description of any person.

(2) No form of proxy shall be used at any meeting except that which is sent out with the notice summoning the meeting, or a substantially similar form.

(3) A form of proxy shall be signed by the principal, or by some person authorised by him (either generally or with reference to a particular meeting). If the form is signed by a person other than the principal, the nature of the person's authority shall be stated.

Use of proxies at meetings

8.3—(1) A proxy given for a particular meeting may be used at **A2–03** any adjournment of that meeting.

(2) Where the official receiver holds proxies for use at any meeting, his deputy, or any other official receiver, may act as a proxy-holder in his place. Alternatively, the official receiver may in writing authorise another officer of the Department to act for him at the meeting and use the proxies as if that other officer were himself proxy-holder.

(3) Where the responsible insolvency practitioner holds proxies to be used by him as chairman of a meeting, and some other person acts as chairman, the other person may use the insolvency practitioner's proxies as if he were himself proxy-holder.

[(4) Where a proxy directs a proxy-holder to vote for or against a resolution for the nomination or appointment of a person as the responsible insolvency practitioner, the proxy-holder may. unless the proxy states otherwise, vote for or against (as he thinks fit) any resolution for the nomination or appointment of that person jointly with another or others.

(5) A proxy-holder may propose any resolution which, if proposed by another, would be a resolution in favour of which by virtue of the proxy he would be entitled to vote.

(6) Where a proxy gives specific directions as to voting, this does not, unless the proxy states otherwise, preclude the proxy-holder from voting at his discretion on resolutions put to the meeting which are not dealt with in the proxy.]

[Rules 8.3(4), (5) and (6) added by SI 1987/1919 (Insolvency (Amendment) Rules) Sch.1(1)(9), para.135.]

Retention of proxies

A2–04   **8.4**—(1) Subject as follows, proxies used for voting at any meeting shall be retained by the chairman of the meeting.

(2) The chairman shall deliver the proxies, forthwith after the meeting, to the responsible insolvency practitioner (where that is someone other than himself).

Right of inspection

A2–05   **8.5**—(1) The responsible insolvency practitioner shall, so long as proxies lodged with him are in his hands, allow them to be inspected, at all reasonable times on any business day, by—

   (a) the creditors, in the case of proxies used at a meeting of creditors, and

   (b) a company's members or contributories, in the case of proxies used at a meeting of the company or of its contributories.

(2) The reference in paragraph (1) to creditors is—

   (a) in the case of a company in liquidation or of an individual's bankruptcy, those creditors who have proved their debts, and

   (b) in any other case, persons who have submitted in writing a claim to be creditors of the company or individual concerned;

   but in neither case does it include a person whose proof or claim has been wholly rejected for purposes of voting, dividend or otherwise.

(3) The right of inspection given by this Rule is also exercisable—

   (a) in the case of an insolvent company, by its directors, and

   (b) in the case of an insolvent individual, by him.

(4) Any person attending a meeting in insolvency proceedings is entitled, immediately before or in the course of the meeting, to inspect the proxies and associated documents [(including proofs) sent or given, in accordance with directions contained in any notice convening the meeting, to the chairman of that meeting or to any other person by a creditor, member or contributory for the purpose of that meeting.]

[*The words in r.8.5(4) were substituted by SI 1987/1919 (Insolvency (Amendment) Rules) Sch.1(1)(9), para.136.*]

Proxy-holder with financial interest

A2–06   **8.6**—(1) A proxy-holder shall not vote in favour of any resolution which would directly or indirectly place him, or any associate of his, in a position to receive any remuneration out of the insolvent estate, unless the proxy specifically directs him to vote in that way.

(1A) Where a proxy-holder has signed the proxy as being authorised to do so by his principal and the proxy specifically directs him to vote in the way mentioned in paragraph (1), he shall nevertheless not vote in that way unless he produces to the chairman of the meeting written authorisation from his principal sufficient to show that the proxy-holder was entitled so to sign the proxy.

(2) This Rule applies also to any person acting as chairman of a meeting and using proxies in that capacity [under Rule 8.3]; and in its application to him, the proxy-holder is deemed an associate of his.

[*The words in r.8.6(2) were inserted by SI 1987/1919 (Insolvency (Amendment) Rules) Sch.1(1)(9), para.137(2).*]

Company representation

8.7—(1)Where a person is authorised under section 375 of the Companies Act to represent a corporation at a meeting of creditors or of the company or its contributories, he shall produce to the chairman of the meeting a copy of the resolution from which he derives his authority. **A2–07**

(2) The copy resolution must be under the seal of the corporation, or certified by the secretary or a director of the corporation to be a true copy.

[(3) Nothing in this Rule requires the authority of a person to sign a proxy on behalf of a principal which is a corporation to be in the form of a resolution of that corporation.]

[*Rule 8.7(3) were inserted by SI 1987/1919 (Insolvency (Amendment) Rules) Sch.1(1)(9), para.138.*]

Interpretation of creditor

[**8.8**—(1) This Rule applies where a member State liquidator has been appointed in relation to a person subject to insolvency proceedings. **A2–08**

(2) For the purposes of rule 8.5(1) (right of inspection of proxies) a member State liquidator appointed in main proceedings is deemed to be a creditor.

(3) Paragraph (2) is without prejudice to the generality of the right to participate referred to in paragraph 3 of Article 32 of the EC Regulation (exercise of creditor's rights).

[*Rule 8.8 added by SI 2002/1307 (Insolvency (Amendment) Rules) r.9(2).*]

A2–09

Rule 8.1

Insolvency Act 1986

Proxy (Company or Individual Voluntary Arrangements)

(TITLE)

Notes to help completion of the form

Please give full name and address for communication

Name of creditor/member _____

Address _____

Please insert name of person (who must be 18 or over) or the "chairman of the meeting" (see note below) If you wish to provide for alternative proxy-holders in the circumstances that your first choice is unable to attend please state the name(s) of the alternative as well

Name of proxy-holder _____

1 _____

_____

2 _____

_____

3 _____

Please delete words in brackets if the proxy-holder is only to vote as directed, *i.e.* he has no discretion

I appoint the above person to be my/the creditor's member's proxy-holder at the meeting of creditor's/members to be held on _____, or at any adjournment of that meeting. The proxy-holder is to propose or vote as instructed below [and in respect of any resolution for which no specific instruction is given, may vote or abstain at his/her discretion].

Voting instructions for resolutions

*Please delete as appropriate

1. For the acceptance/rejection* of the proposed voluntary arrangement [with the following modifications:—]

_____

Any other resolutions which the proxy-holder is to propose or vote in favour of or against should be set out in numbered paragraphs in the space provided below. Paragraph I. It more room is required please use the other side of this form

_____

_____

_____

_____

This form must be signed

Signature _____ Date _____

Name in CAPITAL LETTERS _____

Only to be completed if the creditor/member has not signed in person

Position with creditor/member or relationship to creditor/member or other authority for signature _____

Remember: there may be resolutions on the other side of this form.

Rule 8.1   Insolvency Act 1986   **A2–10**

Proxy Administration

(TITLE)

Notes to help completion of
the form

Please give full name and
address for communication

Name of creditor/member _____

Address _____

_____

_____

Please insert name of person
(who must be 18 or over) or
the "chairman of the
meeting". If you wish to
provide for alternative proxy-
holders in the circumstances
that your first choice is
unable to attend please state
the name(s) of the alternative
as well

Name of proxy-holder _____

1 _____

_____

_____

2 _____

_____

_____

3 _____

_____

Please delete words in
brackets if the proxy-holder is
only to vote as directed, *i.e.*
he has no discretion

I appoint the above person to be my/the creditor's/member's proxy-holder at
the meeting of creditors/members to be held on _____, or
at any adjournment of that meeting. The proxy-holder is to propose or vote
as instructed below [and in respect of any resolution for which no specific
instruction is given, may vote or abstain at his/her discretion].

Voting instructions for resolutions

*Please delete as appropriate

1. For the acceptance/rejection* of the administrator's proposals* as
circulated

_____

_____

_____

2. For the appointment of _____ of _____

_____

_____

representing _____

as a member of the creditors' committee

This form must be signed

Signature _____ Date _____

Name in CAPITAL LETTERS _____

Only to be completed if the
creditor has not signed in
person

Position with creditor/member or relationship to creditor or other authority
for signature

_____

**Remember: there may be resolutions on the other side of
this form.**

A2–11

Rule 8.1

Insolvency Act 1986

Proxy (Administrative Receivership)

(TITLE)

Notes to help completion of
the form

Please give full name and
address for communication

Name of creditor/member _____

Address _____

_____

_____

Please insert name of person
(who must be 18 or over) or
the "chairman of the
meeting". If you wish to
provide for alternative proxy-
holders in the circumstances
that your first choice is
unable to attend please state
the name(s) of the alternative
as well

Name of proxy-holder _____

_____

_____

_____

_____

_____

_____

Please delete words in
brackets if the proxy-holder is
only to vote as directed, *i.e.*
he has no discretion

I appoint the above person to be my/the creditor's/member's proxy-holder at
the meeting of creditor's/members to be held on _____ , or
at any adjournment of that meeting. The proxy-holder is to propose or vote
as instructed below [and in respect of any resolution for which no specific
instruction is given, may vote or abstain at his/her discretion].

Voting instructions for resolutions

for the appointment of _____

of _____

representing _____

representing _____

as a member of the creditors' committee

This form must be signed

Signature _____ Date _____

Name in CAPITAL LETTERS _____

Only to be completed if the
creditor has not signed in
person

Position with creditor or relationship to creditor or other authority for
signature

_____

Remember: there may be resolutions on the other side of
this form.

Rule 8.1   Insolvency Act 1986   **A2–12**

Proxy (Winding up by the Court
or Bankruptcy)

(TITLE)

Notes to help completion of
the form

Please give full name and
address for communication

Name of creditor/member _____

Address _____

_____

_____

Please insert name of person
(who must be 18 or over) or
the "Official Receiver". If
you wish to provide for
alternative proxy-holders in
the circumstances that your
first choice is unable to
attend please state the
name(s) of the alternative as
well

Name of proxy-holder _____

1 _____

_____

_____

2 _____

_____

_____

3 _____

_____

_____

Please delete words in
brackets if the proxy-holder is
only to vote as directed, *i.e.*
he has no discretion

I appoint the above person to be my/the creditor's/contributory's proxy-
holder at the meeting of creditors/contributories to be held on_____ ,
or at any adjournment of that meeting. The proxy-holder is to propose or
vote as instructed below [and in respect of any resolution for which no
specific instruction is given, may vote or abstain at his/her discretion].

Please complete paragraph 1
if you wish to nominate or
vote for a specific person as
trustee/liquidator

Please delete words in
brackets if the proxy-holder is
only to vote as directed, *i.e.*
he has no discretion

Any other resolutions which
the proxy-holder is to
propose or vote in favour of
or against should be set out
in numbered paragraphs in
the space provided below
paragraph 1. If more room is
required please use the other
side of this form

Voting instructions for resolutions

1. For the appointment of _____of _____

as liquidator of the company/trustee of the bankrupt's estate.
[in the event of a person named in paragraph 1 withdrawing or being
eliminated from any vote for the appointment of a liquidator/trustee the
proxy-holder may vote or abstain in any further ballot at his/her discretion]

_____

_____

_____

_____

_____

_____

_____

_____

_____

_____

_____

This form must be signed

Signature _____Date _____

Name in CAPITAL LETTERS _____

Only to be completed if the
credit/member has not signed
in person

Position with creditor/member or relationship to creditor/member or other
authority for signature _____

Remember: there may be resolutions on the other side of
this form.

Rule 8.1   Insolvency Act 1986   **A2–13**

Proxy (Members' or Creditors' Voluntary Winding Up)

(TITLE)

Notes to help completion of
the form

Please give full name and
address for communication

Name of creditor/member _____

Address _____

_____

_____

Please insert name of person
(who must be 18 or over) or
the "chairman of the
meeting" (see note below). If
you wish to provide for
alternative proxy-holders in
the circumstances that your
first choice is unable to
attend please state the
name(s) of the alternative as
well

Name of proxy-holder _____

1 _____

_____

_____

2 _____

_____

_____

3 _____

_____

_____

Please delete words in
brackets if the proxy-holder is
only to vote as directed, *i.e.*
he has no discretion

I appoint the above person to be my/the creditor's/contributory's proxy-holder at the meeting of creditor's/contributories to be held on_____ ,
or at any adjournment of that meeting. The proxy-holder is to propose or
vote as instructed below [and in respect of any resolution for which no
specific instruction is given, may vote or abstain at his/her discretion].

Please complete paragraph 1 if you wish to nominate or vote for a specific person as trustee/liquidator

Voting instructions for resolutions

1. For the appointment of _____ of _____

_____

Please delete words in brackets if the proxy-holder is only to vote as directed, *i.e.* he has no discretion

as liquidator of the company
[in the event of a person named in paragraph 1 withdrawing or being eliminated from any vote for the appointment of a liquidator/trustee the proxy-holder may vote or abstain in any further ballot at his/her discretion]

Any other resolutions which the proxy-holder is to propose or vote in favour of or against should be set out in numbered paragraphs in the space provided below paragraph I. If more room is required please use the other side of this form

_____

_____

_____

_____

_____

_____

_____

_____

_____

This form must be signed

Signature_____ Date_____

Name in CAPITAL LETTERS_____

Only to be completed if the creditor/member has not signed in person

Position with creditor/member or relationship to creditor/member or other authority for signature_____

_____

Please note that if you nominate the chairman of the meeting to be your proxy-holder he will either be a director of the company or the current liquidator.

Remember: there may be resolutions on the other side of this form.

Non-Contentious Probate Rules 1987 rr.31, 35

(SI 1987/2024)

Grants to attorneys

31.—(1) Subject to paragraphs (2) and (3) below, the lawfully **A2–14** constituted attorney of a person entitled to a grant may apply for administration for the use and benefit of the donor, and such grant shall be limited until further representation be granted, or in such other way as the [district judge or] registrar may direct.

(2) Where the donor referred to in paragraph (1) above is an executor, notice of the application shall be given to any other executor unless such notice is dispensed with by the [district judge or] registrar.

[(3) Where the donor referred to in paragraph (1) above lacks capacity within the meaning of the Mental Capacity Act 2005 (c.9) and the attorney is acting under an enduring power of attorney, the application shall be made in accordance with rule 35.]

[The words in square brackets were added by SI 1991/1876 (Non-Contentious Probate (Amendment) (Rules), Pt 2 r.7(1).]

[r.31(3) substituted by SI 2007/1898 (Mental Capacity Act 2005 (Transitional and Consequential Provisions) Order Sch.1, para.13.]

Grants in case of mental incapacity

35.—(1) Unless a district judge or registrar otherwise directs, no **A2–15** grant shall be made under this rule unless all persons entitled in the same degree as the [person who lacks capacity with the meaning of Mental Capacity Act 2006] referred to in paragraph (2) below have been cleared off.

(2) Where a registrar is satisfied that a person entitled to a grant is by reason of [lack of mental capacity] incapable of managing his affairs, administration for his use and benefit, limited until further representation be granted or in such other way as the district judge or registrar may direct, may be granted in the following order of priority—

    (a) to the person authorised by the Court of Protection to apply for a grant;

    (b) where there is no person so authorised, to the lawful attorney of the incapable person acting under a registered enduring power of attorney [or lasting power of attorney].

    (c) where there is no such attorney entitled to act, or if the attorney shall renounce administration for the use and benefit of the [person who lacks capacity within the meaning of the Mental Capacity Act 2005], to the person entitled to the residuary estate of the deceased.

(3) Where a grant is required to be made to not less than two administrators, and there is only one person competent and willing to take a grant under the foregoing provisions of this rule, administration may, unless a registrar otherwise directs, be granted to such person jointly with any other person nominated by him.

(4) Notwithstanding the foregoing provisions of this rule, administration for the use and benefit of the [person who lacks capacity with the meaning of Mental Capacity Act 2005] may be granted to such other person as the registrar may by order direct.

(5) [Unless the applicant is the person authorised in paragraph (2)(a) above,] notice of an intended application under this rule shall be given to the Court of Protection.

[The words in square brackets in r.35(5) inserted by SI 1998/1903 (Non-Contentious Probate (Amendment) Rules), r.9(2).]

[The words in square brackets in rr.35(1)–(4) substituted by SI 2007/1898 (Mental Capacity Act 2005 (Transitional and Consequential Provisions) Order Sch.1, para.13.]

The Land Registration Rules 2003 rr.61–63, Sch.3, forms 1–3

(SI 2003/1417)

PART 6

REGISTERED LAND: APPLICATIONS, DISPOSITIONS AND MISCELLANEOUS ENTRIES

Execution by an attorney

Documents executed by attorney

A2–16   **61.**—(1) If any document executed by an attorney is delivered to the land registry, there must be produced to the registrar—
   (a) the instrument creating the power, or
   (b) a copy of the power by means of which its contents may be proved under section 3 of the Powers of Attorney Act 1971, or
   [(c) a document which under section 4 of the Evidence and Powers of Attorney Act 1940, paragraph 16 of Part 2 of Schedule 1, or paragraph 15(3) of Part 5 of Schedule 4 to the Mental Capacity Act 2005 (c.9) is sufficient evidence of the contents of the power, or"; and]
   (d) a certificate by a conveyancer in Form 1.

[(2) If an order or direction under section 22 or 23 of, or paragraph 16 of Part 5 of Schedule 4 to, the Mental Capacity Act 2005 has been made with respect to a power or the donor of the power or the attorney appointed under it, the order or direction must be produced to the registrar.]

(3) In this rule, "power" means the power of attorney.

[The words in square brackets in rr.61(1)(c) and rr.61(2) substituted by SI 2007/1898 (Mental Capacity Act 2005 (Transitional and Consequential Provisions) Order Sch.1 para.31).]

Evidence of non-revocation of power more than 12 months old

62.—(1) If any transaction between a donee of a power of **A2–17** attorney and the person dealing with him is not completed within 12 months of the date on which the power came into operation, the registrar may require the production of evidence to satisfy him that the power had not been revoked at the time of the transaction.

(2) The evidence that the registrar may require under paragraph (1) may consist of or include a statutory declaration by the person who dealt with the attorney or a certificate given by that person's conveyancer in Form 2.

Evidence in support of power delegating trustees' functions to a beneficiary

63.—(1) If any document executed by an attorney to whom **A2–18** functions have been delegated under section 9 of the Trusts of Land and Appointment of Trustees Act 1996 is delivered to the registrar, the registrar may require the production of evidence to satisfy him that the person who dealt with the attorney—EP

(a) did so in good faith, and

(b) had no knowledge at the time of the completion of the transaction that the attorney was not a person to whom the functions of the trustees in relation to the land to which the application relates could be delegated under that section.

(2) The evidence that the registrar may require under paragraph (1) may consist of or include a statutory declaration by the person who dealt with the attorney or a certificate given by that person's conveyancer either in Form 3 or, where evidence of non-revocation is also required pursuant to rule 62, in Form 2.

SCHEDULE 3

RULE 61

SCHEDULE 3 FORMS REFERRED TO IN RULE 206

Form 1—Certificate as to execution of power of attorney (rule 61)

A2–19 Date of power of attorney: ....

Donor of power of
attorney: ....

Donee of power of
attorney: ....

I/We .... of
....
....

certify that

- the power of attorney ("the power") is in existence [and is made and, where required, has been registered under (*state statutory provisions under which the power is made and, where required, has been registered, if applicable*)],

- the power is dated (*insert date*),

- I am/we are satisfied that the power is validly executed as a deed and authorises the attorney to execute the document on behalf of the donor of that power, and

- I/we hold [the instrument creating the power] *or* [a copy of the power by means of which its contents may be proved under section 3 of the Powers of Attorney Act 1971] *or* [a document which under section 4 of the Evidence and Powers of Attorney Act 1940 [, paragraph 16 of Part 2 of Schedule 1, or paragraph 15(3) of Part 5 of Schedule 4 to the Mental Capacity Act 2005] is sufficient evidence of the contents of the power].

Signature of
conveyancer .... Date ....

Form 2—Statutory declaration/certificate as to non-revocation for powers more than 12 months old at the date of the disposition for which they are used (rule 62)

Date of power of attorney: ....

Donor of power of attorney: ....

I/We .... of
....
....

do solemnly and sincerely [declare] *or* [certify] that at the time of completion of the .... to me/us/my client/I/we/my client had no knowledge—

- of a revocation of the power, or

- of the death or bankruptcy of the donor or, if the donor is a corporate body, its winding up or dissolution, or

- of any incapacity of the donor where the power is not a valid lasting or enduring power, or

[Where the power is in the form prescribed for a lasting power of attorney—

- that a lasting power of attorney was not created, or

- of circumstances which, if the lasting power of attorney had been created, would have terminated the attorney's authority to act as an attorney, or]

Where the power is in the form prescribed for an enduring power of attorney—

- that the power was not in fact a valid enduring power, or

- of an order or direction of the Court of Protection which revoked the power, or

- of the bankruptcy of the attorney, or

Where the power was given under section 9 of the Trusts of Land and Appointment of Trustees Act 1996—

- of an appointment of another trustee of the land in question, or

- of any other event which would have the effect of revoking the power, or

- of any lack of good faith on the part of the person(s) who dealt with the attorney, or

- that the attorney was not a person to whom the functions of the trustees could be delegated under section 9 of the Trusts of Land and Appointment of Trustees Act 1996, or

Where the power is expressed to be given by way of security—

- that the power was not in fact given by way of security, or
- of any revocation of the power with the consent of the attorney, or
- of any other event which would have had the effect of revoking the power.

Where a certificate is given—

Signature of
conveyancer .... Date ....; or

Where a Statutory Declaration is made—

And I/we make this solemn declaration conscientiously believing the same to be true and by virtue of the provisions of the Statutory Declarations Act 1835.

Signature of
Declarant(s) .... Date ....

DECLARED at   before me, a person entitled to administer oaths.

Name ....

Address ....

Qualification ....

Signature ....

[*The words in square brackets substituted by SI 2007/1898 (Mental Capacity Act 2005 (Transitional and Consequential Provisions) Order Sch.1 para.31.*]

Form 3—Statutory declaration/certificate in support of power delegating trustees' functions to a beneficiary (rule 63)

Date of power of attorney: A2–21

Donor of power of
attorney: . . . .

I/We . . . . of
. . . .
. . . .

do solemnly and sincerely [declare] *or* [certify] that at the time of
completion of the . . . . to me/us/my client/I/we/my
client had no knowledge—

- of any lack of good faith on the part of the person(s) who
  dealt with the attorney, or

- that the attorney was not a person to whom the functions of
  the trustees could be delegated under section 9 of the Trusts
  of Land and Appointment of Trustees Act 1996.

Where a certificate is given—

Signature of
conveyancer . . . . Date . . . .; or

Where a Statutory Declaration is made—

And I/we make this solemn declaration conscientiously believing
the same to be true and by virtue of the provisions of the Statutory
Declarations Act 1835.

Signature of
Declarant(s) . . . . Date . . . .

DECLARED at   before me, a person entitled to administer oaths.

Name . . . .

Address . . . .

Qualification . . . .

Signature . . . .

The Lasting Powers of Attorney, Enduring Powers of Attorney and Public Guardian Regulations 2007, regs 1–32, 46–48 and Schs 2–8

(SI 2007/1253)

PART 1

PRELIMINARY

Citation and commencement

A2–22   **1.**—(1) These Regulations may be cited as the Lasting Powers of Attorney, Enduring Powers of Attorney and Public Guardian Regulations 2007.

(2) These Regulations shall come into force on 1 October 2007.

Interpretation

A2–23   **2.**—(1) In these Regulations—

"the Act" means the Mental Capacity Act 2005;

"court" means the Court of Protection;

"LPA certificate", in relation to an instrument made with a view to creating a lasting power of attorney, means the certificate which is required to be included in the instrument by virtue of paragraph 2(1)(e) of Schedule 1 to the Act;

"named person", in relation to an instrument made with a view to creating a lasting power of attorney, means a person who is named in the instrument as being a person to be notified of any application for the registration of the instrument;

"prescribed information", in relation to any instrument intended to create a lasting power of attorney, means the information contained in the form used for the instrument which appears under the heading "prescribed information".

Minimal differences from forms prescribed in these Regulations

A2–24   **3.**—(1) In these Regulations, any reference to a form—

(a) in the case of a form set out in Schedules 1 to 7 to these Regulations, is to be regarded as including a Welsh version of that form; and

(b) in the case of a form set out in Schedules 2 to 7 to these Regulations, is to be regarded as also including—

(i) a form to the same effect but which differs in an immaterial respect in form or mode of expression;

(ii) a form to the same effect but with such variations as the circumstances may require or the court or the Public Guardian may approve; or

(iii) a Welsh version of a form within (i) or (ii).

Computation of time

4.—(1) This regulation shows how to calculate any period of **A2–25** time which is specified in these Regulations.

(2) A period of time expressed as a number of days must be computed as clear days.

(3) Where the specified period is 7 days or less, and would include a day which is not a business day, that day does not count.

(4) When the specified period for doing any act at the office of the Public Guardian ends on a day on which the office is closed, that act will be done in time if done on the next day on which the office is open.

(5) In this regulation—

"business day" means a day other than—

(a) a Saturday, Sunday, Christmas Day or Good Friday; or

(b) a bank holiday under the Banking and Financial Dealings Act 1971, in England and Wales; and

"clear days" means that in computing the number of days—

(a) the day on which the period begins, and

(b) if the end of the period is defined by reference to an event, the day on which that event occurs, are not included.

PART 2

LASTING POWERS OF ATTORNEY

Instruments intended to create a lasting power of attorney

Forms for lasting powers of attorney

5. The forms set out in Parts 1 and 2 of Schedule 1 to these **A2–26** Regulations are the forms which, in the circumstances to which they apply, are to be used for instruments intended to create a lasting power of attorney.

Maximum number of named persons

6. The maximum number of named persons that the donor of a **A2–27** lasting power of attorney may specify in the instrument intended to create the power is 5.

Requirement for two LPA certificates where instrument has no named persons

A2–28   **7.** Where an instrument intended to create a lasting power of attorney includes a statement by the donor that there are no persons whom he wishes to be notified of any application for the registration of the instrument—

    (a) the instrument must include two LPA certificates; and

    (b) each certificate must be completed and signed by a different person.

Persons who may provide an LPA certificate

A2–29   **8.**—(1) Subject to paragraph (3), the following persons may give an LPA certificate—

    (a) a person chosen by the donor as being someone who has known him personally for the period of at least two years which ends immediately before the date on which that person signs the LPA certificate;

    (b) a person chosen by the donor who, on account of his professional skills and expertise, reasonably considers that he is competent to make the judgments necessary to certify the matters set out in paragraph (2)(1)(e) of Schedule 1 to the Act.

  (2) The following are examples of persons within paragraph (1)(b)—

    (a) a registered health care professional;

    (b) a barrister, solicitor or advocate called or admitted in any part of the United Kingdom;

    (c) a registered social worker; or

    (d) an independent mental capacity advocate.

  (3) A person is disqualified from giving an LPA certificate in respect of any instrument intended to create a lasting power of attorney if that person is—

    (a) a family member of the donor;

    (b) a donee of that power;

    (c) a donee of—

      (i) any other lasting power of attorney, or

      (ii) an enduring power of attorney,

    which has been executed by the donor (whether or not it has been revoked);

    (d) a family member of a donee within sub-paragraph (b);

    (e) a director or employee of a trust corporation acting as a donee within sub-paragraph (b);

    (f) a business partner or employee of—

      (i) the donor, or

      (ii) a donee within sub-paragraph (b);

    (g) an owner, director, manager or employee of any care home in which the donor is living when the instrument is executed; or

(h) a family member of a person within sub-paragraph (g).

(4) In this regulation—

"care home" has the meaning given in section 3 of the Care Standards Act 2000;

"registered health care professional" means a person who is a member of a profession regulated by a body mentioned in section 25(3) of the National Health Service Reform and Health Care Professions Act 2002; and

"registered social worker" means a person registered as a social worker in a register maintained by—

    (a) the General Social Care Council;

    (b) the Care Council for Wales;

    (c) the Scottish Social Services Council; or

    (d) the Northern Ireland Social Care Council.

Execution of instrument

9.—(1) An instrument intended to create a lasting power of **A2–30** attorney must be executed in accordance with this regulation.

(2) The donor must read (or have read to him) all the prescribed information.

(3) As soon as reasonably practicable after the steps required by paragraph (2) have been taken, the donor must—

(a) complete the provisions of Part A of the instrument that apply to him (or direct another person to do so); and

(b) subject to paragraph (7), sign Part A of the instrument in the presence of a witness.

(4) As soon as reasonably practicable after the steps required by paragraph (3) have been taken—

(a) the person giving an LPA certificate, or

(b) if regulation 7 applies (two LPA certificates required), each of the persons giving a certificate,

must complete the LPA certificate at Part B of the instrument and sign it.

(5) As soon as reasonably practicable after the steps required by paragraph (4) have been taken—

(a) the donee, or

(b) if more than one, each of the donees,

    must read (or have read to him) all the prescribed information.

(6) As soon as reasonably practicable after the steps required by paragraph (5) have been taken, the donee or, if more than one, each of them—

(a) must complete the provisions of Part C of the instrument that apply to him (or direct another person to do so); and

(b) subject to paragraph (7), must sign Part C of the instrument in the presence of a witness.

(7) If the instrument is to be signed by any person at the direction of the donor, or at the direction of any donee, the signature must be done in the presence of two witnesses.

(8) For the purposes of this regulation—

(a) the donor may not witness any signature required for the power;

(b) a donee may not witness any signature required for the power apart from that of another donee.

(9) A person witnessing a signature must—

(a) sign the instrument; and

(b) give his full name and address.

(10) Any reference in this regulation to a person signing an instrument (however expressed) includes his signing it by means of a mark made on the instrument at the appropriate place.

Registering the instrument

Notice to be given by a person about to apply for registration of lasting power of attorney

A2–31   **10.** Schedule 2 to these Regulations sets out the form of notice ("LPA 001") which must be given by a donor or donee who is about to make an application for the registration of an instrument intended to create a lasting power of attorney.

Application for registration

A2–32   **11.**—(1) Schedule 3 to these Regulations sets out the form ("LPA 002") which must be used for making an application to the Public Guardian for the registration of an instrument intended to create a lasting power of attorney.

(2) Where the instrument to be registered which is sent with the application is neither—

(a) the original instrument intended to create the power, nor

(b) a certified copy of it,

the Public Guardian must not register the instrument unless the court directs him to do so.

(3) In paragraph (2) "a certified copy" means a photographic or other facsimile copy which is certified as an accurate copy by—

(a) the donor; or

(b) a solicitor or notary.

Period to elapse before registration in cases not involving objection or defect

A2–33   **12.** The period at the end of which the Public Guardian must register an instrument in accordance with paragraph 5 of Schedule 1 to the Act is the period of 6 weeks beginning with—

(a) the date on which the Public Guardian gave the notice or notices under paragraph 7 or 8 of Schedule 1 to the Act of receipt of an application for registration; or

(b) if notices were given on more than one date, the latest of those dates.

Notice of receipt of application for registration

13.—(1) Part 1 of Schedule 4 to these Regulations sets out the A2–34 form of notice ("LPA 003A") which the Public Guardian must give to the donee (or donees) when the Public Guardian receives an application for the registration of a lasting power of attorney.

(2) Part 2 of Schedule 4 sets out the form of notice ("LPA 003B") which the Public Guardian must give to the donor when the Public Guardian receives such an application.

(3) Where it appears to the Public Guardian that there is good reason to do so, the Public Guardian must also provide (or arrange for the provision of) an explanation to the donor of—

(a) the notice referred to in paragraph (2) and what the effect of it is; and

(b) why it is being brought to his attention.

(4) Any information provided under paragraph (3) must be provided—

(a) to the donor personally; and

(b) in a way that is appropriate to the donor's circumstances (for example using simple language, visual aids or other appropriate means).

Objection to registration: notice to Public Guardian [to be given by the donee of the power or a named person]

14.—(1) This regulation deals with any objection to the registra- A2–35 tion of an instrument as a lasting power of attorney which is to be made to the Public Guardian [by the donee of the power or a named person].

(2) Where [the donee of the power or a named person]—

(a) is entitled to receive notice under paragraph 6, 7 or 8 of Schedule 1 to the Act of an application for the registration of the instrument, and

(b) wishes to object to registration on a ground set out in paragraph 13(1) of Schedule 1 to the Act,

he must do so before the end of the period of 5 weeks beginning with the date on which the notice is given.

(3) A notice of objection must be given in writing, setting out—

(a) the name and address of the objector;

(b) the name and address of the donor of the power;

(c) if known, the name and address of the donee (or donees); and

(d) the ground for making the objection.

(4) The Public Guardian must notify the objector as to whether he is satisfied that the ground of the objection is established.

(5) At any time after receiving the notice of objection and before giving the notice required by paragraph (4), the Public

Guardian may require the objector to provide such further information, or produce such documents, as the Public Guardian reasonably considers necessary to enable him to determine whether the ground for making the objection is established.

(6) Where—

(a) the Public Guardian is satisfied that the ground of the objection is established, but

(b) by virtue of section 13(7) of the Act, the instrument is not revoked,

the notice under paragraph (4) must contain a statement to that effect.

(7) Nothing in this regulation prevents an objector from making a further objection under paragraph 13 of Schedule 1 to the Act where—

(a) the notice under paragraph (4) indicates that the Public Guardian is not satisfied that the particular ground of objection to which that notice relates is established; and

(b) the period specified in paragraph (2) has not expired.

[Objection to registration: notice to Public Guardian to be given by the donor

14A.—(1) This regulation deals with any objection to the registration of an instrument as a lasting power of attorney which is to be made to the Public Guardian by the donor of the power.

(2) Where the donor of the power—

(a) is entitled to receive notice under paragraph 8 of Schedule 1 to the Act of an application for the registration of the instrument, and

(b) wishes to object to the registration,

he must do so before the end of the period of 5 weeks beginning with the date on which the notice is given.

(3) The donor of the power must give notice of his objection in writing to the Public Guardian, setting out—

(a) the name and address of the donor of the power;

(b) if known, the name and address of the donee (or donees); and

(c) the ground for making the objection.]

[*The words in square brackets in reg.14 and reg.14A inserted by SI 2007/2161 (The Lasting Powers of Attorney, Enduring Powers of Attorney and Public Guardian (Amendment) Regulations 2007 regs 3 and 4.*]

Objection to registration: application to the court

A2–36   **15.**—(1) This regulation deals with any objection to the registration of an instrument as a lasting power of attorney which is to be made to the court.

(2) The grounds for making an application to the court are—

(a) that one or more of the requirements for the creation of a lasting power of attorney have not been met;

(b) that the power has been revoked, or has otherwise come to an end, on a ground other than the grounds set out in paragraph 13(1) of Schedule 1 to the Act;

(c) any of the grounds set out in paragraph (a) or (b) of section 22(3) of the Act.

(3) Where any person—

(a) is entitled to receive notice under paragraph 6, 7 or 8 of Schedule 1 to the Act of an application for the registration of the instrument, and

(b) wishes to object to registration on one or more of the grounds set out in paragraph (2),

he must make an application to the court before the end of the period of 5 weeks beginning with the date on which the notice is given.

(4) The notice of an application to the court, which a person making an objection to the court is required to give to the Public Guardian under paragraph 13(3)(b)(ii) of Schedule 1 to the Act, must be in writing.

Notifying applicants of non-registration of lasting power of attorney

16. Where the Public Guardian is prevented from registering an A2–37 instrument as a lasting power of attorney by virtue of—

(a) paragraph 11(1) of Schedule 1 to the Act (instrument not made in accordance with Schedule),

(b) paragraph 12(2) of that Schedule (deputy already appointed),

(c) paragraph 13(2) of that Schedule (objection by donee or named person on grounds of bankruptcy, disclaimer, death etc),

(d) paragraph 14(2) of that Schedule (objection by donor), or

(e) regulation 11(2) of these Regulations (application for registration not accompanied by original instrument or certified copy),

he must notify the person (or persons) who applied for registration of that fact.

Notice to be given on registration of lasting power of attorney

17.—(1) Where the Public Guardian registers an instrument as a A2–38 lasting power of attorney, he must—

(a) retain a copy of the instrument; and

(b) return to the person (or persons) who applied for registration the original instrument, or the certified copy of it, which accompanied the application for registration.

(2) Schedule 5 to these Regulations sets out the form of notice ("LPA 004") which the Public Guardian must give to the donor and donee (or donees) when the Public Guardian registers an instrument.

(3) Where it appears to the Public Guardian that there is good reason to do so, the Public Guardian must also provide (or arrange for the provision of) an explanation to the donor of—

    (a) the notice referred to in paragraph (2) and what the effect of it is; and

    (b) why it is being brought to his attention.

(4) Any information provided under paragraph (3) must be provided—

    (a) to the donor personally; and

    (b) in a way that is appropriate to the donor's circumstances (for example using simple language, visual aids or other appropriate means).

(5) "Certified copy" is to be construed in accordance with regulation 11(3).

Post-registration

Changes to instrument registered as lasting power of attorney

A2–39   **18.**—(1) This regulation applies in any case where any of paragraphs 21 to 24 of Schedule 1 to the Act requires the Public Guardian to attach a note to an instrument registered as a lasting power of attorney.

(2) The Public Guardian must give a notice to the donor and the donee (or, if more than one, each of them) requiring him to deliver to the Public Guardian—

    (a) the original of instrument which was sent to the Public Guardian for registration;

    (b) any office copy of that registered instrument; and

    (c) any certified copy of that registered instrument.

(3) On receipt of the document, the Public Guardian must—

    (a) attach the required note; and

    (b) return the document to the person from whom it was obtained.

Loss or destruction of instrument registered as lasting power of attorney

A2–40   **19.**—(1) This regulation applies where—

    (a) a person is required by or under the Act to deliver up to the Public Guardian any of the following documents—

        (i) an instrument registered as a lasting power of attorney;

    (ii) an office copy of that registered instrument;

    (iii) a certified copy of that registered instrument; and

  (b) the document has been lost or destroyed.

(2) The person required to deliver up the document must provide to the Public Guardian in writing—

  (a) if known, the date of the loss or destruction and the circumstances in which it occurred;

  (b) otherwise, a statement of when he last had the document in his possession.

Disclaimer of appointment by a donee of lasting power of attorney

20.—(1) Schedule 6 to these Regulations sets out the form **A2–41** ("LPA 005") which a donee of an instrument registered as a lasting power of attorney must use to disclaim his appointment as donee.

(2) The donee must send—

  (a) the completed form to the donor; and

  (b) a copy of it to—

    (i) the Public Guardian; and

    (ii) any other donee who, for the time being, is appointed under the power.

Revocation by donor of lasting power of attorney

21.—(1) A donor who revokes a lasting power to attorney **A2–42** must—

  (a) notify the Public Guardian that he has done so; and

  (b) notify the donee (or, if more than one, each of them) of the revocation.

(2) Where the Public Guardian receives a notice under paragraph (1)(a), he must cancel the registration of the instrument creating the power if he is satisfied that the donor has taken such steps as are necessary in law to revoke it.

(3) The Public Guardian may require the donor to provide such further information, or produce such documents, as the Public Guardian reasonably considers necessary to enable him to determine whether the steps necessary for revocation have been taken.

(4) Where the Public Guardian cancels the registration of the instrument he must notify—

  (a) the donor; and

  (b) the donee or, if more than one, each of them.

Revocation of a lasting power of attorney on death of donor

22.—(1) The Public Guardian must cancel the registration of an **A2–43** instrument as a lasting power of attorney if he is satisfied that the power has been revoked as a result of the donor's death.

(2) Where the Public Guardian cancels the registration of an instrument he must notify the donee or, if more than one, each of them.

PART 3

ENDURING POWERS OF ATTORNEY

Notice of intention to apply for registration of enduring power of attorney

A2–44   **23.**—(1) Schedule 7 to these Regulations sets out the form of notice ("EP1PG") which an attorney (or attorneys) under an enduring power of attorney must give of his intention to make an application for the registration of the instrument creating the power.

(2) In the case of the notice to be given to the donor, the attorney must also provide (or arrange for the provision of) an explanation to the donor of—

(a) the notice and what the effect of it is; and

(b) why it is being brought to his attention.

(3) The information provided under paragraph (2) must be provided—

(a) to the donor personally; and

(b) in a way that is appropriate to the donor's circumstances (for example using simple language, visual aids or other appropriate means).

Application for registration

A2–45   **24.**—(1) Schedule 8 to these Regulations sets out the form ("EP2PG") which must be used for making an application to the Public Guardian for the registration of an instrument creating an enduring power of attorney.

(2) Where the instrument to be registered which is sent with the application is neither—

(a) the original instrument creating the power, nor

(b) a certified copy of it,

the Public Guardian must not register the instrument unless the court directs him to do so.

(3) "Certified copy", in relation to an enduring power of attorney, means a copy certified in accordance with section 3 of the Powers of Attorney Act 1971[5].

Notice of objection to registration

A2–46   **25.**—(1) This regulation deals with any objection to the registration of an instrument creating an enduring power of attorney which is to be made to the Public Guardian under paragraph 13(4) of Schedule 4 to the Act.

(2) A notice of objection must be given in writing, setting out—

(a) the name and address of the objector;
(b) if different, the name and address of the donor of the power;
(c) if known, the name and address of the attorney (or attorneys); and
(d) the ground for making the objection.

Notifying applicants of non-registration of enduring power of attorney

26. Where the Public Guardian is prevented from registering an A2–47 instrument creating an enduring power of attorney by virtue of—
(a) paragraph 13(2) of Schedule 4 to the Act (deputy already appointed),
(b) paragraph 13(5) of that Schedule (receipt by Public Guardian of valid notice of objection from person entitled to notice of application to register),
(c) paragraph 13(7) of that Schedule (Public Guardian required to undertake appropriate enquiries in certain circumstances), or
(d) regulation 24(2) of these Regulations (application for registration not accompanied by original instrument or certified copy),
he must notify the person (or persons) who applied for registration of that fact.

Registration of instrument creating an enduring power of attorney

27.—(1) Where the Public Guardian registers an instrument A2–48 creating an enduring power of attorney, he must—
(a) retain a copy of the instrument; and
(b) return to the person (or persons) who applied for registration the original instrument, or the certified copy of it, which accompanied the application.
(2) "Certified copy" has the same meaning as in regulation 24(3).

Objection or revocation not applying to all joint and several attorneys

28. In a case within paragraph 20(6) or (7) of Schedule 4 to the A2–49 Act, the form of the entry to be made in the register in respect of an instrument creating the enduring power of attorney is a stamp bearing the following words (inserting the information indicated, as appropriate)—

"THE REGISTRATION OF THIS ENDURING POWER OF ATTORNEY IS QUALIFIED AND EXTENDS TO THE APPOINTMENT OF .... (insert name of attorney(s) not affected by ground(s) of objection or revocation) ONLY AS THE ATTORNEY(S) OF .... (insert name of donor)".

Loss or destruction of instrument registered as enduring power of attorney

A2–50   **29.**—(1) This regulation applies where—

(a) a person is required by or under the Act to deliver up to the Public Guardian any of the following documents—

   (i) an instrument registered as an enduring power of attorney;

   (ii) an office copy of that registered instrument; or

   (iii) a certified copy of that registered instrument; and

(b) the document has been lost or destroyed.

(2) The person who is required to deliver up the document must provide to the Public Guardian in writing—

(a) if known, the date of the loss or destruction and the circumstances in which it occurred;

(b) otherwise, a statement of when he last had the document in his possession.

PART 4

FUNCTIONS OF THE PUBLIC GUARDIAN

The registers

Establishing and maintaining the registers

A2–51   **30.**—(1) In this Part "the registers" means—

(a) the register of lasting powers of attorney,

(b) the register of enduring powers of attorney, and

(c) the register of court orders appointing deputies,

which the Public Guardian must establish and maintain.

(2) On each register the Public Guardian may include—

(a) such descriptions of information about a registered instrument or a registered order as the Public Guardian considers appropriate; and

(b) entries which relate to an instrument or order for which registration has been cancelled.

Disclosure of information on a register: search by the Public Guardian

A2–52   **31.**—(1) Any person may, by an application made under paragraph (2), request the Public Guardian to carry out a search of one or more of the registers.

(2) An application must—
(a) state—
  (i) the register or registers to be searched;
  (ii) the name of the person to whom the application relates; and
  (iii) such other details about that person as the Public Guardian may require for the purpose of carrying out the search; and
(b) be accompanied by any fee provided for under section 58(4)(b) of the Act.

(3) The Public Guardian may require the applicant to provide such further information, or produce such documents, as the Public Guardian reasonably considers necessary to enable him to carry out the search.

(4) As soon as reasonably practicable after receiving the application—
(a) the Public Guardian must notify the applicant of the result of the search; and
(b) in the event that it reveals one or more entries on the register, the Public Guardian must disclose to the applicant all the information appearing on the register in respect of each entry.

Disclosure of additional information held by the Public Guardian

32.—(1) This regulation applies in any case where, as a result of **A2–53** a search made under regulation 31, a person has obtained information relating to a registered instrument or a registered order which confers authority to make decisions about matters concerning a person ("P").

(2) On receipt of an application made in accordance with paragraph (4), the Public Guardian may, if he considers that there is good reason to do so, disclose to the applicant such additional information as he considers appropriate.

(3) "Additional information" means any information relating to P—
(a) which the Public Guardian has obtained in exercising the functions conferred on him under the Act; but
(b) which does not appear on the register.

(4) An application must state—
(a) the name of P;
(b) the reasons for making the application; and
(c) what steps, if any, the applicant has taken to obtain the information from P.

(5) The Public Guardian may require the applicant to provide such further information, or produce such documents, as the Public Guardian reasonably considers necessary to enable him to determine the application.

(6) In determining whether to disclose any additional information to P, the Public Guardian must, in particular, have regard to—

(a) the connection between P and the applicant;

(b) the reasons for requesting the information (in particular, why the information cannot or should not be obtained directly from P);

(c) the benefit to P, or any detriment he may suffer, if a disclosure is made; and

(d) any detriment that another person may suffer if a disclosure is made.

Power to require information from donees of lasting power of attorney

A2–54   **46.**—(1) This regulation applies where it appears to the Public Guardian that there are circumstances suggesting that the donee of a lasting power of attorney may—

(a) have behaved, or may be behaving, in a way that contravenes his authority or is not in the best interests of the donor of the power,

(b) be proposing to behave in a way that would contravene that authority or would not be in the donor's best interests, or

(c) have failed to comply with the requirements of an order made, or directions given, by the court.

(2) The Public Guardian may require the donee—

(a) to provide specified information or information of a specified description; or

(b) to produce specified documents or documents of a specified description.

(3) The information or documents must be provided or produced—

(a) before the end of such reasonable period as may be specified; and

(b) at such place as may be specified.

(4) The Public Guardian may require—

(a) any information provided to be verified in such manner, or

(b) any document produced to be authenticated in such manner, as he may reasonably require.

(5) "Specified" means specified in a notice in writing given to the donee by the Public Guardian.

Power to require information from attorneys under enduring power of attorney

A2–55   **47.**—(1) This regulation applies where it appears to the Public Guardian that there are circumstances suggesting that, having regard to all the circumstances (and in particular the attorney's relationship to or connection with the donor) the attorney under a registered enduring power of attorney may be unsuitable to be the donor's attorney.

(2) The Public Guardian may require the attorney—
(a) to provide specified information or information of a specified description; or
(b) to produce specified documents or documents of a specified description.

(3) The information or documents must be provided or produced—
(a) before the end of such reasonable period as may be specified; and
(b) at such place as may be specified.

(4) The Public Guardian may require—
(a) any information provided to be verified in such manner, or
(b) any document produced to be authenticated in such manner, as he may reasonably require.

(5) "Specified" means specified in a notice in writing given to the attorney by the Public Guardian.

Other functions in relation to enduring powers of attorney

48. The Public Guardian has the following functions—   **A2–56**
(a) directing a Court of Protection Visitor—
  (i) to visit an attorney under a registered enduring power of attorney, or
  (ii) to visit the donor of a registered enduring power of attorney,
      and to make a report to the Public Guardian on such matters as he may direct;
(b) dealing with representations (including complaints) about the way in which an attorney under a registered enduring power of attorney is exercising his powers.

SCHEDULES

(Note: Schedule 1 is reproduced in Appendix 5 at p.290 et seq.)

SCHEDULE 2   **Regulation 10**

NOTICE OF INTENTION TO APPLY FOR REGISTRATION OF A LASTING
POWERS OF ATTORNEY: LPA 001

A2–57

LPA 001 | 10.07

Notice of intention to apply for registration of a Lasting Power of Attorney

This notice must be sent to everyone named by the donor in the Lasting Power of Attorney as a person who should be notified of an application to register. Relatives are not entitled to notice unless named in the Lasting Power of Attorney.

The application to register may be made by the donor or the attorney(s).

Where attorneys are appointed to act together they **all** must apply to register.

Details of the named person

Name		Address	
Telephone no.			
		Postcode	

To the named person - You have the right to object to the proposed registration of the Lasting Power of Attorney. You have **five weeks** from the day on which this notice is given to object. Details of how to object and the grounds for doing so are on the back page.

Details of the Lasting Power of Attorney (LPA)

Who is applying to register the LPA? ☐ the donor ☐ the attorney(s)

Which type of LPA is being registered? ☐ Property and Affairs ☐ Personal Welfare
(You must complete separate applications for each LPA you wish to register.)

On what date did the donor sign the LPA? `D D M M Y Y Y Y`

Details of the donor

Full name		Address	
Telephone no.			
		Postcode	

Details of the attorney(s)

Name of 1st attorney

Address

Telephone no.

Postcode

☐ solely   ☐ together and independently
☐ together   ☐ together in some matters and together and independently in others

Name of 2nd attorney

Address

Telephone no.

Postcode

☐ together   ☐ together and independently
☐ together in some matters and together and independently in others

Name of 3rd attorney

Address

Telephone no.

Postcode

☐ together   ☐ together and independently
☐ together in some matters and together and independently in others

Name of 4th attorney

Address

Telephone no.

Postcode

☐ together   ☐ together and independently
☐ together in some matters and together and independently in others

Signature and date ──

This notice must be signed by all parties applying to register the lasting power of attorney.

Signed

Print name

Dated

| D | C | M | M | Y | Y | Y | Y |

How to object to the registering of a Lasting Power of Attorney (LPA)

You can ask the Office of the Public Guardian (OPG) to stop the LPA from being registered if one of the factual grounds at (A) below has occurred. You need to tell us by completing Form LPA7 which is available from the OPG and by providing evidence to accompany it. You must send us the completed LPA7 form **within five weeks** from the date this notice was given. Failure to tell us could result in the LPA being registered.

(A) Factual grounds -- you can ask the Office of the Public Guardian to stop registration if:

- The Donor is bankrupt or interim bankrupt (for property and affairs LPAs only)
- The Attorney is bankrupt or interim bankrupt (for property and affairs LPAs only)
- The Attorney is a trust corporation and is wound up or dissolved (for property and affairs LPAs only)
- The Donor is dead
- The Attorney is dead
- That there has been dissolution or annulment of a marriage or civil partnership between the Donor and Attorney (except if the LPA provided that such an event should not affect the instrument)
- The Attorney(s) lack the capacity to be an attorney under the LPA
- The Attorney(s) have disclaimed their appointment

Form LPA7 is available from the OPG on 0845 330 2900 or www.publicguardian.gov.uk

You have the right to object to the Court of Protection about the registration of the LPA, but only on the grounds mentioned at (B) below. To do this you must contact the Court and complete the application to object form they will send you. Using that form, you must set out your reasons for objecting. They must receive the objection within five weeks from the date this notice was given. You must also notify the OPG when you object to the Court by using the separate form LPA8 that the Court will send you. Failure to notify the OPG of an objection may result in registration of the LPA.

Note: If you are objecting to the appointment of a specific attorney, it will not prevent registration if other attorneys or a substitute attorney have been appointed.

(B) Prescribed grounds -- you can only object to the Court of Protection against registration of the LPA on the following grounds:

- That the power purported to be created by the instrument* is not valid as a LPA. e.g. the person objecting does not believe the donor had capacity to make an LPA.
- That the power created by the instrument no longer exists e.g. the donor revoked it at a time when he/ she had capacity to do so.
- That fraud or undue pressure was used to induce the donor to make the power.
- The attorney proposes to behave in a way that would contravene his authority or would not be in the donor's best interests.

Note: * The instrument means the LPA made by the donor.

The Court will only consider objections made if they are made on the above grounds. To obtain a Court objection form please contact the Court of Protection at Archway Tower, 2 Junction Road, London N19 5SZ or Telephone 0845 330 2900.

SCHEDULE 3   **Regulation 11**

APPLICATION TO REGISTER A LASTING POWERS OF ATTORNEY.
LPA 002

A2–58   Note: this form must be submitted in A4 size.

LPA002 ▮ Office of the Public Guardian
Application to register a
Lasting Power of Attorney

Return your completed form to:
Office of the Public Guardian
Archway Tower
2 Junction Road
London N19 5SZ

Part 1 - The donor

Place a cross (x) against one option

Mr. ☐   Mrs. ☐   Ms. ☐   Miss ☐   Other ☐

If other, please specify ☐☐☐☐☐☐☐☐☐☐☐☐☐☐☐☐

Last name ☐☐☐☐☐☐☐☐☐☐☐☐☐☐☐☐☐☐☐☐☐☐☐☐

First name ☐☐☐☐☐☐☐☐☐☐☐☐☐☐☐☐☐☐☐☐☐☐☐☐

Middle name ☐☐☐☐☐☐☐☐☐☐☐☐☐☐☐☐☐☐☐☐☐☐☐☐

Address 1 ☐☐☐☐☐☐☐☐☐☐☐☐☐☐☐☐☐☐☐☐☐☐☐☐

Address 2 ☐☐☐☐☐☐☐☐☐☐☐☐☐☐☐☐☐☐☐☐☐☐☐☐

Address 3 ☐☐☐☐☐☐☐☐☐☐☐☐☐☐☐☐☐☐☐☐☐☐☐☐

Town/City ☐☐☐☐☐☐☐☐☐☐☐☐☐☐☐☐☐☐☐☐☐☐☐☐

County ☐☐☐☐☐☐☐☐☐☐☐☐☐☐☐☐☐☐☐☐☐☐☐☐

Postcode ☐☐☐☐☐☐   Daytime Tel. no. ☐☐☐☐☐☐☐☐☐☐☐☐☐☐☐☐

Date of birth ☐☐☐☐☐☐☐☐   If the exact date is unknown
D D M M Y Y Y Y   please state the year of birth

e-mail address ☐☐☐☐☐☐☐☐☐☐☐☐☐☐☐☐☐☐☐☐☐☐☐☐☐☐

Please do not write below this line - For office use only

LPA002 Application to register a lasting power of attorney (10 07)   1   © Crown Copyright 2007

Part 2 - The persons making the application

Note: We need to know who is applying and how the attorney(s) have been appointed, please answer the questions in parts two and three carefully.

Place a cross (x) against one option

Is the donor applying to register the Lasting Power of Attorney? ☐ Yes

Is the attorney(s) applying to register the Lasting Power of Attorney? ☐ Yes

Part 3 - How have the attorney(s) been appointed?

The LPA states whether the attorney is to act soley, together or together and independently

Place a cross (x) against one option

There is only one attorney appointed ☐

There are attorneys appointed together and independently ☐

There are attorneys appointed together ☐

There are attorneys appointed together in some matters and together and independently in others ☐

Note: We need to know which, if any of the attorney(s) are making this application to register the LPA. You can tell us this by putting a cross in the box at the start of each attorney(s) details in section 4.

Part 4 - Attorney one

Place a cross (**x**) in this box if attorney one is applying to register ☐

Place a cross (**x**) against one option

Mr. ☐   Mrs. ☐   Ms. ☐   Miss ☐   Other ☐

If other, please specify ☐☐☐☐☐☐☐☐☐☐☐☐☐☐☐☐

Last name ☐☐☐☐☐☐☐☐☐☐☐☐☐☐☐☐☐☐☐☐☐☐☐☐☐☐

First name ☐☐☐☐☐☐☐☐☐☐☐☐☐☐☐☐☐☐☐☐☐☐☐☐☐☐

Middle name ☐☐☐☐☐☐☐☐☐☐☐☐☐☐☐☐☐☐☐☐☐☐☐☐☐☐

Company name (if relevant) ☐☐☐☐☐☐☐☐☐☐☐☐☐☐☐☐☐☐☐☐☐☐☐☐☐☐

Address 1 ☐☐☐☐☐☐☐☐☐☐☐☐☐☐☐☐☐☐☐☐☐☐☐☐☐☐

Address 2 ☐☐☐☐☐☐☐☐☐☐☐☐☐☐☐☐☐☐☐☐☐☐☐☐☐☐

Address 3 ☐☐☐☐☐☐☐☐☐☐☐☐☐☐☐☐☐☐☐☐☐☐☐☐☐☐

Town/City ☐☐☐☐☐☐☐☐☐☐☐☐☐☐☐☐☐☐☐☐☐☐☐☐☐☐

County ☐☐☐☐☐☐☐☐☐☐☐☐☐☐☐☐☐☐☐☐☐☐☐☐☐☐

Postcode ☐☐☐☐☐☐☐   DX number ☐☐☐☐☐☐☐☐☐☐☐

Date of birth ☐☐☐☐☐☐☐☐   DX Exchange ☐☐☐☐☐☐☐☐☐☐☐☐☐☐☐☐
D D M M Y Y Y Y

Daytime Tel. no. ☐☐☐☐☐☐☐☐☐☐☐☐☐☐☐

Occupation ☐☐☐☐☐☐☐☐☐☐☐☐☐☐☐☐☐☐☐☐☐☐☐☐☐☐

e-mail address ☐☐☐☐☐☐☐☐☐☐☐☐☐☐☐☐☐☐☐☐☐☐☐☐☐☐

Place a cross (**x**) against one option that best describes your relationship to the donor

Civil partner / Spouse ☐   Child ☐   Solicitor ☐   Other ☐   Other professional ☐

If 'Other' or 'Other professional', please specify ☐☐☐☐☐☐☐☐☐☐☐☐☐☐

3

Part 4 - Attorney two

Place a cross (x) in this box if attorney two is applying to register ☐

Place a cross (x) against one option

Mr. ☐   Mrs. ☐   Ms. ☐   Miss ☐   Other ☐

If other, please specify ☐☐☐☐☐☐☐☐☐☐☐☐☐☐

Last name ☐☐☐☐☐☐☐☐☐☐☐☐☐☐☐☐☐☐☐☐☐☐☐☐☐☐☐☐

First name ☐☐☐☐☐☐☐☐☐☐☐☐☐☐☐☐☐☐☐☐☐☐☐☐☐☐☐☐

Middle name ☐☐☐☐☐☐☐☐☐☐☐☐☐☐☐☐☐☐☐☐☐☐☐☐☐☐☐☐

Company name *(if relevant)* ☐☐☐☐☐☐☐☐☐☐☐☐☐☐☐☐☐☐☐☐☐☐☐☐☐☐☐☐

Address 1 ☐☐☐☐☐☐☐☐☐☐☐☐☐☐☐☐☐☐☐☐☐☐☐☐☐☐☐☐

Address 2 ☐☐☐☐☐☐☐☐☐☐☐☐☐☐☐☐☐☐☐☐☐☐☐☐☐☐☐☐

Address 3 ☐☐☐☐☐☐☐☐☐☐☐☐☐☐☐☐☐☐☐☐☐☐☐☐☐☐☐☐

Town/City ☐☐☐☐☐☐☐☐☐☐☐☐☐☐☐☐☐☐☐☐☐☐☐☐☐☐☐☐

County ☐☐☐☐☐☐☐☐☐☐☐☐☐☐☐☐☐☐☐☐☐☐☐☐☐☐☐☐

Postcode ☐☐☐☐☐☐☐   DX number ☐☐☐☐☐☐☐☐☐☐☐☐☐

Date of birth ☐☐☐☐☐☐☐☐   DX Exchange ☐☐☐☐☐☐☐☐☐☐☐☐☐
D D M M Y Y Y Y

Daytime Tel. no. ☐☐☐☐☐☐ ☐☐☐☐☐☐☐☐☐

Occupation ☐☐☐☐☐☐☐☐☐☐☐☐☐☐☐☐☐☐☐☐☐☐☐☐☐☐☐☐

e-mail address ☐☐☐☐☐☐☐☐☐☐☐☐☐☐☐☐☐☐☐☐☐☐☐☐☐☐☐☐

Place a cross (x) against one option that best describes your relationship to the donor

Civil partner / Spouse ☐   Child ☐   Solicitor ☐   Other ☐   Other professional ☐

If 'Other' or 'Other professional', please specify ☐☐☐☐☐☐☐☐☐☐☐☐☐

4

Part 4 - Attorney three

Place a cross (x) in this box if attorney three is applying to register ☐

Place a cross (x) against one option

Mr. ☐   Mrs. ☐   Ms. ☐   Miss ☐   Other ☐

If other, please specify ☐☐☐☐☐☐☐☐☐☐☐☐☐☐☐☐☐

Last name ☐☐☐☐☐☐☐☐☐☐☐☐☐☐☐☐☐☐☐☐☐☐☐☐☐

First name ☐☐☐☐☐☐☐☐☐☐☐☐☐☐☐☐☐☐☐☐☐☐☐☐☐

Middle name ☐☐☐☐☐☐☐☐☐☐☐☐☐☐☐☐☐☐☐☐☐☐☐☐☐

Company name *(if relevant)* ☐☐☐☐☐☐☐☐☐☐☐☐☐☐☐☐☐☐☐☐☐☐☐☐☐

Address 1 ☐☐☐☐☐☐☐☐☐☐☐☐☐☐☐☐☐☐☐☐☐☐☐☐☐

Address 2 ☐☐☐☐☐☐☐☐☐☐☐☐☐☐☐☐☐☐☐☐☐☐☐☐☐

Address 3 ☐☐☐☐☐☐☐☐☐☐☐☐☐☐☐☐☐☐☐☐☐☐☐☐☐

Town/City ☐☐☐☐☐☐☐☐☐☐☐☐☐☐☐☐☐☐☐☐☐☐☐☐☐

County ☐☐☐☐☐☐☐☐☐☐☐☐☐☐☐☐☐☐☐☐☐☐☐☐☐

Postcode ☐☐☐☐☐☐☐   DX number ☐☐☐☐☐☐☐☐☐☐☐☐

Date of birth ☐☐☐☐☐☐☐☐
D D M M Y Y Y Y   DX Exchange ☐☐☐☐☐☐☐☐☐☐☐☐☐☐☐☐

Daytime Tel. no. ☐☐☐☐☐☐ ☐☐☐☐☐☐☐☐☐

Occupation ☐☐☐☐☐☐☐☐☐☐☐☐☐☐☐☐☐☐☐☐☐☐☐☐☐

e-mail address ☐☐☐☐☐☐☐☐☐☐☐☐☐☐☐☐☐☐☐☐☐☐☐☐☐

Place a cross (x) against one option that best describes your relationship to the donor

Civil partner / Spouse ☐   Child ☐   Solicitor ☐   Other ☐   Other professional ☐

If 'Other' or 'Other professional', please specify ☐☐☐☐☐☐☐☐☐☐☐☐☐

5

Part 4 - Attorney four

Place a cross (x) in this box if attorney four is applying to register ☐

> If there are additional attorneys, please provide the following details in the 'Additional information' section at the end of this form.

Place a cross (x) against one option

Mr. ☐   Mrs. ☐   Ms. ☐   Miss ☐   Other ☐

If other, please specify

Last name

First name

Middle name

Company name *(if relevant)*

Address 1

Address 2

Address 3

Town/City

County

Postcode   DX number

Date of birth
D D M M Y Y Y Y   DX Exchange

Daytime Tel. no.

Occupation

e-mail address

Place a cross (x) against one option that best describes your relationship to the donor

Civil partner / Spouse ☐   Child ☐   Solicitor ☐   Other ☐   Other professional ☐

If 'Other' or 'Other professional', please specify

6

Part 5 - Notification of named persons

The donor or attorney(s) making the application must give notice to the named persons nominated by the donor in the section of the LPA marked 'Notifying others when an application to register your LPA is made'. The date on which the notice was given **must** be completed (which is the date it was posted or given to the named person). If the donor decided not to notify any named persons, please place a cross in the box provided.

The donor did not specify any named individuals in the LPA ☐

Place a cross (**x**) against one option

☐ I   ☐ We

have given notice to register in the prescribed form (LP1) to the following person(s):

Date notice given
D D M M Y Y Y Y

Last name

First name

Address 1

Address 2

Address 3

Town/City

County

Postcode

Part 5 - continued

Date notice given

D D M M Y Y Y Y

Last name

First name

Address 1

Address 2

Address 3

Town/City

County

Postcode

Date notice given

D D M M Y Y Y Y

Last name

First name

Address 1

Address 2

Address 3

Town/City

County

Postcode

Part 5 - continued

Date notice given
D D M M Y Y Y Y

Last name

First name

Address 1

Address 2

Address 3

Town/City

County

Postcode

Date notice given
D D M M Y Y Y Y

Last name

First name

Address 1

Address 2

Address 3

Town/City

County

Postcode

Part 6 - Fees

Guidelines on fee exemption and remission can be obtained from the Office of the Public Guardian.

Have you enclosed a cheque for the registration fee for this application? ☐ Yes ☐ No

Do you wish to apply for remission of the fee? ☐ Yes ☐ No

Do you wish to apply for exemption of the fee? ☐ Yes ☐ No

Do you wish to apply for postponement of the fee? ☐ Yes ☐ No

If you wish to apply for exemption, remission or postponement of all or part of the fee. You must complete the separate application form available from the Office of the Public Guardian.

Part 7 - Type of power

☐ I ☐ We

apply to register the LPA (the original of which accompanies this application) made by the donor under the provisions of the Mental Capacity Act 2005.

What type of Lasting Power of Attorney are you applying to register?

☐ Property and affairs **OR** ☐ Personal welfare

Date that the **donor** signed the Lasting Power of Attorney
D D M M Y Y Y Y

To your knowledge, has the donor made any other Enduring Powers of Attorney or Lasting Power of Attorney? ☐ Yes ☐ No

If Yes, please give details below including registration date if applicable

Part 8 - Donor declaration

Note: This section should only be completed by the donor if they are applying for the registration of the Lasting Power of Attorney.

I apply to register the Lasting Power of Attorney (the original of which accompanies this application).

I certify that the above information is correct and that to the best of my knowledge and belief, I have completed the application in accordance with the provisions of the Mental Capacity Act 2005 and all statutory instruments made under it.

Signed _____ Date [ ][ ] [ ][ ] [ ][ ][ ][ ]
                                       D D   M M Y Y Y Y

Last name [ ]

First name [ ]

Part 9 - Attorney(s) declaration

Note: This section should only be completed by the attorney(s) if they are applying for the registration of the Lasting Power of Attorney.

[ ] I [ ] We   apply to register the Lasting Power of Attorney (the original of which accompanies this application).

[ ] I [ ] We   certify that the above information is correct to the best of my knowledge and belief.

[ ] I [ ] We   have completed the application within the provisions of the Mental Capacity Act 2005 and all statutory instruments made under it.

Signed _____ Date [ ][ ] [ ][ ] [ ][ ][ ][ ]
                                       D D   M M Y Y Y Y

Last name [ ]

First name [ ]

Signed _____ Date [ ][ ] [ ][ ] [ ][ ][ ][ ]
                                       D D   M M Y Y Y Y

Last name [ ]

First name [ ]

11

Part 9 - continued

Signed [   ] Date [| | | | | | |]
                                                   D D M M Y Y Y Y

Last name [| | | | | | | | | | | | | | | | | | | | | | | | | | | | | |]

First name [| | | | | | | | | | | | | | | | | | | | | | | | | | | | | |]

Signed [   ] Date [| | | | | | |]
                                                   D D M M Y Y Y Y

Last name [| | | | | | | | | | | | | | | | | | | | | | | | | | | | | |]

First name [| | | | | | | | | | | | | | | | | | | | | | | | | | | | | |]

Signed [   ] Date [| | | | | | |]
                                                   D D M M Y Y Y Y

Last name [| | | | | | | | | | | | | | | | | | | | | | | | | | | | | |]

First name [| | | | | | | | | | | | | | | | | | | | | | | | | | | | | |]

Part 10 - Declaration by a trust corporation

If you are a trust corporation making this application please complete this declaration.

[ ] I   [ ] We

certify that the above information is correct and that to the best of my knowledge and belief, I have completed the application in accordance with the provisions of the Mental Capacity Act 2005 and all statutory instruments made under it.

Company name [| | | | | | | | | | | | | | | | | | | | | | | | | | | | | |]

Signature of authorised person(s) [   ]   Company seal (If applicable)
[   ]   [   ]

Last name [| | | | | | | | | | | | | | | | | | | | | | | | | | | | | |]

First name [| | | | | | | | | | | | | | | | | | | | | | | | | | | | | |]

12

Part 11 - Correspondence address

Place a cross (x) against one option

Mr. ☐   Mrs. ☐   Ms. ☐   Miss ☐   Other ☐

If other, please specify ⬚⬚⬚⬚⬚⬚⬚⬚⬚⬚⬚⬚⬚⬚

Last name ⬚⬚⬚⬚⬚⬚⬚⬚⬚⬚⬚⬚⬚⬚⬚⬚⬚⬚⬚⬚⬚⬚⬚⬚⬚

First name ⬚⬚⬚⬚⬚⬚⬚⬚⬚⬚⬚⬚⬚⬚⬚⬚⬚⬚⬚⬚⬚⬚⬚⬚⬚

Middle name ⬚⬚⬚⬚⬚⬚⬚⬚⬚⬚⬚⬚⬚⬚⬚⬚⬚⬚⬚⬚⬚⬚⬚⬚⬚

Company name ⬚⬚⬚⬚⬚⬚⬚⬚⬚⬚⬚⬚⬚⬚⬚⬚⬚⬚⬚⬚⬚⬚⬚⬚⬚

Company reference ⬚⬚⬚⬚⬚⬚⬚⬚⬚⬚⬚⬚⬚⬚⬚⬚⬚⬚⬚⬚⬚⬚⬚⬚⬚

Address 1 ⬚⬚⬚⬚⬚⬚⬚⬚⬚⬚⬚⬚⬚⬚⬚⬚⬚⬚⬚⬚⬚⬚⬚⬚⬚

Address 2 ⬚⬚⬚⬚⬚⬚⬚⬚⬚⬚⬚⬚⬚⬚⬚⬚⬚⬚⬚⬚⬚⬚⬚⬚⬚

Address 3 ⬚⬚⬚⬚⬚⬚⬚⬚⬚⬚⬚⬚⬚⬚⬚⬚⬚⬚⬚⬚⬚⬚⬚⬚⬚

Town/City ⬚⬚⬚⬚⬚⬚⬚⬚⬚⬚⬚⬚⬚⬚⬚⬚⬚⬚⬚⬚⬚⬚⬚⬚⬚

County ⬚⬚⬚⬚⬚⬚⬚⬚⬚⬚⬚⬚⬚⬚⬚⬚⬚⬚⬚⬚⬚⬚⬚⬚⬚

Postcode ⬚⬚⬚⬚⬚⬚⬚   DX number ⬚⬚⬚⬚⬚⬚⬚⬚⬚⬚

DX Exchange ⬚⬚⬚⬚⬚⬚⬚⬚⬚⬚⬚⬚⬚⬚⬚⬚

Daytime Tel. no. ⬚⬚⬚⬚⬚⬚ ⬚⬚⬚⬚⬚⬚⬚⬚

e-mail address ⬚⬚⬚⬚⬚⬚⬚⬚⬚⬚⬚⬚⬚⬚⬚⬚⬚⬚⬚⬚⬚⬚⬚⬚⬚

Part 12 - Additional information

Please write down any additional information to support this application in the space below. If necessary
attach additional sheets.

14

SCHEDULE 4 **Regulation 13**

NOTICE OF RECEIPT OF AN APPLICATION TO REGISTER A LASTING POWER OF ATTORNEY: LPA 003A AND LPA 003B

Part 1: Notice to an Attorney of Receipt of an Application to Register a Lasting Power of Attorney

A2–59

LPA 003A 10 07

Notice to an attorney of receipt of an application to register a Lasting Power of Attorney

Name of attorney

Take notice

An application to register a Lasting Power of Attorney (LPA) has been received by the Office of the Public Guardian.

We are sending you this notice because you are named as an attorney in the LPA and were not involved in the application to register.

You are hereby given notice of the proposed registration. **You have the right to object to the registration.** Details of how to do so are set out on page 2 of this notice. You have five weeks in which to object from the date this notice was given. (We will treat this notice as having been given two days after the date below.)

The names of the donor and the attorney(s) are set out below:

Donor's full name

The following attorney(s) have applied to register an LPA in the name of the above donor.

Attorney's full name

Attorney's full name

Attorney's full name

From   Dated
The Office of the Public Guardian
Archway Tower, 2 Junction Road
London N19 5SZ
Telephone 0845 330 2900

How to object to the registering of a Lasting Power of Attorney (LPA)

You can ask the Office of the Public Guardian (OPG) to stop the LPA from being registered if one of the factual grounds at (A) below has occurred. You need to tell us by completing Form LPA7 which is available from the OPG and by providing evidence to accompany it. You must send us the completed LPA7 form **within five weeks** from the date this notice was given. Failure to tell us could result in the LPA being registered.

(A) Factual grounds – you can ask the Office of the Public Guardian to stop registration if:

- The Donor is bankrupt or interim bankrupt (for property and affairs LPAs only)
- The Attorney is bankrupt or interim bankrupt (for property and affairs LPAs only)
- The Attorney is a trust corporation and is wound up or dissolved (for property and affairs LPAs only)
- The Donor is dead
- The Attorney is dead
- That there has been dissolution or annulment of a marriage or civil partnership between the Donor and Attorney (except if the LPA provided that such an event should not affect the instrument)
- The Attorney lacks the capacity to be an attorney under the LPA
- The Attorney disclaimed their appointment

Form LPA7 is available from the OPG on 0845 330 2900 or www.publicguardian.gov.uk

You have the right to object to the Court of Protection about the registration of the LPA, but only on the grounds mentioned at (B) below. To do this you must contact the Court and complete the application to object form they will send you. Using that form, you must set out your reasons for objecting. They must receive the objection within five weeks from the date this notice was given. You must also notify the OPG when you object to the Court by using the separate form LPA8 that the Court will send you. Failure to notify the OPG of an objection may result in registration of the LPA.

Note: If you are objecting to the appointment of a specific attorney, it will not prevent registration if other attorneys or substitute attorneys have been appointed.

(B) Prescribed grounds – you can only object to the Court of Protection against registration of the LPA on the following grounds:

- That the power purported to be created by the instrument* is not valid as a LPA. e.g. the person objecting does not believe the donor had capacity to make an LPA.
- That the power created by the instrument no longer exists e.g. the donor revoked it at a time when he/ she had capacity to do so.
- That fraud or undue pressure was used to induce the donor to make the power.
- The attorney proposes to behave in a way that would contravene his authority or would not be in the donor's best interests.

Note: * The instrument means the LPA made by the donor.

The Court will only consider objections made if they are made on the above grounds. To obtain a Court objection form please contact the Court of Protection at Archway Tower, 2 Junction Road, London N19 5SZ or telephone 0845 330 2900.

Part 2: Notice to Donor of Receipt of an Application to Register a Lasting Power of Attorney

A2–60

LPA 003B 10.07

Notice to donor of receipt of an application to register a Lasting Power of Attorney

Name of donor

Take notice

An application to register your Lasting Power of Attorney (LPA) has been received by the Office of the Public Guardian (OPG).

We are sending you this notice because your attorney(s) in the LPA has asked the OPG to register your LPA, so that it can be used.

You are hereby given notice of the proposed registration. **You have a right to object to the registration.** You have five weeks in which to object from the date this notice was given. (We will treat this notice as having been given two days after the date below). You can object by using form LPA6, which you can get from the OPG.

The names of your attorney(s) are set out below:

Attorney's full name

Attorney's full name

Attorney's full name

Attorney's full name

Dated

From
The Office of the Public Guardian
Archway Tower, 2 Junction Road
London N19 5SZ

Telephone 0845 330 2900

SCHEDULE 5   **Regulation 17**

NOTICE OF REGISTRATION OF A LASTING POWER OF ATTORNEY: LPA 004

A2–61

LPA 004 10 07

Notice of registration of a Lasting Power of Attorney

This notice is to confirm registration of a Lasting Power of Attorney.

Case no.

The donor

The attorney(s)

The Lasting Power of Attorney was entered into the register on

Notification of registration of the LPA is given as required in Schedule 1 Part 2 Paragraph 15 of the Mental Capacity Act 2005.

SCHEDULE 6

Regulation 20

DISCLAIMER BY DONEE OF A LASTING POWER OF ATTORNEY: LPA 005

A2–62

LPA 005 10.07

Disclaimer by a proposed or acting attorney under a Lasting Power of Attorney

Take notice that

☐ a proposed attorney

☐ an attorney acting under a Lasting Power of Attorney

has disclaimed appointment.

Details of attorney disclaiming appointment ————————————

Name	Address

Telephone no.

Postcode ☐☐☐☐☐☐☐☐

Date of the Lasting Power of Attorney ————————————

On what date was the Lasting Power of Attorney made? ☐☐ ☐☐ ☐☐☐☐

Signature and date ————————————

I disclaim my appointment as attorney under the Lasting Power of Attorney made by the donor.

Signed

Dated ☐☐ ☐☐ ☐☐☐☐

Note: Where the LPA has been registered then a copy of this notice must be sent to the Office of the Public Guardian at: Archway Tower, 2 Junction Road, London N19 5SZ

Call OPG on 0845 330 2900 with any questions.

© Crown copyright 2007

Details of the donor —————————————————————————

Name

Address

Telephone no.

Postcode

Details of the other attorney(s) ——————————————————

Name

Address

Telephone no.

Postcode

Name

Address

Telephone no.

Postcode

Name

Address

Telephone no.

Postcode

APPENDIX 2

SCHEDULE 7   **Regulation 23**

NOTICE OF INTENTION TO APPLY FOR REGISTRATION OF A ENDURING POWER OF ATTORNEY

A2–63

Form EP1PG

Mental Capacity Act 2005
Enduring Power of Attorney

> Notice of intention to apply for registration
> of an Enduring Power of Attorney

To...

Of...

This form may be adapted for use by three or more attorneys	**TAKE NOTICE THAT** I .... of .... and I .... of .... The attorney(s) of ....
Give the name and address of the donor	

....

of ....

....

intend to apply to the Public Guardian for registration of the

enduring power of attorney appointing me (us) attorney(s) and

made by the donor on the ....

1. You have the right to object to the proposed registration on one or more of the grounds set out below. You must notify the Office of the Public Guardian of your objection within five weeks from the day this notice was given to you. You may make an application to the Court of Protection under rule [68] of the Court of Protection Rules 2007 for a decision on the matter. No fee is payable for such an application. If you do not make such an application, the Public Guardian will ask for the court's directions about registration.[1]

> The grounds upon which you can object are limited and are shown at 2 overleaf

EP1PG DRAFT V 2

---

[1] This form was amended by SI 2007/2050 (The Public Guardian (Fees, etc.) Regulations 2007).

Note: The instrument means the document used to make the enduring power of attorney made by the donor, which it is sought to register

The attorney(s) does not have to be a relative. Relatives are not entitled to know of the existence of the enduring power of attorney prior to being given this notice

Our staff will be able to assist with any questions you have regarding the objection (s). However, they cannot provide advice about your particular objection.

Note: Part 4 is addressed only to the donor

Note: This notice should be signed by every one of the attorneys who are applying to register the enduring power of attorney

Note: The attorney(s) must keep a record of the date on which notice was given to the donor and to relatives. This information will be required from the attorney(s) when an application to register the EPA is made

2. The grounds on which you may object to the proposed registration are:

- That the power purported to be created by the instrument is not valid as an enduring power of attorney
- That the power created by the instrument no longer subsists
- That the application is premature because the donor is not yet becoming mentally incapable
- That fraud or undue pressure was used to induce the donor to make the power
- That the attorney is unsuitable to be the donor's attorney (having regard to all the circumstances and in particular the attorney's relationship to or connection with the donor).

3. You can obtain the necessary forms to object by.
- Writing to us at the address on the foot of this form
- Calling us on 0845 330 2900
- Downloading the forms from our website at www.publicguardian.gov.uk

4. You are informed that while the enduring power of attorney remains registered, you will not be able to revoke it until the Court of Protection confirms the revocation.

Signed: .... Dated: ....

Signed: .... Dated: ....

Please write to:
Customer Services
Archway Tower
2 Junction Road
London
N19 5SZ
www.publicguardian.gov.uk

EP1PG - DRAFT V.2

SCHEDULE 8 **Regulation 24**

APPLICATION TO REGISTER AN ENDURING POWER OF ATTORNEY

A2–64 Note: this form must be submitted in A4 size.

Office of the Public Guardian
Mental Capacity Act 2005
Form EP2PG
Application for Registration of an Enduring
Power of Attorney

IMPORTANT: Please complete the form in **BLOCK CAPITALS** using a black ball-point pen. Place a clear cross 'X' mark inside square option boxes ☒ - do not circle the option.

Part One - The Donor

Please state the full name and present address of the donor. State the donor's first name in 'Forename 1' and the donor's other forenames in full in 'Other Forenames'. Company Name should be completed with the name of the nursing/care home or hospital where applicable.

Mr ☐ Mrs ☐ Ms ☐ Miss ☐ Other ☐
Place a cross against one option ☒

If Other, please specify here:

Last Name:

Forename 1:

Other Forenames:

Company Name:

Address 1:

Address 2:

Address 3:

Town/City:

County:

Postcode:

Donor Date of Birth: D D M M Y Y Y Y
If the exact date is unknown please state the year of birth

Please do not write below this line - For Office Use Only

Produced in association with the Office of the Public Guardian   © Crown Copyright 2007   Provider details

Part Two - Attorney One

Please state the full name and present address of the attorney. Professionals e.g, Solicitors or Accountants, should complete the Company Name field.

Mr   Mrs   Ms   Miss   Other

☐   ☐   ☐   ☐   ☐

Place a cross against one option ☒

If Other, please specify here:

Last Name:

Forename 1:

Other Forenames:

Company Name:

Address 1:

Address 2:

Address 3:

Town/City:

County:

Postcode: DX No. (solicitors only):

DX Exchange (solicitors only):

Attorney Date of Birth: Daytime Tel No.:

D D M M Y Y Y Y   (STD Code):

Email Address:

Occupation:

Relationship to donor:

Civil Partner / Spouse   Child   Other Relation   No Relation   Solicitor   Other Professional

☐   ☐   ☐   ☐   ☐   ☐

Place a cross against one option ☒

If 'Other Relation' or 'Other Professional', specify relationship:

Part B of the Enduring Power of Attorney states whether the attorney is to act jointly, jointly and severally, or alone.

Appointment (*Place a cross against one option* ☒):   Jointly   ☐

Jointly and Severally   ☐

Alone   ☐

Part Three - Attorney Two

Please state the full name and present address of the attorney. Professionals e.g. Solicitors or Accountants, should complete the Company Name field.

Mr ☐ Mrs ☐ Ms ☐ Miss ☐ Other ☐
Place a cross against one option ☒
If Other, please specify here: ☐☐☐☐☐☐☐☐☐☐☐☐☐☐☐☐☐

Last Name:

Forename 1:

Other Forenames:

Company Name:

Address 1:

Address 2:

Address 3:

Town/City:

County:

Postcode: DX No. (solicitors only):

DX Exchange (solicitors only):

Attorney Date of Birth: D D M M Y Y Y Y   Daytime Tel No.: (STD Code):

Email Address:

Occupation:

Relationship to donor:

Civil Partner / Spouse ☐ Child ☐ Other Relation ☐ No Relation ☐ Solicitor ☐ Other Professional ☐
Place a cross against one option ☒
If 'Other Relation' or 'Other Professional', specify relationship:

Part Four - Attorney Three

Please state the full name and present address of the attorney. Professionals e.g. Solicitors or Accountants, should complete the Company Name field.

Mr ☐ Mrs ☐ Ms ☐ Miss ☐ Other ☐
Place a cross against one option ☒
If Other, please specify here: ☐☐☐☐☐☐☐☐☐☐☐☐☐☐☐☐☐

Last Name:

Forename 1:

Part Four Continued Overleaf

Part Four - Attorney Three cont'd

Other Forenames:		

Company Name:		

Address 1:

Address 2:

Address 3:

Town/City:

County:

Postcode:		DX No. (solicitors only):

DX Exchange (solicitors only):

Attorney Date of Birth:		Daytime Tel No.:

D D M M Y Y Y Y   (STD Code):

Email Address:

Occupation:

Relationship to donor:

Civil Partner / Spouse	Child	Other Relation	No Relation	Solicitor	Other Professional	If 'Other Relation' or 'Other Professional', specify relationship:
☐	☐	☐	☐	☐	☐	

Place a cross against one option ☒

If there are additional attorneys, please complete the above details in the 'Additional Information' section (at the end of this form).

Part Five - The Enduring Power of Attorney

I (We) the attorney(s) apply to register the Enduring Power of Attorney made by the donor under the Enduring Powers of Attorney Act 1985, the original of which accompanies this application.

I (We) have reason to believe that the donor is or is becoming mentally incapable.

Date that the **Donor** signed the Enduring Power of Attorney. *You can find this in Part B of the Enduring Power of Attorney.*

D D M M Y Y Y Y

To your knowledge, has the Donor made any other Enduring Powers of Attorney?:

Yes No
☐   ☐

Place a cross against one option ☒

If 'Yes', please give details below including registration date if applicable:

Part Six - Notice of Application to Donor

Notice must be given personally to the donor. It should be made clear if someone other than the attorney(s) gives the notice. The date on which the notice was given MUST be completed.

I (We) have given notice of the application to register in the prescribed form (EP1PG) to the donor personally,

on this date: [ ][ ] [ ][ ] [ ][ ][ ][ ]

        D   D   M   M   Y   Y   Y   Y

If someone other than the attorney gives notice to the donor please complete the name and address details below. Please also complete the date above:

Full Name:	
Address 1:	
Address 2:	
Address 3:	
Town/City:	
County:	Postcode:

Part Seven - Notice of Application to Relatives

Please complete details of all relatives entitled to notice.

Please place a cross in the box ☒ if no relatives are entitled to notice: ☐

I (We) have given notice to register in the prescribed form (EP1PG) to the following relatives of the donor:

Full Name:		Relationship to Donor:	
Address:		Date notice given:	
		D D M M Y Y Y Y	

Full Name:		Relationship to Donor:	
Address:		Date notice given:	
		D D M M Y Y Y Y	

Full Name:		Relationship to Donor:	
Address:		Date notice given:	
		D D M M Y Y Y Y	

Full Name:		Relationship to Donor:	
Address:		Date notice given:	
		D D M M Y Y Y Y	

Full Name:		Relationship to Donor:	
Address:		Date notice given:	
		D D M M Y Y Y Y	

If there are additional relatives please complete the Relative Name, Relationship, Address and Date details in the 'Additional Information' section (at the end of this form).

Part Eight - Notice of Application to Co-Attorney(s)

Do not complete this section if it does not apply. If there are additional co-attorneys please complete the Attorney Name, Relationship, Address and Date details in the 'Additional Information' section (at the end of this form).

Are all the attorneys applying to register?   Yes ☐   No ☐   *Place a cross against one option* ☒

If no, I (We) have given notice to my (our) co-attorney(s) as follows:

Full Name:		Relationship to Donor:	

Address:

Date notice given:

D D M M Y Y Y Y

Full Name:		Relationship to Donor:	

Address:

Date notice given:

D D M M Y Y Y Y

Part Nine - Fees

Guidelines on remission and postponement of fees can be obtained from the Office of the Public Guardian.

Have you enclosed a cheque for the registration fee for this application?   Yes ☐   No ☐   *Place a cross against one option* ☒

Do you wish to apply for postponement, exemption or remission of the fee?   Yes ☐   No ☐   *Place a cross against one option* ☒

If yes, please complete the application for exemption or remission form.

Part Ten - Declaration

Note: The application should be signed by all attorneys who are making the application. This must not pre-date the date(s) when the notices were given.

I (We) certify that the above information is correct and that to the best of my (our) knowledge and belief I (We) have complied with the provisions of the Mental Capacity Act 2005.

Signed:

Dated:

D D M M Y Y Y Y

Signed:

Dated:

D D M M Y Y Y Y

Signed:

Dated:

D D M M Y Y Y Y

Part Eleven - Correspondence Address

Solicitors please note: The address to which the correspondence should be sent **MUST** be entered here if this is different to the address of Attorney One. State the full name and present address. Insert the name of the Solicitor's Firm in the Company Name field, if appropriate, and the correspondence reference in the Company Reference field.

Mr   Mrs   Ms   Miss   Other

☐   ☐   ☐   ☐   ☐

Place a cross against one option ☒   If Other, please specify here:

Last Name:

Forename 1:

Other Forenames:

Company Name:

Company Reference:

Address 1:

Address 2:

Address 3:

Town/City:

County:

Postcode: DX No. (solicitors only)

DX Exchange (solicitors only):

Daytime Tel No.:   (STD Code):

Email Address:

Part Twelve - Additional Information

Please write down any additional information to support this application in the space below. If necessary attach additional paper to the end of this form.

APPENDIX 3

FORMS OF DOCUMENT

CONTENTS

25. Special proxy
26. Directors' resolution appointing representative
27. Statutory declaration of nonrevocation for Stock Exchange purposes

A. ORDINARY POWERS OF ATTORNEY

1. Statutory general power

A3–01 **THIS GENERAL POWER OF ATTORNEY** is made this
day of   20
by   of
I appoint   of
[*or*   of
and   of
jointly *or* jointly and severally] to be my attorney[s] in accordance
with section 10 of the Powers of Attorney Act 1971.
Executed as a deed

2. Statutory general power: Welsh version

A3–02   Gwneir y **PŴER ATWRNAI CYFFREDINOL** hwn ar y
dydd o   20   gan AB o
Rwyf yn penodi CD o
[*neu* CD o   a
EF o   ar y cyd *neu*
ar y cyd ac yn unigol] i fod yn atwrnai (atwmeiod) ar fy rhan yn
unol
ag adran 10 Deddf Pŵerau Atwrnai 1971.
     TYSTIWYD GAN

* * *

3. General power: full form

A3–03 1. **THIS POWER OF ATTORNEY** is granted on   20
I,   of
appoint   of
[and   of   ]
to be my attorney[s] [jointly] [jointly and severally] for the following purposes:
     (a) To manage all my land and buildings, and for that purpose
to grant tenancies and licences, accept tenancies, collect rents and
other payments, enforce tenancy and licence terms, comply with
statutory obligations, contract for services and supplies, and pay
outgoings
     (b) To buy, sell, exchange, charge, encumber, or create or accept
any legal or equitable interest in, land of any tenure

(c) To buy, sell and exchange stocks, shares, debentures and other forms of investment dealt with on any stock exchange and to exercise all my rights as owner of those investments, including appointing proxies to attend and vote at meetings on my behalf

(d) To carry on any business of mine and for that purpose to occupy and use my business premises, buy and sell stock, give credit, employ staff, comply with statutory requirements, advertise, and enter into and comply with obligations for administering the business

(e) To sell any of my goods and to buy clothes, accessories, furniture, household goods, motor vehicles and other articles for my use

(f) To open in my name one or more bank accounts of any type and to operate them by depositing, withdrawing and transferring money, and authorising payments direct to the accounts of other people

(f) To borrow money on my behalf from such persons and on such terms, as to interest, repayment and security on my property, as my attorney decides

(h) To mortgage, charge, pledge, create a lien over, deliver as security, or deposit the title deeds of, all or any of my property

(i) To make contracts in my name and to execute and deliver in my name and on my behalf any deed affecting my property or interests, whether or not a deed is necessary in the circumstances

(j) To take, defend, accept service of, and take steps in any legal or arbitration proceedings on my behalf, including applying for or concurring in the appointment of an arbitrator, and for that purpose to appear and instruct solicitors and counsel in any court, tribunal or arbitration

(k) To agree a compromise or settlement of any claim made by or against me, and the terms on which any litigation or arbitration proceedings are to be settled

(l) To accept payment of any money due to me and to give receipts on my behalf to discharge the debtors

(m) To make a proposal for, effect and maintain any policy of insurance against any risk to which I or my property or estate may be exposed

(n) To engage, commission, instruct, direct and discharge any contractor, adviser, broker or agent on my behalf for any purpose, agreeing their terms of engagement and paying them for the services

(o) To employ, give instructions and directions to and to discharge any employee to serve me, fixing his terms of employment, paying him and providing agreed benefits to him

(p) To appoint in writing, with power to revoke any appointment without giving any reason, a substitute to act as my attorney in his stead under this power (but without the substitute having power to appoint a substitute in his turn) without my attorney having any liability for the acts of any substitute

(q) Generally to do all acts on my behalf which I may delegate to an attorney and to manage my affairs as fully as I may myself

2. I undertake to ratify all acts done by my attorney under the authority of this power

Executed as a deed

4. Power for particular purpose

A3–04 **THIS POWER OF ATTORNEY** is granted on   20
I,   of
appoint   of
to be my attorney for the following purposes:

1 To [*special purpose*]

2 For that purpose:

(a) To sign or execute in my name and on my behalf any contract, document or deed

(b) To engage or commission any contractor, advisor or agent, agreeing their terms of engagement and paying them for the services

(c) To do anything else reasonably necessary so that the object can be achieved as effectively as if I had done it myself

And I undertake to ratify whatever my attorney does under the authority or purported authority of this power

Executed as a deed

5. Power granted by owners of jointly owned home

A3–05 **THIS POWER OF ATTORNEY** is granted on   20
WE,   of
and   of
as the joint beneficial owners of   ("the house")
appoint[1]   of
and   of
to be our attorneys jointly to sell/mortgage/let the house, and for that purpose:

(a) To supply information about the house and the ownership and occupation of it

(b) To sign or execute in our names and on our behalves any contract, document or deed

(c) To engage or commission any contractor, advisor, manager or agent, agreeing their terms of engagement and paying them for their services

---

[1] Although both joint owners could appoint the same single attorney, this power is granted to joint attorneys so that there is no difficulty in complying with the two-trustee rules.

(d) To pay the net proceeds to an account in our name at Bank

(e) To do anything else reasonably necessary so that the object can be achieved as effectively as if we had done it ourselves

And we undertake to ratify whatever our attorneys do under the authority or purported authority of this power

Executed as a deed

* * *

6. Power granted by one Joint owner of a home

THIS POWER OF ATTORNEY is granted on   20   A3–06
I,   of
appoint   of
to be my attorney for the following purposes:

1 [Jointly and in consultation with   ]² to sell/mortgage/let the house known as   in which I own a share

2 For that purpose:

(a) To sign or execute in my name and on my behalf any contract, document or deed

(b) To engage or commission any contractor, advisor, manager or agent, agreeing their terms of engagement and paying them for their services

(c) To pay my share of the net proceeds to an account in my name at   Bank

(d) To do anything else reasonably necessary so that the object can be achieved as effectively as if I had done it myself

And I undertake to ratify whatever my attorney does under the authority or purported authority of this power

Executed as a deed

* * *

B. ANCILLARY DOCUMENTS

7. Appointment of substitute

1 I   of   A3–07
was appointed attorney by   of

---

² One joint owner could grant this power in favour of the other. In such a case, the reference to acting jointly and in consultation would not be needed. However, appointing the other joint owner could cause difficulties in complying with the two-trustee rules.

("the Donor") by a Power of Attorney dated   20
("the Power of Attorney")

  2 The Power of Attorney gave me the authority to appoint a substitute to act as attorney instead of me as if he had originally been appointed by the Power of Attorney

  3 I appoint   of
to be my substitute and act as attorney of the Donor under the Power of Attorney

  4 This appointment is subject to the right given to me by the Power of Attorney to revoke any appointments as I think fit

Date   20

Signed

* * *

8. Revocation of appointment of substitute

A3–08 1 I   of
was appointed attorney by   of
("the Donor") by a Power of Attorney dated   20
("the Power of Attorney")

  2 On   20   I appointed   of
("the substitute") to be my substitute as attorney of the Donor

  3 The Power of Attorney gave me authority to revoke any appointment of a substitute

  4 I revoke the appointment of the substitute as attorney under the Power of Attorney

Date   20

Signed

* * *

9. Deed of disclaimer

A3–09 1 I   of   was appointed attorney
[together with   of   ]
by   of   ("the Donor") by a Power of Attorney
dated   20   ("the Power of Authority")

  2 I disclaim the authority conferred on me by the Power of Attorney so that I shall not be capable or entitled to exercise or to join in exercising it

[3 This deed does affect the authority conferred by the Power of Attorney on anyone other than me]

Executed as a deed

* * *

10. Deed of revocation

THIS DEED OF REVOCATION is made on the   day   **A3–10**
of   20
by   of

1 I granted a Power of Attorney dated   20   ("the Power of Attorney") appointing   of   [together with   of   to act] [jointly] [jointly and severally] to be my attorney [s]

2 I revoke the Power of Attorney and the authority granted by it

3 This deed is not to prejudice my undertaking in the Power of Attorney to ratify the acts already done by my attorney[s] under it

Executed as a deed

*   *   *   *

11. Statutory declaration of nonrevocation: ordinary power

[I] [We]   **A3–11**
of
solemnly and sincerely [jointly] declare:
On   20   [I] [we] dealt with
who [was] [were] appointed attorney[s] by a Power of Attorney dated   20   granted by
[I was] [we were] not then aware that the power had been revoked
[I] [We] make this solemn declaration conscientiously believing the same to be true and by virtue of the Statutory Declarations Act 1835
Declared etc

*   *   *

12. Statutory declaration of nonrevocation: enduring power

[1] [WE]   **A3–12**
of
solemnly and sincerely [jointly] declare:

1 On   [I] [we] dealt with
who [was] [were] appointed attorney[s] by a Power of Attorney dated   20   granted by

2 [I] [WE] had then no reason to doubt that the attorney[s] had power to dispose of the property which was the subject of that transaction

[I] [WE] make this solemn declaration conscientiously believing the same to be true and by virtue of the Statutory Declarations Act 1835

Declared etc

*   *   *

13. Statutory declaration: delegation to beneficiaries of trust of land

A3–13   [I] [WE]

of

solemnly and sincerely [jointly] declare:

   1 On   20 [I] [we] dealt with   ("the attorney[s]"),
who [was] [were] appointed attorney[s] by a Power of Attorney
dated   granted by   , in relation to   ("the
land")

   2 [I] [We] dealt in good faith and at the time of the transaction
did not have knowledge that the attorney[s] [was] [were] not [a]
person[s] to whom trustee functions in relation to the land could
have been delegated under section 9(1) of the Trusts of Land and
Appointment of Trustees Act 1996

Declared etc

* * *

14. Statement: trustee/beneficiary

A3–14   AS attorney for   ("the landowner"), appointed under a
power of attorney dated   20,
I state that when I [sold]   on [his] [her] behalf on
20, the landowner had a beneficial interest in that property
Dated   20
Signed

C. TRUSTEES

15. Statutory general trustee power

A3–15   **THIS GENERAL TRUSTEE POWER OF ATTORNEY** is made
on   20
by   of
as trustee of
I appoint   of
to be my attorney [from   20   ] for the period
of   ] in accordance with section 25(5) of the Trustee Act
1925

Executed as a deed

* * *

16. Statutory general trustee power: Welsh version

A3–16   Gweir y **PŴER ATWRNAI YMDDIRIEDOL CYFFREDLNOL**
hwn ar [dyddiad] gan [enw un rhoddwr] o [cyfeiriad y rhoddwr] fel
ymddiriedolwr i [enw neu fanylion un ymddiriedolaeth].

Rwyf yn penodi [enw un rhoddai] o [cyfeiriad y rhoddai] i fod yn
atwrnai i mi [os dymunwch, y dyddiad pan fo'r dirprwyo'n dechrau
neu am ba gyfnod y mae i bara (neu'r ddau)] yn unol ag adran
25(4A) o Ddeddf Ymddiriedolwyr 1925.
[I'w gyflawni fel gweithred).

* * *

17. General trustee power: several trusts

THIS POWER OF ATTORNEY is made on   20   **A3–17**
by   of
as trustee of the following trusts:
I appoint   of
in accordance with section 25 of the Trustee Act 1925 to be my
attorney [from   20   ] [for the period of   ] to
act, jointly with the respective other trustees of the trusts identified
above, as trustee of those trusts and in my name and on my behalf:

   1 To execute or exercise all or any of the trusts powers and
discretions vested in me as trustee of those trusts both by the
respective trust instruments and by statute

   2 For that purpose to execute or sign any deed or document
   And I undertake to ratify whatever my attorney does under the
authority or purported authority of this power
Executed as a deed

* * *

18. Power granted by trustees of land to beneficiary/ies

THIS POWER OF ATTORNEY is made on   20   **A3–18**
by   of
and   of
who are the trustees of   ("the trust")
We appoint   of
[and   of   ]
who [is] [are] [a] beneficiar[y][ies] entitled to an interest in
possession in land subject to the trust to be our attorney[s] [for the
period of   ] [indefinitely] for the following purposes:

   1 To manage the land subject to the trust, and for that purpose,
in relation to the whole or any part of it, to negotiate tenancies of
it, to let it, to accept surrenders of tenancies, to collect rents, to
make and pay for improvements

   2 To negotiate the sale of all or any part of the land subject to
the trust, to contract to sell it and to convey or transfer it a buyer

   3 For those purposes, to engage, employ and remunerate agents,
contractors, advisers and employees, to operate bank accounts in
our names, to take and to defend legal proceedings and to sign and
execute any document or deed

And we undertake to ratify whatever our attorneys do under the authority or purported authority of this power

This power of attorney is granted under section 9 of the Trusts of Land and Appointment of Trustees Act 1996 and may or will be revoked as stated in that section

Executed as a deed

* * *

19. Power of attorney granted by trustees as a body

A3–19 **THIS POWER OF ATTORNEY** is granted on   20
and   of
as the present trustees of   ("the Trust")
appoint   of
to be our attorney for any of the following purposes in relation to the property of the Trust which is for the time being [outside the United Kingdom] [in   ]:

To manage, administer or sell all or any of it for that purpose:

(a) To sign or execute in our name and on our behalf any contract, document or deed

(b) To engage or commission any contractor advisor or agent, agreeing their terms of engagement and paying them for the services

2 This power gives the attorney no authority in relation to:

(a) any property of the trust [within the United Kingdom] [beyond the geographic limits specified above]

(b) Any property belonging to us or to any of us either beneficially or in any capacity other than as trustee of the Trust

And we undertake to ratify whatever our attorney does under the authority or purported authority of this power

Executed as a deed

* * *

20. Notice of grant of power

A3–20 To
I have, by power of attorney, delegated all my trusts, powers and discretions as trustee of
to   of
The power comes into operation on   and lasts for
It was granted because
Date   20
Signed
Name and address

* * *

D. Personal Representatives

21. Power of attorney granted by executor

IN THE HIGH COURT OF JUSTICE   A3–21
Family Division
The [Principal] [District Probate] Registry [at   ]
THIS POWER OF ATTORNEY is granted on   20
by   of
    1   late of   deceased ("the Deceased") died
on   having executed his last will dated   [and codicil
dated   ] which appointed me his executor [executrix]
[together with   as co-executors]
    2 I appoint   of   to be my attorney for the pur-
pose of obtaining letters of administration of the estate of the
Deceased to be granted to him for my use and benefit and until
further representation be granted
    3 I undertake to ratify whatever my attorney does or causes to
be done under the authority of this power
Executed as a deed

* * *

22. Power of attorney granted by person entitled to be administrator

IN THE HIGH COURT OF JUSTICE   A3–22
Family Division
The [Principal] [District Probate] Registry [at   ]
THIS POWER OF ATTORNEY is granted on   20
by   of
    1   late of   deceased ("the Deceased") died
on   20   intestate leaving
    2 I am the lawful   of the Deceased
    3 I appoint   of   to be my attorney for the pur-
pose of obtaining letters of administration of the estate of the
Deceased to be granted to him for my use and benefit and until
further representation be granted
    4 I undertake to ratify whatever my attorney does or causes to
be done under the authority of this power
Executed as a deed

* * *

E. Companies

23. General proxy

I   of   A3–23

a member of   [Limited] [Plc] ("the Company") appoint-
          of   as my proxy to do the following on my behalf:
    (a) To attend, [speak] and vote at meetings of all or any class of
shareholders of the Company which I would be entitled to attend
    (b) To requisition or join in requisitioning any meeting
    (c) To appoint a substitute to act as my proxy instead of him
Dated
Executed as a deed

* * *

24. General proxy for one meeting

A3–24 I   of
a member of   [Limited] [Plc] ("the Company"), appoint as
my proxy to attend, [speak] and vote for me at the [Annual]
[Extraordinary] General Meeting of the Company to be held
on   20   and at any adjournment of it:
          of   , or failing him
of   , or failing him   the Chairman of the meeting
Dated
Signed

* * *

25. Special proxy

A3–25 I   of
a member of   [Limited] [plc] ("the Company"), appoint as
my proxy on my behalf to attend, [speak] and vote in accordance
with the instructions below at the [Annual] [Extraordinary] General Meeting of the Company to be held on   20
and at any adjournment of it:
          of   , or failing him
of   or
failing him the Chairman of the meeting
    My proxy is to vote
For/Against* Resolution No. 1 on the Notice convening the
meeting
For/Against* Resolution No. 2 on the Notice convening the
meeting
etc.
Dated
Signed
* Delete one alternative

* * *

26. Directors' resolution appointing representative

Company shareholder   A3–26
IT IS RESOLVED THAT   be the representative of the
Company to attend any meetings of   [Limited] [plc] or of a
class of members of that company to exercise the rights of the
Company as a shareholder in it
Company creditor
IT IS RESOLVED that   be the representative of the
Company to attend any meeting of the creditors of
[Limited] [Plc] to exercise the rights of the Company as creditor of
it

* * *

27. Statutory declaration of nonrevocation: for Stock Exchange purposes

[I] [WE]   A3–27
of
solemnly and sincerely [jointly] declare:
    1 [I was] [We were] appointed attorney[s] by a Power of
Attorney ("the Power") dated   20   granted by
    2 On   20   [I] [we] executed the following trans-
fer[s] for the purposes of [a] stock exchange transaction[s]:
Security: Transferee[s]:
and on that date the Power had not been revoked.
[I] [WE] make this solemn declaration conscientiously believing
the same to be true and by virtue of the Statutory Declarations Act
1835
Declared etc

* * *

CLAUSES FOR POWERS OF ATTORNEY

A. Appointment

A4–01 Firm as attorney

I appoint the partners for the time being in the firm of ABC & Co solicitors jointly and severally to be my attorneys. This power shall at any time have effect as if it had individually named the then partners in that firm

Nominated partner as attorney

I appoint as my attorney the partner in the firm of ABC & Co solicitors nominated by the firm's then senior partner. No change in the constitution of the firm shall affect the appointment of my attorney, but the then senior partner may at any time revoke a nomination and make another

Company nominee as attorney

I appoint as my attorney the director or employee of XYZ Ltd nominated by resolution of the board of directors of the company. The board may at any time revoke a nomination and make another

One attorney until child attains 21, then eldest child

I appoint as my attorney (a) AB, for the period until one of my children attains the age of 21 years
(b) the first of my children to attain the age of 21 years, for the period beginning when he or she attains that age

Trustees in bankruptcy

I, as the trustee of the estate of AB, a bankrupt, appoint CD of   to be my attorney

B. Authority conferred on attorney

A4–02 To manage property

To manage [all my houses and flats] [my house "Blackacre", Casterbridge,] and for the purpose to grant tenancies and licences, accept tenancies and surrenders of them, collect rents and other payments, enforce tenancy and licence terms, take defend and compromise legal and arbitration proceedings, comply with statutory obligations, contract for services and supplies, pay outgoings and employ agents and professional advisers

To sell house	To sell my house "Blackacre", Casterbridge, by private treaty or public auction for at least £ [gross] [after deduction of sale expenses] and for that purpose to sign and execute all necessary documents and deeds and employ agents and professional advisers
To buy house	To buy ["Blackacre", Casterbridge,] [a house for me to occupy with my family] for no more than £ [including] [excluding] purchase expenses and for that purpose to sign and execute all necessary documents and deeds and employ agents and professional advisers
To take lease	To take a lease or tenancy agreement of living accommodation for my family on such terms and conditions as he thinks fit
To deal in land	To buy, sell, exchange, charge, encumber or create or accept any legal or equitable interest in, land of any tenure and for that purpose to sign and execute all necessary documents and deeds and to employ agents and professional advisers
To manage investments	To buy, sell and exchange stocks, shares, debentures and other forms of investments dealt with on any stock exchange and to exercise all my rights as owner of those investments, including appointing proxies to attend and vote at meetings on my behalf, and for those purposes to sign all necessary documents and employ agents and professional advisers
To consult a stockbroker	To consult a member of a stock exchange before acquiring any investment for me or dealing with any of my investments. No person dealing with my attorney shall be concerned to ensure that he has consulted as required

To carry on business	To carry on my business of at and for that purpose to occupy and use my business premises, buy and sell stock, give credit, employ staff, comply with statutory requirements, advertise, and enter into and comply with obligations for administering the business
To sell chattels	To sell [my motor car number] [all my goods in England] for [a total of] [not less than £] [what he thinks fit] and to pay the net proceeds into my bank account with Bank Plc, Casterbridge, and for that purpose to advertise and employ agents
To operate bank accounts	To open in my name one or more accounts of any type with Bank Plc, Casterbridge, and to operate them by depositing, withdrawing and transferring money, and authorising payments direct to the accounts of other people [but without power to borrow money from the bank for me]
To borrow money	To borrow money on my behalf [for the purposes mentioned above] from such persons and on such terms, as to interest, repayment and security on my property, as my attorney decides
To mortgage	To mortgage, charge, pledge, create a lien over, deliver as security, or deposit the title deeds of, all or any of my property
To execute deeds	To execute and deliver in my name and on my behalf any deed affecting my property or interests, whether or not a deed is necessary in the circumstances
To litigate	To take, defend, accept service of, and take steps in any legal proceedings on my behalf and for that purpose to appear and instruct solicitors and counsel in any court or tribunal
To arbitrate	To agree to arbitrate, concur in the appointment of an arbitrator or the reference of the dispute to one, to take or defend arbitration proceedings and to instruct solicitors and counsel for that purpose
To use alternative dispute resolution	To agree to use, and abide by the determination of, any form of alternative dispute resolution in order to resolve any dispute to which I am a party

To compromise claims	To agree a compromise or settlement of any claim made by or against me, and the terms on which any litigation or arbitration proceedings are to be settled
To give receipts	To accept payment of any money due to me and to give receipts on my behalf to discharge the debtors
To insure	To make a proposal for, effect and maintain any policy of insurance against any risk to which I or my property or estate may be exposed
To employ independent contractors	To engage, commission, instruct, direct and discharge any contractor, adviser or agent on my behalf for any purpose, agreeing their terms of engagement and paying them for the services
To employ servants	To employ, give instructions and directions to and to discharge any employee to serve me, fixing his terms of employment, paying him and providing agreed benefits to him
To charge fees	To charge professional fees for all work done in exercising the authority which I am granting to my attorney by this power, and to pay himself the amount of those fees from any money belonging to me

C. Restrictions on authority

Not to exercise trustee powers	This power of attorney does not give [any of] my attorney[s] power to execute or exercise any trust, power or discretion which I have as trustee	A4–03
Not to benefit or make gifts to attorney[s]	This power of attorney does not give [any of] my attorney[s] power to benefit or make gifts to [himself] [herself] [themselves or any of them] from my property	
Not to make gifts to charity	This power of attorney does not give [any of] my attorney[s] power to make gifts to charity from my property	
Only to benefit or make gifts to relatives	The only people whom my attorney[s] may benefit or make gifts to from my estate are my [wife] [husband] and my relatives of the whole blood	
Limit on value of gifts and benefits	In any one calendar year, my attorney[s] shall not make gifts or confer gratuitous benefits from my estate totalling more than [£5,000] [five per cent of the then total value of my property]	

Spouse's agreement to house sale	Only to sell or mortgage my house "Blackacre", Casterbridge, with the written concurrence of my [wife] [husband]
Delay acting until receipt of confirmation	My attorney shall not exercise the authority this power confers on him until he receives a confirmatory letter signed by me [and witnessed by a consular officer] and attaches the letter to this deed

D. Manner of exercising powers

A4–04	Act in donor's name	My attorney is to act and sign in my name and expressly on my behalf when executing any deed, signing any contract or doing any other act under his authority as my attorney
	Power to appoint substitutes	My attorney may at any time appoint a substitute to act as my attorney, and may revoke any appointment without giving a reason. Every appointment is to be in writing signed by my attorney. Every substitute has full powers as my attorney, as if appointed by this deed, except this power to appoint a substitute
	Limited substitute	My attorney may at any time appoint as a substitute a partner in his solicitor's firm to act as my attorney, and may revoke an appointment at any time. Every appointment is to be in writing signed by my attorney. Every substitute has full power as my attorney, as if appointed by this deed, except this power to appoint a substitute. No one dealing with a substitute shall be concerned to enquire whether he is qualified for appointment
	Corporate attorney's representative	My attorney may at any time by resolution of its board of directors appoint one of its officers to exercise the authority of my attorney in his name but on its behalf, and may be a similar resolution revoke any appointment. Anyone dealing with a person purporting to be appointed by resolution may accept a copy of the resolution certified as a true copy by the secretary of the company as conclusive proof of the appointment.

E. General

A4–05	Ratification	I agree to ratify all acts done, deeds executed and contracts signed by my attorney on my behalf under the authority or purported authority of this power

Irrevocability	This power is given by way of security to secure [a proprietary interest of my attorney] [the performance of an obligation owed to my attorney] and I declare that this deed is irrevocable
Power irrevocable for fixed period	As part of the bargain with my attorney I agreed to grant the authority conferred by this power for the period of [ten years] from the date of this deed. This power of attorney is irrevocable for that period

F. Execution

Person unable to read	SIGNED AS A DEED AND DELIVERED **A4–06** by [the donor], after [I] [someone in my presence] had read and explained to [him] [her] the terms of the deed and [s]he stated that [s]he understood, in the presence of:
Person unable to write or physically disabled	SIGNED AS A DEED AND DELIVERED by AB by direction and in the presence of [the donor] and in the presence also of: [Two witnesses]

APPENDIX 5

LASTING POWERS OF ATTORNEY

The Lasting Powers of Attorney, Enduring Powers of Attorney and Public Guardian Regulations 2007

SI 2001/1253

SCHEDULE 1

SCHEDULE 1   **Regulation 5**

FORM FOR INSTRUMENT INTENDED TO CREATE A LASTING POWER OF
ATTORNEY

Part 1: Form for instrument intended to create a property and affairs Lasting Power of Attorney

LPA PA | 10.07

A5–01

Lasting Power of Attorney Property and Affairs

| For official use only |
| Date of registration |

This is a Lasting Power of Attorney (LPA). It allows you (the donor) to choose someone (the attorney) to make decisions on your behalf. Your attorney(s) can only use the completed LPA after it has been registered with the Office of the Public Guardian (OPG).

Getting started

Before you complete this LPA you **must** read the prescribed information on the next three pages so that you understand the purpose and legal consequences of making an LPA. You should refer to the separate notes on how to complete this LPA when you are directed to because they will help you to complete it.

Things you will need to do to complete this LPA

- decide who to appoint as your attorney(s) in the LPA
- decide if you want to appoint a replacement attorney in case your attorney(s) cannot act for you
- decide whether you want anyone to be notified when an application is made to register your LPA and, if you do, who you want to be notified
- choose at least one independent person to provide a certificate at Part B of the LPA
- fill in part A of the LPA. Your certificate provider(s) will need to complete Part B. Your attorney(s) will need to complete Part C
- have a witness to your signature at the end of Part A of the LPA

What to do after completing this LPA

An LPA can only be used after it has been registered with the OPG, so you will need to think about when you want it to be registered. There is a fee to register an LPA. Further information about how to register an LPA and what happens following registration is available from the OPG.

Information for you, your attorney(s) and your certificate provider(s) is available from the OPG. If you have any questions about how to complete this LPA please contact the OPG.

Office of the Public Guardian

Archway Tower

London N19 5SZ

0845 330 2900

www.publicguardian.gov.uk

OPG STAMP

Important - This form **cannot** be used until it has been registered by the Office of the Public Guardian and stamped on **every** page.

© Crown copyright 2007

PRESCRIBED INFORMATION

Lasting Power of Attorney — Property and Affairs

You must read this information carefully to understand the purpose and legal consequences of making an LPA. You must ask your attorney(s) and certificate provider(s) to read it too.

This form is a legal document known as a Lasting Power of Attorney (LPA). It allows you to authorise someone (the attorney(s)) to make decisions on your behalf about spending your money and managing your property and affairs. Your attorney(s) can only use the LPA after it is registered with the OPG.

If you want someone to make decisions about your personal welfare then you need a different form. You can get a Lasting Power of Attorney — Personal Welfare from the OPG and legal stationers.

Detailed information about why you might find an LPA useful is in the **'Guide for people who want to make a Property and Affairs LPA'.** You can get this from the OPG. You should read this guide before completing this LPA. You should ask your attorney(s) and certificate provider(s) to read it too.

Your attorney(s) cannot do whatever they like. They **must** follow the principles of the Mental Capacity Act 2005 which are:

- a person must be assumed to have capacity unless it is established that the person lacks capacity;

- a person is not to be treated as unable to make a decision unless all practicable steps to help the person to do so have been taken without success;

- a person is not to be treated as unable to make a decision merely because the person makes an unwise decision;

- an act done, or decision made, under the Mental Capacity Act for or on behalf of a person who lacks capacity must be done, or made, in the person's best interests; and

- before the act is done, or the decision is made, regard must be had to whether the purpose for which it is needed can be as effectively achieved in a way that is less restrictive of the person's rights and freedom of action.

Guidance about the principles is in the Mental Capacity Act 2005 Code of Practice. Your attorney(s) will have a duty to have regard to the Code. Copies of the Code can be obtained from Her Majesty's Stationary Office.

1. **CHOOSING YOUR ATTORNEY** Your attorney should be a person you know and trust who is at least 18 or a trust corporation. Your attorney must not be an undischarged or interim bankrupt. You can choose more than one attorney.

2. **CHOOSING MORE THAN ONE ATTORNEY** If you choose more than one attorney you must decide whether your attorneys should act together or together and independently (that is they can all act together but they can also act separately if they wish).
   You may appoint your attorneys together in respect of some matters and together and independently in respect of others. If you appoint more than one attorney and do not state whether they are appointed together or together and independently, when your LPA is registered they will be treated on the basis that they are appointed together. In this LPA, 'together' means jointly 'together and independently' means jointly and severally for the purposes of the Mental Capacity Act 2005.

Please do not detach these notes. They are part of the Lasting Power of Attorney.

PRESCRIBED INFORMATION

3. **CHOOSING A REPLACEMENT ATTORNEY** You can name a replacement(s) in case an attorney is unable to or no longer wishes to continue acting for you. Your attorney(s) can change their mind and may not want to act for you. If this is the case, they must tell you and the OPG.

4. **WHEN AN ATTORNEY CAN ACT** Once your LPA is registered your attorney(s) can act before you lack capacity and after you lack capacity. You may restrict your attorney(s) to act only when you lack capacity in your LPA. There is no one point at which you are treated as having lost capacity to manage your property and affairs. Your attorney(s) must help you to make as many of your own decisions as you can. When decisions have to be taken for you, your attorney(s) must always act in your best interests.

5. **DECISIONS YOUR ATTORNEY CAN MAKE FOR YOU** An attorney for property and affairs may make any decision that you could make about your property and affairs e.g. buy or sell property, manage investments or carry on a business and may access personal information. This is subject to the authority you give them and any decisions excluded by the Mental Capacity Act 2005. Some decisions will also involve personal welfare matters, such as a move to residential care. Your property and affairs attorney(s) will then need to consider your best interests with your attorney(s) for personal welfare (if you have one).

6. **RESTRICTING THE POWERS OF YOUR ATTORNEY(S) OR ADDING CONDITIONS** You can put legally binding restrictions and conditions on your attorney(s)' powers and the scope of their authority in the LPA. But these decisions may still need to be made and other people will have to decide for you. That could involve going to the Court of Protection and a decision being made in your best interests.

7. **GIVING GUIDANCE TO YOUR ATTORNEY** You can also give guidance to your attorney(s) in your LPA. This is not legally binding but should be taken into account when they are making decisions for you.

8. **PAYING ATTORNEYS** An attorney is entitled to be reimbursed for out-of-pocket expenses incurred in carrying out their duties. Professional attorneys, such as solicitors or accountants, charge for their services. You should discuss and record any decision you make about paying your attorney(s) in the LPA.

9. **NOTIFYING OTHER PEOPLE BEFORE REGISTRATION** You can name up to five people to be notified when an application to register your LPA is made. Anyone about to apply for registration of an LPA must notify these people. This gives you an important safeguard because if you lack capacity at the time of registration you will be relying on these people to raise any concerns they may have about the application to register. If you choose not to name anyone to be notified you will need to have two certificate providers under Part B of this form.

10. **CERTIFICATE TO CONFIRM UNDERSTANDING** Once you have filled in Part A of this form an independent person must fill in the certificate at Part B to confirm that, in their opinion, you are making the LPA of your own free and will, that you understand its purpose and the powers you are giving your attorney(s). This is an important safeguard and your LPA cannot be registered unless the certificate is completed.

Please do not detach these notes. They are part of the Lasting Power of Attorney.

PRESCRIBED INFORMATION

11. **REGISTERING THE LPA** *Your LPA cannot be used until it has been registered with the OPG.* Either you or your chosen attorney(s) can apply to register the LPA. If you register it immediately it can be used straightaway unless you have specified that it should only be used when you lack capacity. The form for registering the LPA is available from the OPG together with details of the registration fee.

12. **REGISTER OF LPAs** There is a register of LPAs kept by the OPG. It is possible to access the register of LPAs but access is controlled. On application to the OPG, and payment of a fee, people can find out basic information about your LPA. At the discretion of the OPG and according to the purpose for which they need it, they may be able to find out further information. There is additional guidance available from the OPG on the register.

13. **CHANGING YOUR MIND** You can cancel your LPA even after it is registered if you have the mental capacity to do so. You need to take formal steps to revoke the LPA. You must tell your attorney if you do and, if it is registered, you will need to ask the OPG to remove it from the register of LPAs.

FURTHER NOTICE FOR ATTORNEY(S)
You should read the **'Guide for people taking on the role of Property and Affairs attorney'** under an LPA before you agree to become an attorney and complete Part C of this LPA. The guide contains detailed information about what your role and responsibilities will be.

You must contact the OPG at once if the person you are acting for dies. If you are unable to continue acting you should take steps to disclaim the power and notify the OPG and the donor.

FURTHER NOTICE FOR CERTIFICATE PROVIDER(S)
You should read the separate **'Certificate Providers and witness guidance'** before you agree to become a certificate provider and complete Part B of this LPA. The guidance contains detailed information about your role and responsibilities. You may also like to read the guidance for property and affairs attorneys and donors. If you have any concerns about an LPA you are asked to certify please contact the OPG.

Please do not detach these notes. They are part of the Lasting Power of Attorney.

LPA PA 04 07

Lasting Power of Attorney
Property and Affairs

Important
This LPA form cannot be used until it has been registered by the OPG and stamped on **every** page.

Before you complete this LPA form, you must read the prescribed information on pages 2, 3 and 4 and you should read the guidance produced by the OPG.

To help you complete the form, please refer to the Notes for completing an LPA — Property and Affairs.

PART A – Donor's statement

Your details

1. My name and date of birth are:

☐ Mr. ☐ Mrs. ☐ Ms. ☐ Miss ☐ Other _____

First name	
Middle name(s)	
Last name	
Date of birth	

Any other names you are known by or have been known by in the past (e.g. maiden name)

2. My contact details and e-mail are:

Address	
	Postcode
Telephone no.	
Mobile no.	
E-mail address	

The details of the attorney(s) you are appointing

3. I appoint the following attorney(s) in accordance with the provisions of the Mental Capacity Act 2005:

`See Note 4`

Attorney

☐ Mr. ☐ Mrs. ☐ Ms. ☐ Miss ☐ Other _____

`See Note 5`

First name(s)

Last name

Attorney

☐ Mr. ☐ Mrs. ☐ Ms. ☐ Miss ☐ Other _____

First name(s)

Last name

Appointment of a trust corporation as attorney

`See Note 6`

Company name

Note: (You do not have to appoint a trust corporation as one of your attorneys)

How your attorney(s) is to act for you

If you only have one attorney please cross through this page.

4. If you are appointing more than one attorney, how do you wish them to act?
   (If you do not choose an option your attorneys will be appointed together)

        ☐ together

        ☐ together and independently

        ☐ together in respect of some matters and together and independently in respect of others

If together in respect of some matters and together and independently in respect of others, details are as follows:

Replacement attorney(s)

5. I wish to appoint a replacement attorney: (You do not have to appoint a replacement attorney). ◁ See Note 9

    ☐ Yes ☐ No

If Yes, I appoint the following replacement attorney:

    ☐ Mr. ☐ Mrs. ☐ Ms. ☐ Miss ☐ Other _____ ◁ See Note 10

First name(s)

Last name

Restrictions on the appointment of a replacement attorney: (If you do not complete this section your first replacement will replace the first attorney who needs replacing). ◁ See Note 11

Placing restrictions and/or conditions on the attorney(s) you are appointing

You can use this section to specify that your LPA is only to be used when you lack capacity. If you decide to specify this, you should specify anything you want the attorney(s) to do to confirm that you lack capacity to make the decision in question.

You may also use this section to place restrictions on the ability of your attorney(s) to use your property and affairs to make gifts. Any restrictions and/or conditions you set out below **must** be followed by the attorney(s).

6. I wish to place restrictions and/or conditions on my attorney(s) in relation to my property and affairs:

See Note 12

☐ Yes   ☐ No

If Yes, the restrictions and conditions are as follows:

Guidance for your attorney(s) to consider   ◁ See Note 13

Your attorney(s) **should** consider the guidance set out below when making decisions in your best interests.

7. I wish my attorney(s) to consider the following guidance:

8. I have agreed to pay my attorney(s) a fee to act as my attorney(s):   ◁ See Note 14

    ☐ Yes ☐ No

If Yes, the following is additional information about fees that I have agreed with my attorney(s):

Notifying others when an application to register your LPA is made   See Note 15

9. I wish the following people, 'the named persons', to be notified when an application to register my LPA is made:

☐ Mr.   ☐ Mrs.   ☐ Ms.   ☐ Miss   ☐ Other _____

Full name

Address

Postcode

Telephone no.

E-mail address

☐ Mr.   ☐ Mrs.   ☐ Ms.   ☐ Miss   ☐ Other _____

Full name

Address

Postcode

Telephone no.

E-mail address

☐ Mr.   ☐ Mrs.   ☐ Ms.   ☐ Miss   ☐ Other _____

Full name

Address

Postcode

Telephone no.

E-mail address

☐ Mr.   ☐ Mrs.   ☐ Ms.   ☐ Miss   ☐ Other _____

Full name

Address

Postcode

Telephone no.

E-mail address

☐ Mr.   ☐ Mrs.   ☐ Ms.   ☐ Miss   ☐ Other _____

Full name

Address

Postcode

Telephone no.

E-mail address

If you do not include anyone here you **must** have two certificate providers at Part B.

10. I confirm that

☐ I have read the prescribed information on pages 2, 3 and 4 of this LPA.

or

☐ The prescribed information has been read to me by

See Note 16

11. I confirm that

☐ I intend to give my attorney(s) authority to make decisions on my behalf, including in circumstances when I lack capacity subject to any restrictions I have made.

See Note 17

12. I confirm that

☐ the persons named in paragraph 9 are to be notified when an application to register this LPA is made

or

☐ I do not want anyone to be notified when an application to register this LPA is made and I understand that I need **two** people to provide a separate certificate each at Part B of this LPA.

See Note 18

13. I confirm that

☐ I have chosen my certificate provider(s) myself.

See Note 19

14. Signed by me as a deed

See Note 20

15. Date signed (delivered as a deed)

If you are unable to sign the form, please refer to the notes for completion and turn to page 14 of this LPA.

In the presence of

16. Signature of witness

See Note 21

17. Full name of witness

18. Address of witness

Postcode

Important - This form **cannot** be used until it has been registered by the Office of the Public Guardian and stamped on **every** page.

If you are unable to sign or make a mark, then you must ask someone else to sign for you in your presence and the presence of two witnesses. Please refer to notes 22 and 23.

I am signing this LPA at the donor's direction and in the donor's presence: ◄ See Note 22

19. Signed as a deed

20. Date signed (delivered as a deed)

21. Full name

22. Address

Postcode

In the presence of

23. Signature of witness ◄ See Note 23

24. Full name of witness

25. Address of witness

Postcode

26. Signature of witness

27. Full name of witness

28. Address of witness

Postcode

PART B – Certificate provider's statement   See Note 24

Who can provide a certificate?
The donor can choose someone they have known personally over the last two years (Category A) or someone who, because of their relevant professional skills and expertise, considers themselves able to provide the certificate (Category B).

Note: Category B providers are entitled to charge a fee for providing this certificate.

Who cannot provide a certificate?   See Note 25
A certificate provider must not be:
• a member of the donor's or attorney's family;
• a business partner or paid employee of the donor or attorney(s);
• an attorney appointed in this form or another LPA or any EPA made by the donor;
• the owner, director, manager, or an employee of a care home in which the donor lives or their family member or partner;
• a director or employee of a trust corporation appointed as an attorney in this LPA.

You, the certificate provider, **must** read Part A and B of this LPA, and the prescribed information on pages 2, 3 and 4. You should also read the separate '**Certificate provider and witness guidance**' produced by the OPG before completing the certificate. You must discuss the LPA with the donor without the attorney(s) present.   See Note 26

☐ I confirm that I am acting independently of the person making this LPA (the donor) and the person(s) appointed under the LPA and in particular I am not a person listed in the above section 'Who cannot provide a certificate?'.   See Note 27

☐ I am aged 18 or over.   See Note 28

The certificate provider

Name and contact details of certificate provider

☐ Mr.   ☐ Mrs.   ☐ Ms.   ☐ Miss   ☐ Other _____   See Note 29

First name

Middle name(s)

Last name

Address

Postcode ☐☐☐☐☐☐☐

Telephone no.   See Note 30

Mobile no.

E-mail address

The OPG may need to contact you to verify the information you provide.

Category of certificate provider – choose from category A or B – do not complete both ◄ See Note 31

Category A – Knowledge certification ◄ See Note 32

☐ I have known the donor personally over the last two years.

How do you know them?

_____

Category B - Skills certification ◄ See Note 33

I am:

☐ a registered healthcare professional (includes GP)

☐ a barrister, solicitor or advocate

☐ a registered social worker

☐ an Independent Mental Capacity Advocate (IMCA)

☐ none of the above but consider that I have the relevant professional skills and expertise to be a certificate provider.

My relevant professional skills and expertise are:

_____

I confirm and understand

☐ I confirm that I have read Parts A and B of this LPA, and the prescribed information on pages 2, 3 and 4. ◄ See Note 34

☐ I confirm that I have discussed the contents of this LPA with the donor and that the attorney(s) was not present. ◄ See Note 35

☐ I understand that I should make efforts to discuss this LPA with the donor without anyone present; and ◄ See Note 36

☐ I have discussed this LPA with the donor without anyone else present

or

☐ I have discussed this LPA with the donor in the presence of:

_____

because

_____

☐ I confirm that I am completing this certificate straight after discussing this LPA with the donor. ◄ See Note 37

Core certification

I certify

I certify that in my opinion, at the time when the donor is making this LPA, that: See Note 34

☐ the donor understands the purpose of this LPA and the scope of the authority under it;

☐ no fraud or undue pressure is being used to induce the donor to create this LPA; and

☐ there is nothing else that would prevent this LPA being created.

Do not sign this certificate if you have any doubt about any of the above. You should bring any concerns you have to the attention of the OPG.

Signature of certificate provider   Date signed   See Note 35

D	D	M	M	Y	Y	Y	Y	

Full name of certificate provider

Additional certificate provider's statement

This additional certificate only needs to be completed if there are no notified persons listed in the LPA

Who can provide a certificate?
The donor can choose someone they have known personally over the last two years (Category A) or someone who, because of their relevant professional skills and expertise, considers themselves able to provide the certificate (Category B).

Note: Category B providers are entitled to charge a fee for providing this certificate.

Who cannot provide a certificate? See Note 40
A certificate provider must not be
- a member of the donor's or attorney's family;
- a business partner or paid employee of the donor or attorney(s);
- an attorney appointed in this form or another LPA or any EPA made by the donor;
- the owner, director, manager or an employee of a care home in which the donor lives or their family member or partner;
- a director or employee of a trust corporation appointed as an attorney in this LPA

You, the certificate provider, **must** read Part A and B of this LPA, and the prescribed information on pages 2, 3 and 4. You should also read the separate **'Certificate provider and witness guidance'** produced by the OPG before completing the certificate. You must discuss the LPA with the donor without the attorney(s) present.

☐ I confirm that I am acting independently of the person making this LPA (the donor) and the person(s) appointed under the LPA and in particular I am not a person listed in the above section 'Who cannot provide a certificate?'.

☐ I am aged 18 or over.

The certificate provider

Name and contact details of certificate provider

☐ Mr. ☐ Mrs. ☐ Ms. ☐ Miss ☐ Other _____

First name

Middle name(s)

Last name

Address

Postcode

Telephone no.

Mobile no.

E-mail address

The OPG may need to contact you to verify the information you provide.

Category of certificate provider – choose from category A **or** B – do not complete both

Category A – Knowledge certification

☐ I have known the donor personally over the last two years.

How do you know them?

Category B - Skills certification

I am:

☐ a registered healthcare professional (includes GP)

☐ a barrister, solicitor or advocate

☐ a registered social worker

☐ an Independent Mental Capacity Advocate (IMCA)

☐ none of the above but consider that I have the relevant professional skills and expertise to be a certificate provider.

My relevant professional skills and expertise are:

I confirm and understand

☐ I confirm that I have read Parts A and B of this LPA, and the prescribed information on pages 2, 3 and 4.

☐ I confirm that I have discussed the contents of this LPA with the donor and that the attorney(s) was not present.

☐ I understand that I should make efforts to discuss this LPA with the donor without anyone present; and

☐ I have discussed this LPA with the donor without anyone else present

or

☐ I have discussed this LPA with the donor in the presence of:

because

☐ I confirm that I am completing this certificate straight after discussing this LPA with the donor.

Core certification

I certify

I certify that in my opinion, at the time when the donor is making this LPA, that:

☐ the donor understands the purpose of this LPA and the scope of the authority under it;

☐ no fraud or undue pressure is being used to induce the donor to create this LPA; and

☐ there is nothing else that would prevent this LPA being created.

Do not sign this certificate if you have any doubt about any of the above. You should bring any concerns you have to the attention of the OPG.

Signature of additional certificate provider   Date signed

Full name of additional certificate provider

PART C – Attorney's statement (Every attorney must complete a copy of this Part)   See Note 41

29. My contact details and date of birth are:

Attorney

☐ Mr.   ☐ Mrs.   ☐ Ms.   ☐ Miss   ☐ Other _____   See Note 42

First name

Middle name(s)

Last name

Date of birth

Telephone no.   Mobile

E-mail address   See Note 43

30. ☐ I have read the prescribed information on pages 2, 3 and 4 or have had the prescibed information read to me.   See Note 44

31. ☐ I understand the duties imposed on me under this Lasting Power of Attorney including the obligation to act in accordance with the principles of the Mental Capacity Act 2005 and the duty to have regard to the Code of Practice issued under the Act.   See Note 45

32. ☐ I am not an undischarged bankrupt or an interim bankrupt.   See Note 46

33. ☐ I understand that I cannot act under this Lasting Power of Attorney until this form has been registered by the Public Guardian.   See Note 47

34. Signed by me as a deed *(You must not sign until after the donor has signed at paragraph 14 and the certificate provider has signed the certificate)*   See Note 48

35. Date signed (delivered as a deed)

In the presence of

36. Signature of witness   See Note 49

37. Full name of witness

38. Address of witness

Postcode

Important - This form **cannot** be used until it has been registered by the Office of the Public Guardian and stamped on **every** page.

PART C – Attorney's statement (Every attorney must complete a copy of this Part)   See Note 41

29. My contact details and date of birth are:

Attorney

☐ Mr.   ☐ Mrs.   ☐ Ms.   ☐ Miss   ☐ Other _____   See Note 4

First name

Middle name(s)

Last name

Date of birth D D / M M / Y Y Y Y

Telephone no.   Mobile

E-mail address   See Note 43

30. ☐ I have read the prescribed information on pages 2, 3 and 4 or have had the prescibed information read to me.   See Note 44

31. ☐ I understand the duties imposed on me under this Lasting Power of Attorney including the obligation to act in accordance with the principles of the Mental Capacity Act 2005 and the duty to have regard to the Code of Practice issued under the Act.   See Note 45

32. ☐ I am not an undischarged bankrupt or an interim bankrupt.   See Note 46

33. ☐ I understand that I cannot act under this Lasting Power of Attorney until this form has been registered by the Public Guardian.   See Note 47

34. Signed by me as a deed *(You must not sign until after the donor has signed at paragraph 14 and the certificate provider has signed the certificate)*   See Note 48

35. Date signed (delivered as a deed) D D / M M / Y Y Y Y

In the presence of

36. Signature of witness   See Note 49

37. Full name of witness

38. Address of witness

Postcode

Important - This form **cannot** be used until it has been registered by the Office of the Public Guardian and stamped on **every** page

LPA_PA_1007_final.indd   22   22/06/2007   14:03:47

See Note 50

PART C – Attorney's statement – Trust Corporation

(This section only needs to be completed where the donor has chosen a trust corporation to be an attorney)

39. Name and address of a trust corporation   See Note 51

A trust corporation

Company name

Address

Postcode

Company seal (if applicable)

Company Registration no.

40. ☐ I have read the prescribed information on pages 2, 3 and 4 or had the prescribed   See Note 52
    information read to me.

41. ☐ I understand the duties imposed on me under this Lasting Power of Attorney including the
    obligation to act in accordance with the principles of the Mental Capacity Act 2005 and
    the duty to have regard to the Code of Practice issued under the Act.

This should not be executed until after the donor has signed at paragraph 14 and the   See Note 53
certificate provider has signed the certificate.

Note: The statements above are made by the trust corporation not the individuals above.

PART C – Replacement Attorney's statement   ◁ See Note 54

(To be completed by a replacement attorney if appointed. Only complete this if you are a replacement attorney chosen at paragraph 5.)

42. My contact details and date of birth are:

Attorney

☐ Mr.   ☐ Mrs.   ☐ Ms.   ☐ Miss   ☐ Other _____   ◁ See Note 55

First name

Middle name(s)

Last name

Date of birth

Telephone no.   Mobile

E-mail address   ◁ See Note 56

43. ☐ I have read the prescribed information on pages 2, 3 and 4 or had the prescribed information read to me.   ◁ See Note 57

44. ☐ I understand that if an original attorney's appointment is terminated I will replace the original attorney if I am still eligible to act as an attorney.   ◁ See Note 58

45. ☐ I understand that I do not have the authority to act under this LPA until such time as a relevant attorney's appointment is terminated.   ◁ See Note 59

46. ☐ I understand the duties imposed on me under this Lasting Power of Attorney including the obligation to act in accordance with the principles of the Mental Capacity Act 2005 and the duty to have regard to the Code of Practice issued under the Act.   ◁ See Note 60

47. ☐ I am not an undischarged bankrupt or an interim bankrupt.   ◁ See Note 61

48. ☐ I understand that I cannot act under this Lasting Power of Attorney until this form has been registered by the Public Guardian.   ◁ See Note 62

49. Signed by me as a deed *(You must not sign until after the donor has signed at paragraph 14 and the certificate provider has signed the certificate).*   ◁ See Note 63

50. Date signed (delivered as a deed)

(Continued over the page)

In the presence of

51. Signature of
    witness

See Note 64

52. Full name
    of witness

53. Address of
    witness

Postcode

Important - This form **cannot** be used until it has been registered by
the Office of the Public Guardian and stamped on **every** page.

A5–05

LPA PW 10.07

Lasting Power of Attorney
Personal Welfare

For official use only
Date of registration

This is a Lasting Power of Attorney (LPA). It allows you (the donor) to choose someone (the attorney) to make decisions on your behalf where you lack capacity to make those decisions yourself. Your attorney(s) can only use the completed LPA after it has been registered with the Office of the Public Guardian (OPG).

Getting started

Before you complete this LPA you **must** read the prescribed information on the next three pages so that you understand the purpose and legal consequences of making an LPA. You should refer to the separate notes on how to complete this LPA when you are directed to because they will help you to complete it.

Things you will need to do to complete this LPA

- decide who to appoint as your attorney(s) in the LPA
- decide if you want to appoint a replacement attorney in case your attorney(s) cannot act for you
- decide whether you want anyone to be notified when an application is made to register your LPA and, if you do, who you want to be notified
- choose at least one independent person to provide a certificate at Part B of the LPA
- fill in part A of the LPA. Your certificate provider(s) will need to complete Part B. Your attorney(s) will need to complete Part C
- have a witness to your signature at the end of Part A of the LPA

What to do after completing this LPA

An LPA can only be used after it has been registered with the OPG, so you will need to think about when you want it to be registered. There is a fee to register an LPA. Further information about how to register an LPA and what happens following registration is available from the OPG.

Information for you, your attorney(s) and your certificate provider(s) is available from the OPG. If you have any questions about how to complete this LPA please contact the OPG.

Office of the Public Guardian

Archway Tower

London N19 5SZ

0845 330 2900

www.publicguardian.gov.uk

OPG
STAMP

> **Important** - This form **cannot** be used until it has been registered by the Office of the Public Guardian and stamped on **every** page.

© Crown copyright 2007

PRESCRIBED INFORMATION

You must read this information carefully to understand the purpose and legal consequences of making an LPA. You must ask your attorney(s) and certificate provider(s) to read it too.

This form is a legal document known as a Lasting Power of Attorney (LPA). It allows you to authorise someone (the attorney(s)) to make decisions on your behalf about your personal welfare including your healthcare, if you lack capacity to make those decisions. Your attorney(s) can only use the LPA after it is registered with the OPG.

If you want someone to make decisions about your property and affairs then you need a different form. You can get a Lasting Power of Attorney — Property and Affairs from the OPG and legal stationers.

Detailed information about why you might find an LPA useful is in the **'Guide for people who want to make a personal welfare LPA'**. You can get this from the OPG. You should read this guide before completing this LPA. You should ask your attorney(s) and certificate provider(s) to read it too.

Your attorney(s) cannot do whatever they like. They **must** follow the principles of the Mental Capacity Act 2005 which are:

- a person must be assumed to have capacity unless it is established that the person lacks capacity;

- a person is not to be treated as unable to make a decision unless all practicable steps to help the person to do so have been taken without success;

- a person is not to be treated as unable to make a decision merely because the person makes an unwise decision;

- an act done, or decision made, under the Mental Capacity Act for or on behalf of a person who lacks capacity must be done, or made, in the person's best interests; and

- before the act is done, or the decision is made, regard must be had to whether the purpose for which it is needed can be as effectively achieved in a way that is less restrictive of the person's rights and freedom of action.

Guidance about the principles is in the Mental Capacity Act 2005 Code of Practice. Your attorney(s) will have a duty to have regard to the Code. Copies of the Code can be obtained from Her Majesty's Stationary Office.

1. **CHOOSING YOUR ATTORNEY** Your attorney should be a person you know and trust who is at least 18. You can choose more than one attorney.

2. **CHOOSING MORE THAN ONE ATTORNEY** If you choose more than one attorney you must decide whether your attorneys should act together or together and independently (that is they can all act together but they can also act separately if they wish).
You may appoint your attorneys together in respect of some matters and together and independently in respect of others. If you appoint more than one attorney and do not state whether they are appointed together or together and independently, when your LPA is registered they will be treated on the basis that they are appointed together. In this LPA form, 'together' means jointly and 'together and independently' means jointly and severally for the purposes of the Mental Capacity Act 2005.

Please do not detach these notes. They are part of the Lasting Power of Attorney.

PRESCRIBED INFORMATION

3. **CHOOSING A REPLACEMENT ATTORNEY** You can name a replacement(s) in case an attorney is unable to or no longer wishes to continue acting for you. Your attorney(s) can change their mind and may not want to act for you. If this is the case, they must tell you and the OPG.

4. **WHEN AN ATTORNEY CAN ACT** An attorney for personal welfare can only act when you lack the capacity to make a particular decision yourself. There is no one point at which you are treated as having lost capacity to make decisions about your personal welfare. You may have capacity to make some decisions but not others: for example, you may be able to decide what to wear but not to consent to an operation. Your attorney(s) must help you to make as many of your own decisions as you can. When decisions have to be taken for you, your attorney(s) must always act in your best interests.

5. **DECISIONS YOUR ATTORNEY CAN MAKE FOR YOU** An attorney for personal welfare may make any decision that you could make about your welfare e.g. where you live and with whom, accessing your personal information like medical records, deciding what you wear, what you eat and how you spend your day. This is subject to the authority you give them and any decisions excluded by the Mental Capacity Act 2005. They will also be able to give and refuse consent to medical treatment according to your best interests. Your attorney(s) will only be able to make these decisions where you lack capacity to make them yourself. Some decisions will also involve property and affairs, such as a move to residential care. Your personal welfare attorney(s) will then need to consider your best interests with your attorney(s) for property and affairs (if you have one).

6. **LIFE-SUSTAINING TREATMENT** Your attorney(s) cannot make decisions about life-sustaining treatment for you unless you expressly state that in your LPA. Life-sustaining treatment means any treatment that a doctor considers necessary to sustain your life. Life-sustaining treatment is not a category of treatment. Whether or not a treatment is life-sustaining will depend on the circumstances of a particular situation. Some treatments will be life-sustaining in some situations but not in others; the important factor is if the treatment is needed to keep you alive. In the LPA you must specify whether you are giving your attorney(s) this power.

7. If you do not say that your attorney(s) can make decisions about life-sustaining treatment, the doctor in charge of your treatment will make the decision in your best interests. Where practicable and appropriate, your doctor will take into account the views of your attorney(s) and other people interested in your welfare as part of the best interests assessment. This is what happens in all cases where there is nobody authorised to take decisions on your behalf. However, if you have a separate valid and applicable advance decision, that should be followed by the doctor.

8. **RESTRICTING THE POWERS OF YOUR ATTORNEY(S) OR ADDING CONDITIONS** You can put legally binding restrictions and conditions on your attorney(s)' powers and the scope of their authority in the LPA. But these decisions may still need to be made and other people will have to decide for you. That could involve going back to your doctor or care worker or the Court of Protection and a decision being made in your best interests.

9. **GIVING GUIDANCE TO YOUR ATTORNEY** You can also give guidance to your attorney(s) in your LPA. This is not legally binding but should be taken into account when they are making decisions for you.

Please do not detach these notes. They are part of the Lasting Power of Attorney.

PRESCRIBED INFORMATION

10. PAYING ATTORNEYS An attorney is entitled to be reimbursed for out-of-pocket expenses incurred in carrying out their duties. Professional attorneys, such as solicitors or accountants, charge for their services. You should discuss and record any decision you make about paying your attorney(s) in the LPA.

11. NOTIFYING OTHER PEOPLE BEFORE REGISTRATION You can name up to five people to be notified when an application to register your LPA is made. Anyone about to apply for registration of an LPA must notify these people. This gives you an important safeguard because if you lack capacity at the time of registration you will be relying on these people to raise any concerns they may have about the application to register. If you choose not to name anyone to be notified you will need to have two certificate providers under Part B of this form.

12. CERTIFICATE TO CONFIRM UNDERSTANDING Once you have filled in Part A of this form an independent person must fill in the certificate at Part B to confirm that, in their opinion, you are making the LPA of your own free will, and that you understand its purpose and the powers you are giving your attorney(s). This is an important safeguard and your LPA cannot be registered unless the certificate is completed.

13. REGISTERING THE LPA *Your LPA cannot be used until it has been registered with the OPG.* Either you or your chosen attorney(s) can apply to register the LPA. If you register it immediately it is ready to be used when you lack capacity. The form for registering the LPA is available from the OPG together with details of the registration fee.

14. REGISTER OF LPAs There is a register of LPAs kept by the OPG. It is possible to access the register of LPAs but access is controlled. On application to the OPG, and payment of a fee, people can find out basic information about your LPA. At the discretion of the OPG and according to the purpose for which they need it, they may be able to find out further information. There is additional guidance available from the OPG on the register.

15. CHANGING YOUR MIND You can cancel your LPA even after it is registered if you have the mental capacity to do so. You need to take formal steps to revoke the LPA. You must tell your attorney if you do and, if it is registered, you will need to ask the OPG to remove it from the register of LPAs.

FURTHER NOTICE FOR ATTORNEY(S)
You should read the **'Guide for people taking on the role of Personal Welfare attorney'** under an LPA before you agree to become an attorney and complete Part C of this LPA. The guide contains detailed information about what your role and responsibilities will be.

You must contact the OPG at once if the person you are acting for dies. If you are unable to continue acting you should take steps to disclaim the power and notify the OPG and the donor.

FURTHER NOTICE FOR CERTIFICATE PROVIDER(S)
You should read the separate **'Certificate Providers and witness guidance'** before you agree to become a certificate provider and complete Part B of this LPA. The guidance contains detailed information about your role and responsibilities. You may also like to read the guidance for personal welfare attorneys and donors. If you have any concerns about an LPA you are asked to certify please contact the OPG.

Please do not detach these notes. They are part of the Lasting Power of Attorney.

4

A5–06

LPA PW 04.07

Lasting Power of Attorney – Personal Welfare

Important
This LPA form cannot be used until it has been registered by the OPG and stamped on **every** page.

Before you complete this LPA form, you must read the prescribed information on pages 2, 3 and 4 and you should read the guidance produced by the OPG.

To help you complete the form, please refer to the Notes for completing an LPA – Personal Welfare.

PART A – Donor's statement

Your details

1. My name and date of birth are: ◄ See Note 1

☐ Mr. ☐ Mrs. ☐ Ms. ☐ Miss ☐ Other _____

First name [   ]

Middle name(s) [   ]

Last name [   ]

Date of birth [D D | M M | Y Y Y Y]

Any other names you are known by or have been known by in the past ◄ See Note 2
(e.g. maiden name)

[   ]

2. My contact details are: ◄ See Note 3

Address [   ]

Postcode [   ]

Telephone no. [   ]

Mobile no. [   ]

E-mail address [   ]

The details of the attorney(s) you are appointing

3. I appoint the following attorney(s) in accordance with the provisions of the
Mental Capacity Act 2005:

See Note 4

Attorney

☐ Mr.   ☐ Mrs.   ☐ Ms.   ☐ Miss   ☐ Other _____

See Note 5

First name(s)

Last name

Attorney

☐ Mr.   ☐ Mrs.   ☐ Ms.   ☐ Miss   ☐ Other _____

First name(s)

Last name

How your attorney(s) is to act for you

If you only have one attorney please cross through this part.

4. If you are appointing more than one attorney, how do you wish them to act?

See Note 6

(If you do not choose an option your attorneys will be appointed together)

☐ together

See Note 7

☐ together and independently

☐ together in respect of some matters and together and independently in respect of others

If together in respect of some matters and together and independently in respect of others,
details are as follows:

Replacement attorney(s)

5. I wish to appoint a replacement attorney: (You do not have to appoint a replacement attorney). ◄ See Note 8

☐ Yes ☐ No

If Yes, I appoint the following replacement attorney:

☐ Mr. ☐ Mrs. ☐ Ms. ☐ Miss ☐ Other [ ] ◄ See Note 9

First name(s)

Last name

Restrictions on the appointment of a replacement attorney: (If you do not complete this section your first replacement will replace the first attorney who needs replacing). ◄ See Note 10

Life-sustaining treatment

6. You **must** choose **one** of the two options below:

> If you cannot sign or make a mark, please read the notes for completion.

See Note 11

Option A

I want to give my attorney(s) authority to give or refuse consent to life-sustaining treatment on my behalf

Your signature	

Date signed	D D M M Y Y Y Y

Option B

I **do not** want to give my attorney(s) authority to give or refuse consent to life-sustaining treatment on my behalf

Your signature	

Date signed	D D M M Y Y Y Y

In the presence of

See Note 12

Signature of witness	

Full name of witness	

Address of witness	

Postcode	

Placing restrictions and/or conditions on the attorney(s) you are appointing

Any restrictions and/or conditions you set out below **must** be followed by the attorney(s). For example, if you have given your attorney(s) powers with regard to life-sustaining treatment you can comment further here about any restrictions you want to add.

7. I wish to place restrictions and/or conditions on my attorney(s) in relation to my personal welfare:

See Note 13

☐ Yes ☐ No

If Yes, the restrictions and conditions are as follows:

Guidance for your attorney(s) to consider   See Note 14

Your attorney(s) **should** consider the guidance set out below when making decisions in your best interests.

8. I wish my attorney(s) to consider the following guidance:

9. I have agreed to pay my attorney(s) a fee to act as my attorney(s):   See Note 15

  ☐ Yes   ☐ No

If Yes, the following is additional information about fees that I have agreed with my attorney(s):

Notifying others when an application to register your LPA is made — See Note 16

10. I wish the following people, 'the named persons', to be notified when an application to register my LPA is made:

☐ Mr. ☐ Mrs. ☐ Ms. ☐ Miss ☐ Other _____

Full name _____

Address _____

Postcode ☐☐☐☐☐☐☐☐

Telephone no. _____

E-mail address _____

☐ Mr. ☐ Mrs. ☐ Ms. ☐ Miss ☐ Other _____

Full name _____

Address _____

Postcode ☐☐☐☐☐☐☐☐

Telephone no. _____

E-mail address _____

☐ Mr. ☐ Mrs. ☐ Ms. ☐ Miss ☐ Other _____

Full name _____

Address _____

Postcode ☐☐☐☐☐☐☐☐

Telephone no. _____

E-mail address _____

☐ Mr.　☐ Mrs.　☐ Ms.　☐ Miss　☐ Other _____

Full name

Address

Postcode

Telephone no.

E-mail address

☐ Mr.　☐ Mrs.　☐ Ms.　☐ Miss　☐ Other _____

Full name

Address

Postcode

Telephone no.

E-mail address

If you do not include anyone here you **must** have two certificate providers at Part B.

11. I confirm that

☐ I have read the prescribed information on pages 2, 3 and 4 of this LPA   ◄ See Note 17

or

☐ the prescribed information has been read to me by [   ]

12. I confirm that

☐ I give my attorney(s) authority to make decisions on my behalf in circumstances when I lack capacity.   ◄ See Note 18

13. I confirm that

☐ I have chosen between Option A and option B with regard to life-sustaining treatment in paragraph 6 of this LPA.   ◄ See Note 19

14. I confirm that

☐ the person(s) named in paragraph 10 are to be notified when this LPA is registered   ◄ See Note 20

or

☐ I do not want anyone to be notified when an application to register this LPA is made and I understand that I need **two** people to provide a separate certificate each at Part B of this LPA.

15. I confirm that

☐ I have chosen my certificate provider(s) myself.   ◄ See Note 21

16. Signed by me as a deed [   ]   ◄ See Note 22

17. Date signed (delivered as a deed) [D D M M Y Y Y Y]

> If you are unable to sign the form, please refer to the notes for completion and turn to page 14 of this LPA.

In the presence of

18. Signature of witness [   ]   ◄ See Note 23

19. Full name of witness [   ]

20. Address of witness [   ]

Postcode [   ]

> **Important** - This form **cannot** be used until it has been registered by the Office of the Public Guardian and stamped on **every** page.

If you are unable to sign or make a mark, then you must ask someone else to sign for you in your presence and the presence of two witnesses. Please refer to notes 24 and 25.

I am signing this LPA at the donor's direction and in the donor's presence and I confirm that I have signed at paragraph 6 according to the donor's direction.   ◀ See Note 24

21. Signed as a deed

22. Date signed (delivered as a deed)   `D D M M Y Y Y Y`

23. Full name

24. Address

Postcode

In the presence of   ◀ See Note 25

25. Signature of witness

26. Full name of witness

27. Address of witness

Postcode

28. Signature of witness

29. Full name of witness

30. Address of witness

Postcode

A5–07

PART B - Certificate provider's statement
See Note 26

Who can provide a certificate?
The donor can choose someone they have known personally over the last two years (Category A) or someone who, because of their relevant professional skills and expertise, considers themselves able to provide the certificate (Category B).

Note: Category B providers are entitled to charge a fee for providing this certificate.

Who cannot provide a certificate?
See Note 27
A certificate provider must not be:
• a member of the donor's or attorney's family;
• a business partner or paid employee of the donor or attorney(s);
• an attorney appointed in this form or another LPA or any EPA made by the donor;
• the owner, director, manager, or an employee of a care home in which the donor lives or their family member.

You, the certificate provider, **must** read Parts A and B of this LPA, and the prescribed information on pages 2, 3 and 4. You should also read the separate **'Certificate provider and witness guidance'** produced by the OPG before completing the certificate. You must discuss the LPA with the donor without the attorney(s) present.
See Note 28

☐ I confirm that I am acting independently of the person making this LPA (the donor) and the person(s) appointed under the LPA and in particular I am not a person listed in the above section 'Who cannot provide a certificate?'.
See Note 29

☐ I am aged 18 or over.
See Note 30

The certificate provider

Name and contact details of the certificate provider

☐ Mr.　☐ Mrs.　☐ Ms.　☐ Miss　☐ Other
See Note 31

First name

Middle name(s)

Last name

Address

Postcode

Telephone no.
See Note 32

Mobile no.

E-mail address

The OPG may need to contact you to verify the information you provide.

Category of certificate provider – choose from category A **or** B – do not complete both. See Note 33

Category A – Knowledge certification See Note 34

☐ I have known the donor personally over the last two years.

How do you know them?

Category B - Skills certification See Note 35

I am:

☐ a registered healthcare professional (includes GP)

☐ a barrister, solicitor or advocate

☐ a registered social worker

☐ an Independent Mental Capacity Advocate (IMCA)

☐ none of the above but consider that I have the relevant professional skills and expertise to be a certificate provider.

My relevant professional skills and expertise are:

I confirm and understand

☐ I confirm that I have read Parts A and B of this LPA and the prescribed information on pages 2, 3 and 4. See Note 36

☐ I confirm that I have discussed the contents of this LPA with the donor and that the attorney(s) was not present. See Note 37

☐ I understand that I should make efforts to discuss this LPA with the donor without anyone present; and See Note 38

☐ I have discussed this LPA with the donor without anyone else present

or

☐ I have discussed this LPA with the donor in the presence of:

because

☐ I confirm that I am completing this certificate straight after discussing this LPA with the donor. See Note 39

Core certification

I certify

See Note 40

I certify that in my opinion, at the time when the donor is making this LPA, that:

☐ the donor understands the purpose of this LPA and the scope of the authority under it;

☐ no fraud or undue pressure is being used to induce the donor to create this LPA; and

☐ there is nothing else that would prevent this LPA being created.

Do not sign this certificate if you have any doubt about any of the above. You should bring any concerns you have to the attention of the OPG.

Signature of certificate provider   Date signed   See Note 41

| | D | D | M | M | Y | Y | Y | Y |

Full name of certificate provider

Additional certificate provider's statement

See Note 42

This additional certificate only needs to be completed if there are no notified persons listed in the LPA.

Who can provide a certificate?
The donor can choose someone they have known personally over the last two years (Category A) or someone who, because of their relevant professional skills and expertise, considers themselves able to provide the certificate (Category B).

Note: Category B providers are entitled to charge a fee for providing this certificate.

Who cannot provide a certificate?
A certificate provider must not be:
- a member of the donor's or attorney's family;
- a business partner or paid employee of the donor or attorney(s);
- an attorney appointed in this form or another LPA or any EPA made by the donor;
- the owner, director, manager, or an employee of a care home in which the donor lives or their family member.

You, the certificate provider, **must** read Part A and B of this LPA, and the prescribed information on pages 2, 3 and 4. You should also read the separate **'Certificate provider and witness guidance'** produced by the OPG before completing the certificate. You must discuss the LPA with the donor and without the attorney(s) present.

☐ I confirm that I am acting independently of the person making this LPA (the donor) and the person(s) appointed under the LPA and in particular I am not a person listed in the above section 'Who cannot provide a certificate?'.

☐ I am aged 18 or over.

The certificate provider

Name and contact details of certificate provider

☐ Mr.   ☐ Mrs.   ☐ Ms.   ☐ Miss   ☐ Other _____

First name _____

Middle name(s) _____

Last name _____

Address _____

Postcode ☐☐☐☐☐☐☐☐

Telephone no. _____

Mobile no. _____

E-mail address _____

The OPG may need to contact you to verify the information you provide.

Category of certificate provider – choose from category A or B – do not complete both

Category A – Knowledge certification

☐ I have known the donor personally over the last two years.

How do you know them?

>

Category B - Skills certification

I am:

☐ a registered healthcare professional (includes GP)   ☐ a barrister, solicitor or advocate

☐ a registered social worker   ☐ an Independent Mental Capacity Advocate (IMCA)

☐ none of the above but consider that I have the relevant professional skills and expertise to be a certificate provider.

My relevant professional skills and expertise are:

>

I confirm and understand

☐ I confirm that I have read Parts A and B of this LPA and the prescribed information on pages 2, 3 and 4.

☐ I confirm that I have discussed the contents of this LPA with the donor and that the attorney(s) was not present.

☐ I understand that I should make efforts to discuss this LPA with the donor without anyone present; and

     ☐ I have discussed this LPA with the donor without anyone else present

     or

     ☐ I have discussed this LPA with the donor in the presence of:

>

     because

>

☐ I confirm that I am completing this certificate straight after discussing this LPA with the donor.

Core certification

I certify

I certify that in my opinion, at the time when the donor is making this LPA, that:

☐ the donor understands the purpose of this LPA and the scope of the authority under it;

☐ no fraud or undue pressure is being used to induce the donor to create this LPA; and

☐ there is nothing else that would prevent this LPA being created.

Do not sign this certificate if you have any doubt about any of the above. You should bring any concerns you have to the attention of the OPG.

Signature of certificate provider

Date signed

D D M M Y Y Y Y

Full name of certificate provider

A5–08

PART C – Attorney's statement (Every attorney must complete a copy of this Part)   See Note 43

31. My contact details and date of birth are:

Attorney

☐ Mr.   ☐ Mrs.   ☐ Ms.   ☐ Miss   ☐ Other _____   See Note 44

First name

Middle name(s)

Last name

Date of birth   D D M M Y Y Y Y

Telephone no.   Mobile

E-mail address   See Note 45

32. ☐ I have read the prescribed information on pages 2, 3 and 4 or have had the prescribed information read to me.   See Note 46

33. ☐ I understand the duties imposed on me under this Lasting Power of Attorney including the obligation to act in accordance with the principles of the Mental Capacity Act 2005 and the duty to have regard to the Code of Practice issued under that Act.   See Note 47

34. ☐ I understand that I cannot act until this form has been registered by the Public Guardian.   See Note 48

35. ☐ I understand that I cannot act under this Lasting Power of Attorney until the donor lacks capacity.   See Note 49

36. Signed by me as a deed *(You must not sign until after the donor has signed at paragraph 16 and the certificate provider has signed the certificate)*   See Note 50

37. Date signed (delivered as a deed)   D D M M Y Y Y Y

In the presence of   See Note 51

38. Signature of witness

39. Full name of witness

40. Address of witness

Postcode

Important - This form **cannot** be used until it has been registered by the Office of the Public Guardian and stamped on **every** page.

PART C – Attorney's statement (Every attorney must complete a copy of this Part) ◁ See Note 43

31. My contact details and date of birth are:

Attorney

☐ Mr.   ☐ Mrs.   ☐ Ms.   ☐ Miss   ☐ Other _____   ◁ See Note 44

First name _____

Middle name(s) _____

Last name _____

Date of birth [D][D][M][M][Y][Y][Y][Y]

Telephone no. _____   Mobile _____

◁ See Note 45

E-mail address _____

32. ☐ I have read the prescribed information on pages 2, 3 and 4 or have had the prescribed information read to me.   ◁ See Note 46

33. ☐ I understand the duties imposed on me under this Lasting Power of Attorney including the obligation to act in accordance with the principles of the Mental Capacity Act 2005 and the duty to have regard to the Code of Practice issued under that Act.   ◁ See Note 47

34. ☐ I understand that I cannot act until this form has been registered by the Public Guardian.   ◁ See Note 48

35. ☐ I understand that I cannot act under this Lasting Power of Attorney until the donor lacks capacity.   ◁ See Note 49

36. Signed by me as a deed *(You must not sign until after the donor has signed at paragraph 16 and the certificate provider has signed the certificate)*   ◁ See Note 50

_____

37. Date signed (delivered as a deed) [D][D][M][M][Y][Y][Y][Y]

In the presence of   ◁ See Note 51

38. Signature of witness _____

39. Full name of witness _____

40. Address of witness _____

Postcode [ ][ ][ ][ ][ ][ ][ ]

Important - This form **cannot** be used until it has been registered by the Office of the Public Guardian and stamped on **every** page.

APPENDIX 5

PART C – Replacement attorney's statement `See Note 52`

(To be completed by a replacement attorney if appointed. Only complete this if you are a replacement attorney chosen at paragraph 5.)

41. My contact details and date of birth are:

Attorney

☐ Mr.　☐ Mrs.　☐ Ms.　☐ Miss　☐ Other `See Note 53`

First name

Middle name(s)

Last name

Date of birth `D D M M Y Y Y Y`

Telephone no. 　　　　　　　　　　Mobile

E-mail address `See Note 54`

42. ☐ I have read the prescribed information on pages 2, 3 and 4 or have had the prescribed information read to me. `See Note 55`

43. ☐ I understand that if an original attorney's appointment is terminated I will replace the original attorney if I am still eligible to act as an attorney. `See Note 56`

44. ☐ I understand that I do not have the authority to act under this LPA until such time as a relevant attorney's appointment is terminated. `See Note 57`

45. ☐ I understand the duties imposed on me under this Lasting Power of Attorney including the obligation to act in accordance with the principles of the Mental Capacity Act 2005 and the duty to have regard to the Code of Practice issued under that Act. `See Note 58`

46. ☐ I understand that I cannot act under this Lasting Power of Attorney until this form has been registered by the Public Guardian. `See Note 59`

47. ☐ I understand that I cannot act until the donor lacks capacity. `See Note 60`

48. Signed by me as a deed *(You must not sign until after the donor has signed at paragraph 16 and the certificate provider has signed the certificate)* `See Note 61`

49. Date signed
    (delivered as
    a deed)　`D D M M Y Y Y Y`

In the presence of   See Note 62

50. Signature of
    witness

51. Full name
    of witness

52. Address of
    witness

Postcode

> **Important** - This form **cannot** be used until it has been registered
> by the Office of the Public Guardian and stamped on **every** page.

Guidance for Forms LPA PA 10.07 and LPA PW 10.07 is reproduced below

This Guidance from the Office of the Public Guardian should be read in conjunction with the form.

A5–09   `LPA PA Notes` `10.07`

Lasting Power of Attorney Property and Affairs

Notes for completing an LPA – Property and Affairs

Important information

These notes will help you to fill in a Lasting Power of Attorney – Property and Affairs (LPA PA).

If you are making a Lasting Power of Attorney – Personal Welfare (LPA PW) you should **not** use these completion notes. Please refer to the notes for completing an LPA – Personal Welfare.

Before you complete the LPA

You must read the prescribed information at pages 2, 3 and 4 of the LPA form before you make the LPA. You should read the blank LPA form and these completion notes all the way through before you begin to make an LPA so that you know what you need to do. Your certificate provider and attorney(s) should also read these notes. There is more information about LPAs available from the Office of the Public Guardian (OPG) and you are advised to read this before making the LPA.

Completing the LPA

If there is not enough room for you to express your intentions in any Part or paragraph of the LPA, you should continue on a separate sheet and **attach it securely** at the back of the LPA. You should sign and date any continuation sheets and note clearly which Part and paragraph of the LPA they relate to.

If you make a minor mistake you should correct it and clearly initial the correction. You cannot make any changes at all to an LPA that has been signed, witnessed and certified.

These notes state which paragraphs and boxes **must** be completed. Failure to complete mandatory paragraphs and boxes may result in a delay when the LPA is sent for registration or may even result in the LPA being invalid in some cases. Where you are asked to cross through a part of the LPA that you are not using this is to stop anyone else filling in it. You must complete or cross through every part of the LPA.

When you are required to make a choice or confirm something you must be sure that you understand what you are choosing or confirming.

If you are unsure about the requirements of this LPA form, contact the OPG at the address given on the front of the LPA form. The OPG can help you in completing the form, but cannot give you legal advice.

Please use black or blue ink when filling in the form.

Part A – Donor's statement (Page 5 of LPA PA)

Your details

Note 1 ▶ Place a cross in the appropriate title box and enter your first name, middle name, last name and date of birth. If you do not have a middle name, clearly cross through that box.

Note 2 ▶ You must enter any other names you are known by or have been known by in the past, for example, your maiden name. If you are not known by any other names or have not been known by any other names in the past, clearly cross through this box.

Note 3 ▶ Enter your contact details. You must enter your address and postcode. You should enter your telephone number and mobile phone number (if you have one) but you do not have to. You may also like to enter your e-mail address (if you have one). The more contact options you complete the easier it will be for the OPG, your attorney(s) or other people who may be relying on your LPA to contact you. If you leave a box blank clearly cross through that box.

The details of the attorney(s) you are appointing (Page 6 of LPA PA)

Note 4 ▶ There are two attorney spaces on the form but you do not have to appoint two attorneys. You can appoint as many or as few attorneys as you want. If you are not using both of the attorney boxes, clearly cross through those that you are not using. You should do this to avoid other people completing blank boxes. If you want to appoint more than two attorneys, follow the instructions on page 1 of these notes about continuation sheets.

Note 5 ▶ Place a cross in the appropriate title box and enter the first name and last name of the attorney(s) you are appointing. **You must check with the person(s) you would like to appoint as your attorney(s) that they agree to act as attorney(s) for you before completing this page.**

Note 6 ▶ You can choose a trust corporation to be your attorney or one of your attorneys but you do not have to. If you are not appointing a trust corporation to be an attorney, clearly cross through that box. There is more information on the appointment of a trust corporation in the OPG guidance on LPAs.

How your attorney(s) is to act for you (Page 7 of LPA PA)

Note 7 ▶ If you are only appointing one attorney cross through the entirety of this page. If you are appointing more than one attorney you must decide how your attorneys are to act and place a cross in one of the three small boxes to indicate your choice. You must only place a cross in one box. If you cross more than one box or fail to cross any of the boxes then your attorneys will be appointed together by default.

If you appoint your attorneys 'together' this means that all of them have to take decisions and act together for you. If you appoint your attorneys 'together and independently' this means that they can all take decisions and act together for you **and** they can also take decisions and act separately for you. You can also specify that your attorneys should act together in respect of some matters and together and independently in respect of others. You must think carefully about the practical implications of appointing attorneys to act in different ways.

2

Note 8 ▶ If you decide to appoint your attorneys together in respect of some matters and together and independently in respect of others (by placing a cross in the relevant small box) you must then specify in the large text box on which matters your attorneys are to act together and on which matters they are to act together and independently.

In this LPA form, 'together' means jointly and 'together and independently' means jointly and severally for the purposes of the Mental Capacity Act 2005.

Replacement attorney(s) (Page 8 of LPA PA)

Note 9 ▶ You must choose box 'Yes' or box 'No'. You can choose to appoint a replacement attorney to act if one or any of your attorneys cannot continue to be your attorney. You do not have to appoint a replacement attorney. There is more information on replacement attorneys in the OPG guidance on LPAs.

If you are not appointing a replacement attorney, place a cross in the 'No' box and clearly cross through the rest of this page. If you decide to appoint a replacement attorney, place a cross in the 'Yes' box. **You should check with the person you would like to appoint as your replacement attorney that they agree before completing this page.**

If you want to appoint more than one replacement attorney you must follow the instructions above about using continuation sheets. If you do not specify clearly which attorneys your replacements are to replace then the first replacement to be named in your LPA will replace the first attorney who needs replacing.

Note 10 ▶ Place a cross in the appropriate title box and enter the first name and last name of your replacement attorney.

Note 11 ▶ You do not have to complete this large text box. If you do not complete this box your replacement attorney will replace the first attorney who needs replacing. You can use this box to specify that your replacement should only replace a specific named attorney. Or you can specify that the replacement can replace any of your attorneys except a specific named attorney.

Placing restrictions and/or conditions on the attorney(s) you are appointing (Page 9 LPA PA)

Note 12 ▶ You must choosebox 'Yes' or box 'No'. If you do not want to place any restrictions and/or conditions on your attorney(s), place a cross in the 'No' box and clearly cross through the rest of this page.

If you do not place any restrictions and/or conditions on your attorney(s) they will be able to take any decisions about your property and affairs that you can take. If you place restrictions or conditions on the decisions your attorney(s) can make or the matters which they can deal with, these must be followed by your attorney(s).

If you want to place restrictions and/or conditions on your attorney(s), place a cross in the 'Yes' box. If you choose this option you must specify in the large text box what those restrictions and/or conditions are. **You can restrict your attorney(s) or any of your attorneys in whatever manner you see fit but you should ensure that your restrictions and/or conditions will work in practice.** There is more information on the placing restrictions and/or conditions on your attorney in the OPG guidance on LPAs.

3

Guidance for your attorney(s) to consider (Page 10 LPA PA)

Note 13 ▶ You do not have to complete this paragraph. If you do not want to give your attorney(s) any guidance in your LPA, clearly cross through this large text box.

Any guidance you give to your attorney(s) is for their information only. Your attorney(s) should consider your guidance when making decisions for you in your best interests.

If you want to give your attorney(s) guidance, complete the large text box. There is more information on giving guidance to your attorney in the OPG guidance on LPAs.

Paying attorney(s) (Page 10 LPA PA)

Note 14 ▶ You must choose one of the two small option boxes in this paragraph. This will reflect whether you have agreed to pay your attorney(s) a fee. You do not have to pay your attorney(s) a fee. If you have more than one attorney you may make different decisions about fees for different attorneys. If you place a cross in the 'Yes' box you may give additional information about the fees you have agreed with your attorney in the text box provided.

If you place a cross in the 'No' box you should clearly cross through the rest of this paragraph.

Notifying others when an application to register your LPA is made (Page 11 and 12 of LPA PA)

Note 15 ▶ You can choose up to five people to be notified when an application to register your LPA is made. You can choose anyone you want. **This is an important safeguard because it gives the people you have chosen the right to object to registration of the LPA.** You do not have to choose anyone to be notified but if you do not, you will need to have two certificate providers at Part B of the LPA. If at all possible, you should choose at least one person to be notified when an application is made to register the LPA.

If you are not choosing anyone to be notified, clearly cross through the entirety of this and the following page.

If you choose a person(s) to be notified you should let them know that you have chosen them to perform this role.

For each person you want to be notified place a cross in the appropriate title box and enter their name and address including their postcode. You do not have to enter a telephone number and e-mail for these people but it will be easier to contact them if you do. If you leave a box blank, clearly cross through that box.

Things to confirm (Page 13 of LPA PA)

Note 16 ▶ You **must** read the prescribed information on pages 2, 3 and 4 of the LPA form or have it read to you before completing the LPA. You must confirm this by placing a cross in the appropriate box. If the information has been read to you by somebody else their name should be printed in the space provided. This person should **not** be one of your attorneys.

Note 17 ▶ By making an LPA you are giving your attorney(s) the legal authority to make decisions on your behalf including in circumstances when you lack capacity. You must place a cross in the box to confirm that you are giving your attorney(s) that authority.

Note 18 ▶ When making an LPA you must either choose a person or people to be notified when an application to register your LPA is made or you must select two people to provide a separate Part B certificate each. Confirm which one of these you are doing by placing a cross in the appropriate box.

Note 19 ▶ Your certificate provider(s) independently verifies the circumstances in which you are making your LPA. It is important that you choose them, not your attorney(s) or any other person. You must place a cross in the box to confirm that you have chosen your certificate provider(s) yourself.

Signing the LPA (Page 13 of LPA PA)

Note 20 ▶ Sign the document or make your mark in the signature box and enter the date on which it is signed or marked. If you are unable to sign or mark the LPA, see completion note 22 and page 13 of the LPA form. 'Signed by me as a deed' and 'delivered' as a deed are legal formalities. They just mean you need to sign and date.

Witness (Page 13 of the LPA PA)

Note 21 ▶ Your signature must be witnessed. Your witness must be at least 18 years of age and must not be your attorney(s). Your witness can be your Part B certificate provider. The witness must sign the LPA, enter their full name, their address and their postcode.

If you are unable to sign or make a mark (Page 14 of LPA PA)

Note 22 ▶ **This page should only be completed if you cannot sign or make a mark.** If you cannot sign the form or make a mark you can direct someone else to sign it for you. You can 'direct' someone in whatever way you choose to communicate. This person must be at least 18 years of age and must not be your attorney(s) or your Part B certificate provider(s). The person you are directing to sign must sign and date the form.

Witnesses (Page 14 of LPA PA)

Note 23 ▶ There must be two witnesses to this person's signature. Your Part B certificate provider(s) may be a witness to this person's signature. Your attorney(s) must not be a witness to this person's signature. The witnesses must each sign the LPA, enter their full names and their addresses including their postcodes.

5

LASTING POWERS OF ATTORNEY, ETC REGS 2007 345

Part B – Certificate provider's statement (Page 15 of LPA PA) A5–11

Note 24 ➤ You must choose someone to be the certificate provider for your LPA. Both you and your certificate provider must read the certificate before beginning to complete any of it.

The rest of this note on completing Part B is for the certificate provider. If you do not feel able to complete any of the Part B certificate do not complete it and raise any concerns you have with the OPG. There is separate guidance available, 'Certificate Provider and Witness Guidance'.

Who cannot provide a certificate? (Page 15 of LPA PA)

Note 25 ➤ You must not fall into one of these categories. If you do and you provide a certificate, the LPA will **not** be valid.

Note 26 ➤ You must read the whole of Parts A and B of this LPA, including the prescribed information on pages 2 – 4 before completing the certificate. The OPG has guidance on the role and responsibilities of the certificate provider and you should also read this before completing the certificate.

Note 27 ➤ You must be acting independently of the person making the LPA and the attorney(s) appointed under the LPA. You must not fall into the categories listed under 'Who cannot provide a certificate'. Once you are certain that you are not one of these people you must confirm by placing a cross in the box.

Note 28 ➤ You must be 18 or over to provide this certificate. You must confirm this by placing a cross in the box. Only after you have confirmed this should you continue to complete the rest of the certificate.

Note 29 ➤ Place a cross in the appropriate title box and enter your first name, middle name and last name. If you do not have a middle name, clearly cross through that box. Enter your address and postcode.

Note 30 ➤ You should enter your telephone number and mobile number (if you have one) but you do not have to. You may also like to enter your e-mail address (if you have one). The more contact options you complete the easier it will be for the OPG or other people to contact you. If you leave a box blank, clearly cross through that box.

Who can provide a certificate? (Page 16 of LPA PA)

Note 31 ➤ You must identify yourself as either a category A certificate provider or a category B certificate provider. Do not fill in both category A and B. You must choose only one.

Knowledge certification (Page 16 of LPA PA)

Note 32 ➤ Place a cross in the small box to show that you have known the donor personally over the last two years. 'Personally' means that the donor is known to you as more than a passing acquaintance. Specify how you know them. This need not be in detail.

6

Skills certification (Page 16 of LPA PA)

Note 33 ▶ There are five boxes for skills certification. Choose one of the boxes by placing a cross in it. If you place a cross in the last box which begins, 'I am none of the above...' you must describe what you consider your relevant skills and expertise are in the text box titled 'My relevant professional skills and expertise are:'.

I confirm and understand (Page 16 of LPA PA)

Note 34 ▶ You must read Part A and B of this LPA including the prescribed information on pages 2 – 4 before you certify. Place a cross in the box to confirm that you have done so.

Note 35 ▶ You must discuss the contents of this LPA with the donor in order to be sure of the matters you are certifying. **The attorney(s) must not be present.** Place a cross in the box to confirm that you have discussed this LPA with the donor and that the attorney(s) was not present.

Note 36 ▶ You should make efforts to discuss this LPA with the donor without anyone present. Place a cross in the box to confirm that you understand that you should try to do this.

There may, however, be situations where there has to be someone else there, for example where you need someone to assist you to communicate with the donor. You must choose (by placing a cross in the appropriate box) between confirming that you discussed the LPA with the donor alone or that there was another person or person(s) present. Print the name of the person or people who was or were present and explain why they needed to be there.

Note 37 ▶ You are certifying certain matters at a particular point in time, so it is important that you complete the certificate straight after discussing the LPA with the donor. Place a cross in the box to confirm this.

Core certification (Page 17 of LPA PA)

Note 38 ▶ You are required to certify three things. You are certifying in your opinion having read the LPA and discussed the contents with the donor. You must consider whether you can certify these matters and, if you can, you must place a cross in the three boxes.

Note 39 ▶ The certification process is complete when you sign the certificate. **Do not sign the certificate if you have any doubt about any of the matters you are being asked to certify.** Sign the document in the signature box and enter the date on which you are signing. Print your full name in the box below the signature box.

Additional certificate provider's statement (Page 18 LPA PA)

Note 40 ▶ Only complete page 18 when there are no people listed at paragraph 9 to be notified of an application for registration. If this additional certificate is required it should not be completed by the same person as the first certificate on pages 15 – 17. See notes 24 to 39 above for guidance.

7

Part C – Attorney's statement (Page 21 LPA PA)

Note 41 Every attorney named in Part A of the form must complete a separate attorney's statement at Part C. They are identical and therefore notes 41 to 49 can be used by all attorneys.

There is a different statement at page 23 to use if a trust corporation is being appointed as an attorney. If there is a replacement attorney they must complete the replacement attorney's statement at page 24.

The rest of this note on completing Part C is for the attorney(s).
You must read this LPA, including the prescribed information on pages 2 – 4, before completing your statement. The OPG has guidance on the role and responsibilities of an attorney and you should also read this before completing the statement so that you understand the nature of the role you are taking on. You should also discuss with the donor the duties you are assuming.

Note 42 Place a cross in the appropriate title box and enter your first name, middle name, last name and date of birth. You must be at least 18 to be an attorney. If you do not have a middle name, clearly cross through that box.

Note 43 You should enter your telephone number and mobile number (if you have one) but you do not have to. You may also like to enter your e-mail address (if you have one). The more options you complete the easier it will be for the OPG or other people to contact you. If you leave a box blank, clearly cross through that box.

Note 44 You **must** read the prescribed information on pages 2 – 4 of the LPA. Place a cross in the box to confirm that you have done.

Note 45 You **must** read the LPA, and the separate guidance for attorneys and you must familiarise yourself with the wishes and feelings of the donor. As an attorney you have a legal duty to act in accordance with the principles of the Mental Capacity Act 2005. You also have a duty to have regard to the Code of Practice. The Code of Practice has practical guidance about the Act and your role as an attorney. Place a cross in the box to confirm that you understand the duties you have as an attorney.

Note 46 An attorney acting under an LPA – Property and Affairs must not be an undischarged bankrupt or an interim bankrupt. Place a cross in the box to confirm that you are neither.

Note 47 **You cannot and must not use the LPA form and the powers in it until it has been registered by the Public Guardian.** Place a cross in the box to confirm that you understand this.

Note 48 Sign the LPA in the signature box and enter the date on which you sign. You **must not** sign until the donor has signed at paragraph 14 of the LPA and the certificate provider has signed the certificate. 'Signed by me as a deed' and 'delivered by me as a deed' are legal formalities. They just mean you need to sign and date.

A5–13 Note 49 Your signature must be witnessed. Your witness must be at least 18. Your witness may be a Part B certificate provider or another attorney. The witness must sign the LPA, enter their full name, their address and their postcode.

Part C – Attorney's statement – Trust Corporation (Page 23 LPA PA)

Note 50 This page need only be completed where the donor has chosen a trust corporation to be an attorney. In order for a trust corporation to be an attorney they must comply with the requirements of company and trust law.

Note 51 Enter the company name, the company address and postcode and the company registration number.

Note 52 Representatives of the company must cross the two boxes to confirm these matters. Please refer to notes 45 and 46.

Note 53 Please use this space to execute as a deed in accordance with company and trust law requirements.

A5–14 Part C – Replacement attorney's statement (Page 24 LPA PA)

Note 54 This page only needs to be completed if the donor has appointed a replacement attorney at paragraph 5 of the LPA. The rest of this note is addressed to the replacement attorney. You must read this LPA, including the prescribed information on pages 2 – 4 before completing your statement. The OPG has guidance on the role and responsibilities of an attorney (including a replacement attorney) and you should also read this before completing the statement so that you understand the nature of the role you are taking on. You should also discuss with the donor the duties you are taking on.

Note 55 Place a cross in the appropriate title box and enter your first name, middle name, last name and date of birth. You must be at least 18 years of age to be an attorney. If you do not have a middle name, clearly cross through that box.

Note 56 You should enter your telephone number and mobile number (if you have one) but you do not have to. You may also like to enter your e-mail address (if you have one). The more contact options you complete the easier it will be for the OPG or other people to contact you. If you leave a box blank, clearly cross through that box.

Note 57 You **must** read the prescribed information on pages 2 – 4 of the LPA. Place a cross in the box to confirm that you have done.

Note 58 You will only replace an attorney if you are needed and you will only be eligible to replace that attorney if you are still legally able to do so. Place a cross in the box to confirm that you understand this.

Note 59 You do not have any authority to act under the LPA until an original attorney's appointment is terminated. Place a cross in the box to confirm that you understand this.

Note 60 ▶ You **must** read the LPA, and the relevant guidance and you must familiarise yourself with the wishes and feelings of the donor. If you are called upon to act as an attorney you have a duty to act in accordance with the principles of the Mental Capacity Act 2005. You also have a duty to have regard to the Code of Practice. The Code of Practice has practical guidance about the Act and your role as an attorney. Place a cross in the box to confirm that you understand the duties you have as an attorney.

Note 61 ▶ An attorney acting under an LPA – Property and Affairs must not be an undischarged bankrupt or an interim bankrupt. Place a cross in the box to confirm that you are neither.

Note 62 ▶ **You cannot and must not use the LPA form and the powers under it until it has been registered by the Public Guardian.** Place cross in the box to confirm that you understand this.

Note 63 ▶ Sign the LPA in the signature box and enter the date on which you sign. You must not sign until the donor has signed at paragraph 14 of the LPA and the certificate provider has signed the certificate. 'Signed by me as a deed' and 'delivered by me as a deed' are legal formalities. They just mean you need to sign and date.

Note 64 ▶ Your signature must be witnessed. Your witness must be 18 or over. Your witness may be a Part B certificate provider or another attorney. The witness must sign the LPA, enter their full name, their address and their postcode.

A5–15 `LPA PW Notes 10.07`

Lasting Power of Attorney Personal Welfare

Notes for completing an LPA – Personal Welfare

Important information

These notes will help you to fill in a Lasting Power of Attorney – Personal Welfare (LPA PW).

If you are making a Lasting Power of Attorney – Property and Affairs (LPA PA) you should not use these completion notes. Please refer to the notes for completing an LPA – Property and Affairs instead.

Before you complete the LPA

You must read the prescribed information at pages 2, 3 and 4 of the LPA form before you make the LPA. You should read the blank LPA form and these completion notes all the way through before you begin to make an LPA so that you know what you need to do. Your certificate provider and attorney(s) should also read these notes. There is more information about LPAs available from the Office of the Public Guardian (OPG) and you are advised to read this before making the LPA.

Completing the LPA

If there is not enough room for you to express your intentions in any Part or paragraph of the LPA, you should continue on a separate sheet and **attach it securely** at the back of the LPA. You should sign and date any continuation sheets and note clearly which Part and paragraph of the LPA they relate to.

If you make a minor mistake you should correct it and clearly initial the correction. You cannot make any changes at all to an LPA that has been signed, witnessed and certified.

These notes state which paragraphs and boxes **must** be completed. Failure to complete mandatory paragraphs and boxes may result in a delay when the LPA is sent for registration or may even result in the LPA being invalid in some cases. Where you are asked to cross through a part of the LPA that you are not using this is to stop anyone else filling it in. You must complete or cross through every part of the LPA.

When you are required to make a choice or confirm something you must be sure that you understand what you are choosing or confirming.

If you are unsure about the requirements of this LPA form, contact the OPG at the address given on the front of the LPA form. The OPG can help you in completing the form, but cannot give you legal advice.

Please use black or blue ink when filling in the form.

Part A – Donor's statement (Page 5 of LPA PW)

Your details

`Note 1` ▶ Place a cross in the appropriate title box and enter your first name, middle name, last name and date of birth. If you do not have a middle name, clearly cross through this box.

`Note 2` ▶ You must enter any other names you are known by or have been known by in the past, for example, your maiden name. If you are not known by any other names or have not been known by any other names in the past, clearly cross through that box.

`Note 3` ▶ Enter your contact details. You must enter your address and postcode. You should enter your telephone number and mobile phone number (if you have one) but you do not have to. You may also like to enter your e-mail address (if you have one). The more contact options you complete the easier it will be for the OPG, your attorney(s) or other people who may be relying on your LPA to contact you. If you leave a box blank, clearly cross through that box.

The details of the attorney(s) you are appointing (Page 6 of LPA PW)

`Note 4` ▶ There are two attorney spaces on the form but you do not have to appoint two attorneys. You can appoint as many or as few attorneys as you want. If you are not using both of the attorney boxes, clearly cross through those that you are not using. You should do this to avoid other people completing blank boxes. If you want to appoint more than two attorneys, follow the instructions on page 1 of these notes about continuation sheets.

`Note 5` ▶ Place a cross in the appropriate title box and enter the first name and last name of the attorney(s) you are appointing. **You must check with the person(s) you would like to appoint as your attorney(s) that they agree to act as attorney(s) for you before completing this page.**

How your attorney(s) is to act for you (Page 6 of LPA PW)

`Note 6` ▶ If you are only appointing one attorney cross through the whole of paragraph 4 of this page. If you are appointing more than one attorney you must decide how your attorneys are to act and place a cross in one of the three small boxes to indicate your choice. You must only place a cross in one box. If you cross more than one or fail to cross any of the boxes then your attorneys will be appointed together by default.

If you appoint your attorneys 'together' this means that all of them have to take decisions and act together for you. If you appoint your attorneys 'together and independently' this means that they can all take decisions and act together for you **and** they can also take decisions and act separately for you. You can also specify that your attorneys should act together in respect of some matters and together and independently in respect of others.

2

Note 7 ▶ If you decide to appoint your attorneys together in respect of some matters and together and independently in respect of others (by placing a cross in the relevant small box), you must then specify in the large text box on which matters your attorneys are to act together and on which matters they are to act together and independently. You must think carefully about the practical implications of appointing attorneys to act in different ways.

In this LPA form, 'together' means jointly and 'together and independently' means jointly and severally for the purposes of the Mental Capacity Act 2005.

Replacement attorney(s) (Page 7 of LPA PW)

Note 8 ▶ You must choose box 'Yes' or box 'No'. You can choose to appoint a replacement attorney to act if one or any of your attorneys cannot continue to be your attorney. You do not have to appoint a replacement attorney. There is more information on replacement attorneys in the OPG guidance on LPAs.

If you are not appointing a replacement attorney, place a cross in the 'No' box and clearly cross through the rest of this page. If you decide to appoint a replacement attorney, place a cross in the 'Yes' box. **You should check with the person you would like to appoint as your replacement attorney that they agree before completing this page.**

If you want to appoint more than one replacement attorney you must follow the instructions above about using continuation sheets. If you do not specify clearly which attorneys your replacements are to replace then the first replacement to be named in your LPA will replace the first attorney who needs replacing.

Note 9 ▶ Place a cross in the appropriate title box and enter the first name and last name of your replacement attorney.

Note 10 ▶ You do not have to complete this large text box. If you do not complete this box your replacement attorney will replace the first attorney who needs replacing. You can use this box to specify that your replacement should only replace a specific named attorney. Or you can specify that the replacement can replace any of your attorneys except a specific named attorney.

3

Life-sustaining treatment (Page 8 of LPA PW)

Note 11 ►

In your LPA – Personal Welfare you are giving your attorney(s) the authority to make any decisions about your personal welfare that you can make subject to any restrictions or conditions you place on them on page 9 of the form. The law requires you to specifically choose whether you want your attorney to have the authority to give or refuse consent to life-sustaining treatment on your behalf when you lack capacity or not. You **must** specify your decision on this page of the form. This is because there should be no ambiguity about the choice you are making. If you do not complete this paragraph the process of registering your LPA will be held up and your LPA may not be able to be registered at all.

You should read the information on life-sustaining treatment in the OPG guidance on LPAs before you make your choice. You may also want to discuss this with your doctor, and you should discuss this with your attorney. You must choose either Option A or Option B on this page. You must sign or mark one of the options. **Do not** sign or mark both of them. Enter the date your choice is signed or marked.

If you choose Option A you are choosing to give your attorney the authority to make decisions about life-sustaining treatment on your behalf.

If you choose Option B you are choosing to withhold from your attorney the authority to make decisions about life-sustaining treatment on your behalf.

If you are not able to sign please see notes 24 and 25 and page 14 of the LPA.

Witness of signature and selection of options (Page 8 of LPA PW)

Note 12 ►

Your selection and signature must be witnessed. Your witness must be at least 18 years of age and must not be your attorney(s). Your witness can be your Part B certificate provider. The witness must sign the LPA enter their full name, their address and postcode.

Placing restrictions and/or conditions on the attorney(s) you are appointing (Page 9 of LPA PW)

Note 13 ►

You must choose box 'Yes' or box 'No'. If you do not want to place any restrictions and/or conditions on your attorney(s), place a cross in the 'No' box and clearly cross through the rest of this page.

If you do not place any restrictions and/or conditions on your attorney(s) they will be able to take any decisions about your personal welfare that you can take. If you place restrictions or conditions on the decisions your attorney(s) can make or the matters which they can deal with, these must be followed by your attorney(s).

If you want to place restrictions and/or conditions on your attorney(s), place a cross in the 'Yes' box. If you choose this option you must specify in the large text box what those restrictions and/or conditions are. **You can restrict your attorney(s) or any of your attorneys in whatever manner you see fit but you should ensure that your restrictions and/or conditions will work in practice.** There is more information on the placing restrictions and/or conditions on your attorney in the OPG guidance on LPAs.

4

Guidance for your attorney(s) to consider (Page 10 of LPA PW)

Note 14 ▶ You do not have to complete this paragraph. If you do not want to give your attorney(s) any guidance in your LPA, clearly cross through this large text box.

Any guidance you give to your attorney(s) is for their information only. Your attorney(s) should consider your guidance when making decisions for you in your best interests.

If you want to give your attorney(s) guidance, complete the large text box. There is more information on giving guidance to your attorney in the OPG guidance on LPAs.

Paying your attorney(s) (Page 10 LPA PW)

Note 15 ▶ You must choose one of the two small option boxes in this paragraph. This will reflect whether you have agreed to pay your attorney(s) a fee. You do not have to pay your attorney(s) a fee. If you have more than one attorney you may make different decisions about fees for different attorneys. If you place a cross in the 'Yes' box you may give additional information about the fees you have agreed with your attorney in the text box provided.

If you place a cross in the 'No' box you should clearly cross through the rest of this paragraph.

Notifying others when an application to register your LPA is made (Page 11 and 12 of LPA PW)

Note 16 ▶ You can choose up to five people to be notified when an application to register your LPA is made. You can choose anyone you want. **This is an important safeguard because it gives the people you have chosen the right to object to registration of the LPA.** You do not have to choose anyone to be notified but if you do not, you will need to have two certificate providers at Part B of the LPA. If at all possible, you should choose at least one person to be notified when an application is made to register the LPA.

If you are not choosing anyone to be notified, clearly cross through the entirety of this and the following page.

If you choose a person(s) to be notified you should let them know that you have chosen them to perform this role.

For each person you want to be notified place a cross in the appropriate title box and enter their name and address including their postcode. You do not have to enter a telephone number and email for these people but it will be easier to contact them if you do. If you leave a box blank clearly cross through that box.

Things to confirm (Page 13 of LPA PW)

Note 17 ▶ You **must** read the prescribed information on pages 2, 3 and 4 of the LPA form or have it read to you before completing the LPA. You must confirm this by placing a cross in the appropriate box. If the information has been read to you by somebody else their name should be printed in the space provided. This person should **not** be one of your attorneys.

Note 18 ► By making an LPA PW you are giving your attorney(s) the legal authority to make decisions on your behalf in circumstances when you lack capacity. You must place a cross in the box to confirm that you are giving your attorney(s) that authority.

Note 19 ► You must choose between Option A and Option B with regard to life-sustaining treatment in paragraph 6 of the LPA by signing the option you choose. You must place a cross in the box to confirm that you have made a choice.

Note 20 ► When making an LPA you must either choose a person or people to be notified when an application to register your LPA is made or you must select two people to provide a separate Part B certificate each. Confirm which one of these you are doing by placing a cross in the appropriate box.

Note 21 ► Your certificate provider(s) independently verifies the circumstances in which you are making your LPA. It is important that you choose them, not your attorney(s) or any other person. You must place a cross in the box to confirm that you have chosen your certificate provider(s) yourself.

Signing the LPA (Page 13 of LPA PW)

Note 22 ► Sign the document or make your mark in the signature box and enter the date on which it is signed or marked. If you are unable to sign or mark the LPA, see completion note 24 and page 14 of the LPA form. The words 'signed by me as a deed' and 'delivered as a deed' are legal formalities. They just mean you need to sign and date.

Witness (Page 13 of LPA PW)

Note 23 ► Your signature must be witnessed. Your witness must be at least 18 years of age and must not be your attorney(s). Your witness can be your Part B certificate provider. The witness must sign the LPA, enter their full name, their address and their postcode. This can be the same witness as is required at page 8 of the LPA.

If you are unable to sign or make a mark (Page 14 of LPA PW)

Note 24 ► **This page should only be completed if you cannot sign or make a mark.** If you cannot sign the form or make a mark you can direct someone else to sign it for you. You can 'direct' someone in whatever way you choose to communicate. This person must be at least 18 years of age or over and must not be your attorney(s) or your Part B certificate provider(s). The person you are directing to sign must sign and date the form.

You must also direct this person to sign your choice of Option A or B at paragraph 6 of the form with regard to life-sustaining treatment.

Witness (Page 14 of LPA PW)

Note 25 ► There must be two witnesses to this person's signature. Your Part B certificate provider(s) may be a witness to this person's signature. Your attorney(s) must not be a witness to this person's signature. The witnesses must each sign the LPA, enter their full names and their addresses including their postcodes. The witnesses are signing both to confirm that they have witnessed the direction and the person's signature on this page and at paragraph 6.

A5–19 Part B – Certificate provider's statement (Page 15 of LPA PW)

Note 26 ▶ You must choose someone to be the certificate provider for your LPA.
Both you and your certificate provider must read the certificate before beginning to complete any of it.

The rest of this note on completing Part B is for the certificate provider. If you do not feel able to complete any of the Part B certificate do not complete it and raise any concerns you have with the OPG. There is separate guidance available, 'Certificate Provider and Witness Guidance'.

Who cannot provide a certificate? (Page 15 of LPA PW)

Note 27 ▶ You must not fall into one of these categories. If you do and you provide a certificate, the LPA will **not** be valid.

Note 28 ▶ You must read the whole of Parts A and B of this LPA, including the prescribed information on pages 2 – 4 before completing the certificate. The OPG has guidance on the role and responsibilities of the certificate provider and you should also read this before completing the certificate.

Note 29 ▶ You must be acting independently of the person making the LPA and the attorney(s) appointed under the LPA. You must not fall into the categories listed under 'Who cannot provide a certificate'. Once you are certain that you are not one of these people you must confirm this by placing a cross in the box.

Note 30 ▶ You must be 18 or over to provide this certificate. You must confirm this by placing a cross in the box. Only after you have confirmed this should you continue to complete the rest of the certificate.

Note 31 ▶ Place a cross in the appropriate title box and enter your first name, middle name and last name. If you do not have a middle name, clearly cross through that box. Enter your address and postcode.

Note 32 ▶ You should enter your telephone number and mobile number (if you have one) but you do not have to. You may also like to enter your e-mail address (if you have one). The more contact options you complete the easier it will be for the OPG or other people to contact you. If you leave a box blank, clearly cross through that box.

Who can provide a certificate? (Page 16 of LPA PW)

Note 33 ▶ You must identify yourself as either a category A certificate provider or a category B certificate provider. Do not fill in both category A and B. You must choose only one.

Knowledge certification (Page 16 of LPA PW)

Note 34 ▶ Place a cross in the small box to show that you have known the donor personally over the last two years. 'Personally' means that the donor is known to you as more than a passing acquaintance. Specify how you know them. This need not be in detail.

Skills certification (Page 16 of LPA PW)

`Note 35` ▶ There are five boxes for skills certification. Choose one of the boxes by placing a cross in it. If you place a cross in the box which begins, 'I am none of the above...' you must describe what you consider your relevant skills and expertise are in the text box titled 'My relevant skills and expertise are:'.

I confirm and understand (Page 16 of LPA PW)

`Note 36` ▶ You must read Part A and B of this LPA including the prescribed information on pages 2 – 4 before you certify. Place a cross in the box to confirm that you have done so.

`Note 37` ▶ You must discuss the contents of this LPA with the donor in order to be sure of the matters you are certifying. **The attorney(s) must not be present.** Place a cross in the box to confirm that you have discussed this LPA with the donor and that the attorney(s) was not present.

`Note 38` ▶ You should make efforts to discuss this LPA with the donor without anyone present. Place a cross in the box to confirm that you understand that you should try to do this.

There may, however, be situations where there has to be someone else there, for example where you need someone to assist you to communicate effectively with the donor. You must choose (by placing a cross in the appropriate box) between confirming that you discussed the LPA with the donor alone or that there was another person or person(s) present. Print the name of the person or people who was or were present and explain why they needed to be there.

`Note 39` ▶ You are certifying certain matters at a particular point in time, so it is important that you complete the certificate straight after discussing the LPA with the donor. Place a cross in the box to confirm this.

Core certification (Page 17 of LPA PW)

`Note 40` ▶ You are required to certify three things. You are certifying in your opinion having read the LPA and discussed the contents with the donor. You must consider whether you can certify these matters and, if you can, you must place a cross in the three boxes.

`Note 41` ▶ The certification process is complete when you sign the certificate. **Do not sign the certificate if you have any doubt about any of the matters you are being asked to certify.** Sign the document in the signature box and enter the date on which you are signing. Print your full name in the box below the signature box.

Additional certificate provider's statement (Page 18 of LPA PW)

`Note 42` ▶ Only complete page 18 when there are no people listed at paragraph 10 to be notified of an application for registration. If this additional certificate is required it should not be completed by the same person as the first certificate on pages 15 – 17. See notes 26 to 41 above for guidance.

A5–20 Part C – Attorney's statement (Page 21 of LPA PW)

Note 43 ▶	Every attorney named in Part A of the form must complete a separate attorney's statement at Part C. They are identical and therefore notes 43 to 51 can be used by all attorneys.

If there is a replacement attorney they must complete the replacement attorney's statement at page 23.

The rest of this note on completing Part C is for the attorney(s). You must read this LPA, including the prescribed information on pages 2 – 4 before completing your statement. The OPG has guidance on the role and responsibilities of an attorney and you should also read this before completing the statement so that you understand the nature of the role you are taking on. You should also discuss with the donor the duties you are assuming.

Note 44 ▶	Place a cross in the appropriate title box and enter your first name, middle name, last name and date of birth. You must be at least 18 to be an attorney. If you do not have a middle name, clearly cross through that box.

Note 45 ▶	You should enter your telephone number and mobile number (if you have one) but you do not have to. You may also like to enter your e-mail address (if you have one). The more options you complete the easier it will be for the OPG or other people to contact you. If you leave a box blank, clearly cross through that box.

Note 46 ▶	You **must** read the prescribed information on pages 2 – 4 of the LPA. Place a cross in the box to confirm that you have done.

Note 47 ▶	You **must** read the LPA, and the separate guidance for attorneys and you must familiarise yourself with the wishes and feelings of the donor. As an attorney you have a legal duty to act in accordance with the principles of the Mental Capacity Act 2005. You also have a duty to have regard to the Code of Practice. The Code of Practice has practical guidance about the Act and your role as an attorney. Place a cross in the box to confirm that you understand the duties you have as an attorney.

Note 48 ▶	**You cannot and must not use the LPA form and the powers in it until it has been registered by the Public Guardian.** Place a cross in the box to confirm that you understand this.

Note 49 ▶	**You cannot and must not act under this LPA until the donor lacks capacity.** Place a cross in the box to confirm that you understand this.

Note 50 ▶	Sign the LPA in the signature box and enter the date on which you sign. You **must not** sign until the donor has signed at paragraph 16 of the LPA and the certificate provider has signed the certificate. 'Signed by me as a deed' and 'delivered as a deed' are legal formalities. They just mean you need to sign and date.

Note 51 ▶	Your signature must be witnessed. Your witness must be at least 18. Your witness may be a Part B certificate provider or another attorney. The witness must sign the LPA, enter their full name, their address and their postcode.

Part C – Replacement attorney's statement (Page 23 of LPA PW)   A5–21

Note 52 ► This page only needs to be completed if the donor has appointed a replacement attorney at paragraph 5 of the LPA. The rest of this note is addressed to the replacement attorney. You must read this LPA, including the prescribed information on pages 2 – 4 before completing your statement. The OPG has guidance on the role and responsibilities of an attorney (including a replacement attorney) and you should also read this before completing the statement so that you understand the nature of the role you are taking on. You should also discuss with the donor the duties you are taking on.

Note 53 ► Place a cross in the appropriate title box and enter your first name, middle name, last name and date of birth. You must be 18 or over to be an attorney. If you do not have a middle name, clearly cross through that box.

Note 54 ► You should enter your telephone number and mobile number (if you have one) but you do not have to. You may also like to enter your e-mail address (if you have one). The more contact options you complete the easier it will be for the OPG or other people to contact you. If you leave a box blank, clearly cross through that box.

Note 55 ► You **must** read the prescribed information on pages 2 – 4 of the LPA. Place a cross in the box to confirm that you have done.

Note 56 ► You will only replace an attorney if you are needed and you will only be eligible to replace that attorney if you are still legally able to do so. Place a cross in the box to confirm that you understand this.

Note 57 ► You do not have any authority to act under the LPA until an original attorney's appointment is terminated. Place a cross in the box to confirm that you understand this.

Note 58 ► You **must** read the LPA, and the relevant guidance and you must familiarise yourself with the wishes and feelings of the donor. If you are called upon to act as an attorney you have a duty to act in accordance with the principles of the Mental Capacity Act 2005. You also have a duty to have regard to the Code of Practice. The Code of Practice has practical guidance about the Act and your role as an attorney. Place a cross in the box to confirm that you understand the duties you have as an attorney.

Note 59 ► **You cannot and must not use the LPA form and the powers under it until it has been registered by the Public Guardian.** Place a cross in the box to confirm that you understand this.

Note 60 ► **You cannot and must not act under this LPA until the donor lacks capacity.** Place a cross in the box to confirm that you understand this.

Note 61 ► Sign the LPA in the signature box and enter the date on which you sign. You must not sign until the donor has signed at paragraph 16 of the LPA and the certificate provider has signed the certificate. 'Signed by me as a deed' and 'delivered as a deed' are legal formalities. They just mean you need to sign and date.

Your signature must be witnessed. Your witness must be 18 or over. Your witness may be a Part B certificate provider or another attorney. The witness must sign the LPA, enter their full name, their address and their postcode.

Part B. Clauses for Insertion

1. Restrictions and conditions

[Form LPA PA (property and affairs), para.6, and form LPA PW **A5–22** (personal welfare), para.7]

Ethical investment	My money is not to be invested in any company which produces, sells or supplies weapons, armaments or tobacco products
No charitable gifts	My attorney(s) is/are not to make any gifts to charity from my estate
Sale of home	Before disposing of my house ... my attorney(s) shall obtain the written consent of my wife/husband/civil partner
Contact with donor	My attorney(s) do not have authority to decide who shall be permitted to visit or contact me

2. Guidance for attorneys

[Form LPA PA (property and affairs), para.7, and form LPA PW **A5–23** (personal welfare), para.8]

Religious conviction	In exercising authority under this power of attorney, my attorney(s) should always take into account the doctrine and teaching of the Roman Catholic church to which I have always sought to be true
Disabled child	My daughter ... suffers from ... which involves costly care, treatment and special facilities and accommodation. I have always strived to give her special support and my attorney(s) should give her needs preference over those of other members of my family
Supporting charities	I have for a long time made regular gifts to certain charities (in particular ...) and I hope it will possible for my attorney(s) to continue this support from my estate
Choice of home	In deciding where I should live, my attorney(s) should take account of my life-long love of gardens and the countryside
Attorney(s) to act independently	I prefer not to be troubled by routine decisions about financial transactions and hope that my attorney(s) will therefore not consult me unnecessarily

APPENDIX 6

ENDURING POWERS OF ATTORNEY

The Enduring Powers of Attorney
(Prescribed Form)
Regulations 1986

(SI 1986/126)

The Lord Chancellor, in exercise of the powers conferred on him by section 2(2) of the Enduring Powers of Attorney Act 1985 hereby makes the following Regulations:—

Citation and Operation

A6–01   **1.** These Regulations may be cited as the Enduring Powers of Attorney (Prescribed Form) Regulations 1986 and shall come into operation on March 10, 1986.

Interpretation

A6–02   **2.** In these Regulations unless the context otherwise requires expressions used to have the same meaning as in the Act (as herein defined):—

"the Act" means the Enduring Powers of Attorney Act 1985;

"attorney" means an attorney appointed under an enduring power of attorney;

"donor" means a person who has created an enduring power of attorney:

"enduring power of attorney" means a power of attorney which complies with these Regulations.

Prescribed Form

A6–03   **3.**—(1) Subject to regulations 3(2) and 5 of these Regulations, and enduring power of attorney in the form set out in the Schedule to these Regulations, together with such additions, variations or restrictions as the donor may decide, shall operate to confer on the attorney authority to do on behalf of the donor anything which the attorney can lawfully do by virtue of the Act or the contents of the enduring powers of attorney itself.

(2) An enduring power of attorney which seeks to exclude any provision contained in these Regulations, and in particular in the Schedule to these Regulations, is not a valid enduring power of attorney.

Execution

4. An enduring power of attorney in the form set out in the **A6–04** Schedule to these Regulations shall be executed by both the donor and the attorney, although not necessarily at the same time, in the presence of a witness but not necessarily the same witness, who will state his full name, address and occupation. The donor and an attorney may not witness the signature of each other. Where more than one attorney is appointed to act jointly and severally, then at least one of the attorneys so appointed must execute the instrument for it to take effect, but only those attorneys who have executed the instrument shall be able to act under the enduring power of attorney if the donor becomes mentally incapable.

Explanatory Information

5. The prescribed Explanatory Information, set out in the **A6–05** Schedule, shall be endorsed on the enduring power of attorney when the donor executes the instrument.

January 16, 1986 *Hailsham of St Marylebone, C.*

SCHEDULE

ENDURING POWER OF ATTORNEY

(PRESCRIBED FORM

THIS ENDURING POWER OF ATTORNEY is made
this day of 19 by
of
Date of birth
I appoint of
(and of

jointly *or* jointly and severally) to be my attorney(s)for the Enduring Powers of Attorney Act 1985

with general authority to act on the behalf   *or*
with authority to do the following on my behalf:

in relation to   **(a)**

all my property and affairs   *or*

the following property and affairs: **(b)(c)**

(subject to the following restrictions and conditions):

I intend that this power shall continue even if I become mentally incapable.

I have read *or* had read to me the explanatory information which is endorsed on and explains this document.

IN WITNESS whereof I have hereunto set my hand
and seal this   day of   in the
presence of:—

)

)(f)(g)

I/WE, the attorney(s) named in their power, understand that under the Enduring Powers of Attorney Act 1985 we have a duty to make application to the Court for the registration of the instrument and have a limited power (subject to any restrictions or conditions specified in this instrument) to make gifts of property or otherwise to benefit myself/ourselves and other persons and exercise the donor's trust functions. I am/we are not minor.

(h) IN WITNESS whereof the attorney [name] has hereunto set his/her hand and seal this   day of   19
in the presence of:—

IN WITNESS whereof the attorney [name] has hereunto set his/her hand and seal this   day of   19   in the presence of:—

EXPLANATORY INFORMATION

A6–06   (a) If general authority is given, section 3 of the Enduring Powers of Attorney Act 1985 (the Act) will have the effect, subject to any restrictions or conditions specified in the instrument, of enabling the attorney to do anything the donor can do by an attorney including, for example, selling any house or other property belonging to the donor. He will be able to make gifts and use the donor's property to benefit himself or others, but only to the extent described in notes (e) and (f) below. He may also exercise the donor's trust powers.

(b) If the alternative of giving only limited authority is adopted, the attorney will be able to do only the things specified. However, he will be able to make gifts and use the donor's property to benefit himself or others, but only to the extent described in notes (e) and (f) below or exercise the donor's trust powers, unless the enduring power of attorney restricts this authority.

(c) These further provisions can include, for example, a provision for paying the attorney for his service as attorney.

(d) The duty to apply for the registration of the instrument arises under section 4 of the Act as soon as the attorney has reason to believe the donor is becoming or has become mentally incapable of managing his affairs and is a duty to apply (or join with the other joint attorneys in applying) for the registration of the instrument with the Court of Protection. The Act contains requirements for the notification of the donor and certain of his relatives by the attorney before the instrument can be registered. Details of these requirements are contained in Part 1 of Schedule 1 of the Act.

(e) The donor's property can be given away under an enduring power of attorney within the limits set out in section 3(5) of the Act but it includes power (within those limits) for the attorney to benefit himself by gifts and to exercise the donor's trust powers. The donor can attach conditions to these powers or restrict them further than those limits by inserting the conditions or restrictions in the instrument at the place indicated for any restrictions or conditions. This can include a restriction that the enduring power of attorney is not to come into operation until the attorney has reason to believe that the donor is becoming mentally incapable.

(f) The donor's property can be used to benefit other persons, including the attorney, within the limits set out in section 3(4) of the Act. See also note (e) above as to further restrictions or conditions.

(g) After an instrument has been registered the attorney should notify the Court of Protection of the death or recovery of the donor.

(f) It is inadvisable for a married person to witness the signature to the power of attorney of his or her spouse.

[*The statutory references above have been corrected from the version originally printed*]

The Enduring Powers of Attorney (Prescribed Form) Regulations 1987

(SI 1987/1612)

The Lord Chancellor, in exercise of the power conferred on him by section 2(2) of the Enduring Powers of Attorney Act 1985, hereby makes the following Regulations:

Citation and commencement

A6–07   **1.** These Regulations may be cited as the Enduring Powers of Attorney (Prescribed Form) Regulations 1987 and shall come into force on November 1, 1987.

Prescribed Form

A6–08   **2.**—(1) Subject to paragraph (2) and (3) of this regulation and to regulation 4, an enduring power of attorney must be in the form set out in the Schedule to these Regulations and must include all the explanatory information headed "About using this form" in Part A of the Schedule and all the relevant marginal notes to Parts B and C. It may also include such additions or restrictions as the donor may decide.

(2) In completing the form of enduring power of attorney, the donor shall exclude (either by omission or deletion) one and only one of any pair of alternatives. When one of a pair of alternatives is omitted or deleted, the corresponding marginal note may be omitted or deleted.

(3) The form of execution by an attorney of an enduring power of attorney may be adapted to provide for sealing by a trust corporation with its common seal.

(4) Subject to paragraph (1), (2) and (3) of this regulation and to regulation 4, an enduring power of attorney which seeks to exclude any provision contained in these Regulations is not a valid enduring power of attorney.

Execution

A6–09   **3.** An enduring power of attorney in the form set out in the Schedule to these Regulations shall be executed by both the donor and the attorney, although not necessarily at the same time, in the presence of a witness, but not necessarily the same witness, who shall give his full name and address. The donor and an attorney shall not witness the signature of each other nor one attorney the signature of another. Where more than one attorney is appointed and they are to act jointly and severally, then at least one of the attorneys so appointed must execute the instrument for it to take effect as an enduring power of attorney, but only those attorneys who have executed the instrument shall be able to act under the enduring power of attorney in the event of the donor's mental incapacity or of the registration of the power, whichever first occurs.

Revocation

4. The Enduring Powers of Attorney (Prescribed Form) Regulations 1986 are hereby revoked, except that a power executed in the form prescribed by those Regulations and executed before July 1, 1988 shall be capable of being a valid enduring power of attorney. **A6–10**

SCHEDULE

ENDURING POWER OF ATTORNEY

Part A: About using this form **A6–11**

1. You may choose one attorney or more than one. If you choose more than one, you must decide whether they are to be able to act:
- Jointly (that is, they must all act together and cannot act separately) or
- Jointly and severally (that is, they can all act together but they can also act separately if they wish.)

On the form, at the place marked **1**, show what you have decided by crossing out one of the alternatives.

2. If you give your attorney(s) general power, in relation to all your property and affairs, it means that they will be able to deal with your money or property and may be able to sell your house.

3. If you don't want your attorney(s) to have such wide powers, you can include any restrictions you like, For example, you can include a restriction that your attorney(s) must not act on your behalf until they have reason to believe that you are becoming mentally incapable; or a restriction that your attorney(s) may not sell your house. Any restrictions you choose must be written or typed on the form in the place marked **2**.

4. Unless you put in a restriction preventing it your attorney(s) will be able to use any of your money or property to benefit themselves or other people by doing what you yourself might be expected to do to provide for their needs. Your attorney(s) will also be able to use your money to make gifts, but only for reasonable amounts in relation to the value of your money and property.

5. Your attorney(s) can recover the out-of-pocket expenses of acting as your attorney(s). If your attorney(s) are professional people, for example solicitors or accountants, they may be able to charge for their professional services as well.

6. If your attorney(s) have reason in the future to believe that you have become or art becoming mentally incapable of managing your affairs, your attorney(s) will have to apply to the Court of Protection for registration of this power.

7. Before applying to the Court of Protection for Registration of this power, your attorney(s) must give written notice that this is what they are going to do, to you and your nearest relatives as defined in the Enduring Powers of Attorney Act 1985. You or your relatives will be able to object if you or they disagree with registration.

8. This is a simplified explanation of what the Enduring Powers of Attorney Act 1985 and the Rules and Regulations say. If you need more guidance, you or your advisers will need to look at the Act itself and the Rules and Regulations. The Rules are the Court of Protection (Enduring Powers of Attorney) Rules 1986 (Statutory Instrument 1986 No. 127). The Regulations are the Enduring Powers of Attorney (Prescribed Form) Regulations 1987 (Statutory Instrument 1987 No. 1612).

9. *Note to Attorney(s)* After the power has been registered the attorney(s) should notify the Court of Protection if the donor dies or recovers.

You can cancel this power at any time before it has to be registered.

Part B: To be completed by the 'donor' (the person appointing the attorney(s))

A6–12   **Don't sign this form unless you understand what it means**
Please read the notes
in the margin

Donor's name and address	I _____ of _____
Donor's date of birth	born on _____
Attorney(s) name(s) and address(es)	appoint _____ of _____

See note 1 on the front of this form. If you are appointing only one attorney you should cross out everything between the square brackets

● [and _____

  of _____

Cross out the one which does not apply (see note 1) on the front of this form)

1. ● jointly
   ● jointly and severally

to be my attorney(s) for the purpose of the Enduring Powers of Attorney Act 1985

Cross out the which does not apply (see note 2 on the front of this form)

● with general authority to act on my behalf
● with authority to do the following on my behalf:

If you don't want the attorney(s) to have general power, you must give details here of what authority you are giving the attorney(s)

in relation to

Cross out the one which does not apply

● all my property and affairs
● the following property and affairs:

Please read the notes in the margin

A6–13

If there are restrictions or conditions, insert them here; if not, cross out these words (See note 3 on the front of this form)

2 ● subject to the following restrictions and conditions:

I intend that this power shall continue even if I become mentally incapable.

I have read or have had read to me the notes in Part A which are part of, and explain, this form.

Your signature

Signed, sealed and delivered by me _____ L.S.

Date | on _____

Someone must wit-
ness your signature

Signature of witness | In the presence of _____

Your attorney(s) can-
not be your witness.
If you are married it
is not advisable for
your husband or wife
to be your witness

Full name of witness _____

Address of witness _____

_____

_____

_____

Part C: To be completed by the attorney(s)

A6–14 Note ● This form may be adapted to provide for sealing by a corporation with its common seal

● If there are more than two attorneys attach an additional Part C

Don't sign this form
before the donor has
signed Part B

I understand that I have a duty to apply to the Court for the registration of this form under the Enduring Powers of Attorney Act 1985 when the donor is becoming or has become mentally incapable.

I also understand my limited power to use the donor's property to benefit persons other than the donor.

I am not a minor

Signature of attorney

Signed, sealed and delivered by me _____ L.S.

Date | on _____

Signature of witness | in the presence of _____

Each attorney must
sign the form and
each signature must
be witnessed. The
donor may not be the
witness and one
attorney may not wit-
ness the signature of
the other

Full name of witness _____

Address of witness _____

_____

_____

_____

To be completed only if there is a second attorney	I understand that I have a duty to apply to the Court for the registration of this form under the Enduring Powers of Attorney Act 1985 when the donor is becoming or has become mentally incapable.
	I also understand my limited power to use the donor's property to benefit persons then the donor.
	I am not a minor.
Signature of attorney	Signed, sealed and delivered by me _____ L.S.
Date	on _____
Signature of witness	in the presence of _____
Each attorney must sign the form and each signature must be witnessed. The donor may not to the witness and one attorney may not witness the signature of the other	Full name of witness _____
	Address of witness _____
	_____
	_____

The Enduring Powers of Attorney (Prescribed Form) Regulations 1990

(SI 1990/1376)

The Lord Chancellor, in exercise of the powers conferred on him by section 2(2) of the Enduring Powers of Attorney act 1985 hereby makes the following Regulations:

Citation and commencement

1. These Regulations may be cited as the Enduring Powers of **A6–15** Attorney (Prescribed Form) Regulations 1990 and shall come into force on July 31, 1990.

Prescribed form

2.—(1) Subject to paragraphs (2) and (3) of this regulation and **A6–16** to regulation 4: an enduring power of attorney must be in the form set out in the Schedule to these Regulations and must include all the explanatory information headed "About using this form" in Part A of the Schedule and all the relevant marginal notes to Parts B and C. It may also include such additions (including paragraph numbers) or restrictions as the donor may decide.

(2) In completing the form of enduring power of attorney—

(a) there shall be excluded (either by omission or deletion)—

(i) where the donor appoints only one attorney, everything between the square brackets on the first page of Part B; and

(ii) one and only one of any pair of alternatives;

(b) there may also be so excluded—

(i) the words on the second page of Part B "subject to the following restrictions and conditions", if those words do not apply;

(ii) the attestation details for a second witness in Parts B and C if a second witness is not required: and

(iii) any marginal notes which correspond with any words excluded under the provisions of this paragraph and the two notes numbered 1 and 2 which appear immediately under the heading to Part C.

(3) The form of execution by the donor or by an attorney may be adapted to provide—

(a) for a case where the donor or an attorney signs by means of a mark: and

(b) for the case (dealt with in regulation 3) where the enduring power of attorney is executed at the discretion of the donor or of an attorney;

and the form of execution by an attorney may be adapted to provide for execution by a trust corporation.

(4) Subject to paragraphs (1), (2) and (3) of this regulation and to regulation 4, an enduring power of attorney which seeks to exclude any provision contained in these Regulations is not a valid enduring power of attorney.

Execution

A6–17   3.—(1) An enduring power of attorney in the form set out in the Schedule to these Regulations shall be executed by both the donor and the attorney, although not necessarily at the same time, in the presence of a witness, but not necessarily the same witness, who shall sign the form and give his full name and address.

(2) The donor and an attorney shall not witness the signature of each other nor one attorney the signature of another.

(3) Where an enduring power of attorney is executed at the direction of the donor—

(a) it must be signed in the presence of two witnesses who shall each sign the form and give their full name and addresses; and

   (b) a statement that the enduring power of attorney has been executed at the direction of the donor must be inserted in Part B;

   (c) it must not be signed by either an attorney or any of the witnesses to the signature of either the donor or an attorney.

(4) Where an enduring power of attorney is executed at the direction of an attorney—

   (a) paragraph (3)(a) above applies; and

   (b) a statement that the enduring power of attorney has been executed at the direction of the attorney must be inserted in Part C;

   (c) it must not be signed by either the donor, an attorney or any of the witnesses to the signature of either the donor or an attorney.

4. Where more than one attorney is appointed and they are to act jointly and severally, then at least one of the attorneys so appointed must execute the instrument for it to take effect as an enduring power of attorney, and only those attorneys who have executed the instrument shall have the functions of an attorney under an enduring power of attorney in the event of the donor's mental incapacity or of the registration of the power, whichever first occurs.

Revocation

5. The Enduring Powers of Attorney (Prescribed Form) Regulations 1987 are hereby revoked, except that— **A6–18**

   (a) a power executed in the form prescribed by those Regulations and executed by the donor before July 31, 1991 shall be capable (whether or not seals are affixed to it) of being a valid enduring power of attorney;

   (b) regulation 3(3) shall apply to a power executed by the donor before July 31, 1991 under the provisions of those Regulations and the form of enduring power of attorney prescribed by those Regulations may be modified accordingly.

Dated July 5, 1990   *Mackay of Clashfern*, C.

SCHEDULE

Enduring Power of Attorney

Part A: About using this form

A6–19   **1. You may choose one attorney or more than one.** If you choose one attorney then you must delete everything between the square brackets on the first page of the form. If you choose more than one, you must decide whether they are to be able to act:

- Jointly (that is, they must all act together and cannot act separately) or

- Jointly and severally (that is, they can all act together but they can also act separately if they wish).

On the first page of the form, show what you have decided by crossing out one of the alternatives.

2. If you give your attorney(s) general power in relation to all your property and affairs, it means that they will be able to deal with your money or property and may be able to sell your house.

3. If you don't want your attorney(s) to have such wide powers, you can include any restrictions you like. For example, you can include a restriction that your attorney(s) must not act on your behalf until they have reason to believe that you are becoming mentally incapable; or a restriction as to what your attorney(s) may do. Any restrictions you choose must be written or typed where indicated on the second page of the form.

4. If you are a trustee (and please remember that co-ownership of a home involves trusteeship), you should seek legal advice if you want your attorney(s) to act as trustee on your behalf.

5. Unless you put in a restriction preventing it you attorney(s) will be able to use any of your money or property to make any provision which you yourself might be expected to make for their own needs or the needs of other people. Your attorney(s) will also be able to use your money to make gifts, but only for reasonable amounts in relation to the value of your money and property.

6. Your artorney(s) can recover the out-of-pocket expenses of acting as your attorney(s). If your attorney(s) are professional people, for example solicitors or accountants, they may be able to charge for their professional services as well. You may wish to provide expressly for the remuneration of your attorney(s) (although if they are trustees they may not be allowed to accept it).

7. If your attorney(s) have reason to believe that you have become or are becoming mentally incapable of managing your affairs, your attorney(s) will have to apply to the Court of Protection for registration of this power.

8. Before applying to the Court of Protection for registration of this power, your attorney(s) must give written notice that that is what they are going to do, to you and your nearest relatives as defined in the Enduring Powers of Attorney Act 1985. You or your relatives will be able to object if you or they disagree with registration.

9. This is a simplified explanation of what the Enduring Powers of Attorney Act 1985 and the Rules and Regulations say. If you need more guidance, you or your advisers will need to look at the Act itself and the Rules and Regulations. The Rules are the Court of Protection (Enduring Powers of Attorney) Rules 1986 (Statutory Instrument 1986 No. 127). The Regulations are the Enduring Powers of Attorney (Prescribed Form) Regulations 1990 (Statutory Instrument 1990 No. 1376).

10. Note to Attorney(s)

After the power has been registered you should notify the Court of Protection if the donor dies or recovers.

11. Note to Donor

Some of these explanatory notes may not apply to the form you are using if it has already been adapted to suit your particular requirements.

YOU CAN CANCEL THIS POWER AT ANY TIME BEFORE IT HAS TO BE REGISTERED.

Part B: To be completed by the "donor" (the person appointing the attorney(s))

Don't sign this form unless you understand what it means   A6–20

Please read the notes
in the margin which
follow and which are
part of the form itself

Donor's name and   I _____
address
                          of _____

Donor's date of birth   born on

                          appoint

                          of

See note 1 on the front of this form. If you are appointing only one attorney you should cross out everything between the square brackets. If appointing more than two attorneys please give the additional name(s) on an attached sheet

● [and _____
of _____

Cross out the one which does not apply (see note 1 on the front of this form)

● jointly
● jointly and severally

to be my attorney(s) for the purpose of the Enduring Powers of Attorney Act 1985

Cross out the which does not apply (see note 2 on the front of this form). Add any additional powers

● with general authority to act on my behalf
● with authority to do the following on my behalf

If you don't want the attorney(s) to have general power, you must give details here of what authority you are giving the attorney(s)

Cross out the one which does not apply

in relation to
● all my property and affairs
● the following property and affairs:

A6–21 Please read the notes in the margin which follow and which are part of the form itself.

If there are restrictions or conditions, insert them here; if not, cross out these words if you wish (see note 3 on the front of this form)

● subject to the following restrictions and conditions:

If this form is being signed at your diretion:
- the person signing must not be an attorney or any witness (to Parts B or C)
- you must add a statement that this form has been signed at your discretion
- a second witness is necessary (please see below)

I intend that this power shall continue even if I become mentally incapable

I have read or have had read to me the notes in Part A which are part of, and explain, this form.

Your signature (or mark)

Signed by me as a deed and delivered

Date

on _____

Signature of witness

In the presence of _____

Your attorney(s) cannot be your witness. [It is not advisable for your husband or wife to be your witnes][1]

Full name of witness _____

Address of witness _____

_____

_____

Please read the notes in the margin which follow and which are part of the form itself

Dont's sign this form before the donor has signed Part B or if, in your opinion, donor was already mentally incapable at the time of signing Part B

I understand that I have a duty to apply to the Court for the registration of this form under the Enduring Powers of Attorney Act 1985 when the donor is becoming or has become mentally incapable.

I also understand any limited power to use the donor's property to benefit persons other than the donor.

---

[1] Deleted by the Enduring Powers of Attorney (Prescribed Form) (Amendment) Regulations 2005 (SI 2005/3116).

If this form is being signed at your direction:
● the person signing must not be an attorney or any witness (to Parts B or C)
● You must add a statement that this form has been signed at your direction
● A second witness is necessary (please see below)

Signature (or mark) of attorney.

Signed by me as a deed _____ amd delivered

Date

on _____

Signature of witness

In the presence of _____

The attorney must sign the form and his signature must be witnessed. The donor may not be the witness and one attorney may not witness the signature of the other

Full name of witness _____

Address of witness _____

_____

_____

A second witness is only necessary if this form is not being signed by you personally but at your direction (for example, if a physical disability prevents you from signing)

Signature of second witness

in the presence of _____

Full name of witness _____

Address of witness _____

_____

_____

Part C: To be completed by the attorney(s)

Note: A6–22
1. This form may be adapted to provide for execution by a corporation
2. If there is more than one attorney additional sheets in the form as shown below must be added to this Part C

The Enduring Powers of Attorney (Welsh Language Prescribed Form) Regulations 2005

(SI 2005/3125)

(Note: The 2005 Regulations revoke and replace the 2000 Regulations with minor amendments)

The Lord Chancellor makes the following Regulations in exercise of the powers conferred by section 2(2) of the Enduring Powers of Attorney Act 1985 as extended by section 26(3) of the Welsh Language Act 1993:

Citation and commencement

1. These Regulations may be cited as the Enduring Powers of A6–23 Attorney (Welsh Language Prescribed Form) Regulations 2005 and shall come into force on 5th December 2005.

Welsh language prescribed form

2. The form of words in the Schedule to these Regulations may A6–24 be used instead of than set out in the Schedule to the Enduring Powers of Attorney (Prescribed Form) Regulations 1990.

Revocation

3. The Enduring Powers of Attorney (Welsh Language Pre- A6–25 scribed Form) Regulations 2000 are revoked except that a power executed in the form prescribed in the Schedule to those Regulations and executed by the donor before 1st April 2007 shall be capable (whether or not seals are affixed to it) of being a valid enduring power of attorney.

SCHEDULE 1

Regulation 2

ATWRNEIAETH BARHAUS

Rhan A: Ynghylch defnyddio'r ffurflen hon

A6–26   **1. Cewch ddewis un atwrnai neu fwy nag un.** Os mai un atwrnai a ddewiswch, rhaid i chi ddileu popeth rhwng y bracedi sgwâr ar dudalen gyntaf y ffurflen. Os dewiswch chi fwy nag un, rhaid i chi benderfynu a ydyn nhw'n gallu gweithredu:

Ar y cyd (hynny yw, rhaid iddyn nhw i gyd weithredu gyda'i gilydd ac ni chânt weithredu ar wahân) neu

Ar y cyd ac ar wahân (hynny yw, cânt oll weithio gyda'i gilydd ond cânt hefyd weithredu ar wahân os ydyn nhw'n dymuno gwneud hynny).

Ar dudalen gyntaf y ffurflen, nodwch eich penderfyniad chi trwy groesi un o'r dewisiadau allan.

2. Os rhowch chi bŵer cyffredinol i'ch atwrnai yng nghyswllt eich holl eiddo a'ch busnes, mae hynny'n golygu y byddan nhw'n gallu delio gyda'ch arian a'ch eiddo ac, o bosib, yn gallu gwerthu eich tŷ.

3. Os nad ydych chi'n dymuno i'ch atwrnai feddu ar bwerau mor eang, cewch gynnwys unrhyw gyfyngiadau a fynnwch chi. Er enghraifft, cewch gynnwys cyfyngiad na chaiff ei atwrnai(eiod) weithredu ar eich rhan nes bod ganddyn nhw sail dros gredu eich bod yn feddyliol analluog: neu gyfyngiad ynghylch yr hyn y caiff eich atwrnai(eiod) ei wneud. Rhaid ysgrifennu neu deipio unrhyw gyfyngiadau y dewiswch eu nodi yn y man priodol ar ail dudalen y ffurflen.

4. Os ydych chi'n ymddiriedolwr (a chofiwch hefyd bod cyd-berchnogi cartref yn golygu eich bod yn ymddiriedolwr), dylech ofyn am gyngor cyfreithiol os ydych chi'n dymuno i'r atwrnai(eiod) weithredu fel ymddiriedolwr ar eich rhan.

5. Oni bai eich bod yn cynnwys cyfyngiad i rwystro hynny, bydd eich atwrnai(eiod) yn gallu defnyddio eich arian neu'ch eiddo i wneud darpariaeth y gellid disgwyl i chi eich hun ei gwneud at eu hanghenion eu hunain neu at anghenion pobl eraill. Bydd eich atwrnai(eiod) hefyd yn gallu defnyddio eich arian fel rhoddion, ond dim ond am symiau rhesymol yng nghyswllt gwerth eich arian a'ch eiddo.

6. Caiff eich atwrnai(eiod) adennill y mân-gostau o weithredu fel atwrnai(eiod) ar eich rhan. Os yw eich atwmai(eiod) yn weithwyr proffesiynol, er enghraifft cyfreithwyr neu gyfrifwyr, mae'n bosib y gallan nhw godi am eu gwasanaethau proffesiynol hefyd. Mae'n bosib y byddwch yn dymuno gwneud darpariaeth arbennig ar gyfer rhoi cydnabyddiaeth am waith eich atwrnai(eiod) (er, os ydyn nhw'n ymddiriedolwyr, mae'n bosib na fydd ganddyn nhw'r hawl i'w derbyn).

7. Os yw eich atwrnai(eiod) o'r farn eich bod, neu eich bod ar fin bod, yn feddyliol analluog i gadw trefn ar eich busnes, bydd yn rhaid i'ch atwrnai(eiod) gyflwyno cais i'r Llys Nodded er mwyn cofrestru ei bŵer.

8. Cyn cyflwyno cais i'r Llys Nodded ar gyfer cofrestru'r pŵer hwn, bydd yn rhaid i'ch atwrnai(eiod) roi rhybudd ysgrifenedig o'u bwraid, i chi ac i'ch perthnasau agos, yn ôl diffiniad Deddf Atwrneiaeth Barhaus 1985. Byddwch chi neu'ch perthnasau yn gallu gwrthwynebu os ydych chi, neu os ydyn nhw, yn anghytuno gyda'r cofrestriad hwn.

9. Mae hwn yn esboniad syml o'r hyn sydd gan Ddeddf Atwrneiaeth Barhaus 1985 a'r Rheolau a'r Rheoliadau i'w ddweud. Os oes angen rhagor o arweiniad arnoch, bydd gofyn i chi, neu'ch cynghorwyr, edrych ar y Ddeddf ei hun ac ar y Rheolau a'r Rheoliadau. Y Rheolau yw Rheolau y Llys Nodded (Atwrneiaeth Barhaus) 1986 (Offeryn Statudol 1986 Rhif 127). Y Rheoliadau yw Rheoliadau Atwrneiaeth Barhaus (Ffurf Benodedig) 1990 (Offeryn Statudol 1990 Rhif 1376).

10. Nodyn i'r Atwrnai(eiod)
Ar ôl cofrestru'r pŵer, dylech roi gwybod i'r Llys Nodded os yw'r rhoddwr yn marw neu'n gwella.

11. Nodyn i'r Rhoddwr
Mae'n bosib na fydd rhywfaint o'r nodiadau esboniadol yn berthnasol i'r ffurflen y byddwch chi'n ei defyddio os yw eisoes wedi'i haddasu i gyd-fynd â'ch gofynion penodol chi.
CEWCH GANSLO'R PŴER HWN UNRHYW BRYD CYN BOD YN RHAID EI GOFRESTRU.

Rhan B: I'w llenwi gan y rhoddmr (y sawl sy'n penodi'r A6–27 atwrnai(eiod)).

Peidiwch â llofnodi'r ffurflen hon nes eich bod yn deall beth mae hynny'n ei olygu

A fyddech gystal â darllen y nodiadau isod ar ymyl y dudalen sy'n rhan o'r ffurflen ei hun.

Enw a chyfeiriad y Rhoddwr.	Yr wyf fi
	o
Dyddiad geni y Rhoddwr.	a anwyd ar
	yn penodi

Gweler nodyn 1 ar flaen y ffurflen hon.
Os mai dim ond un atwrnai yr ydych yn ei
benodi, dylech ddileu popeth arall sy'n
ymddangos rhwng y bracedi sgwâr trwy'i
groesi allan. Os ydych chi'n penodi mwy
na dau atwrnai, nodwch yr enw(au) ar y
ddalen sydd ynghlwm.
Dilëwch ba un bynnag sy'n amherthnasol
trwy'i groesi allan (gweler nodyn 1 ar
flaen y ffurflen hon).

o
[●
o

● ar y cyd
● ar y cyd ac ar
wahân]

i fod yn atwrnai (eiod)
at ddibenion Deddf

Atwrneiaeth Barhaus
1985
● gydag awdurdod
cyffredinol   I
weithredu ar fy

rhan

Dilëwch ba un bynnag sy'n amherthnasol
trwy'i groesi allan (gweler nodyn 2 ar
flaen y ffurflen hon). Nodwch unrhyw
bwerau ychwanegol.
Os nad ydych chi'n dymuno i'r
atwrnai(eiod) feddu ar bŵer cyffredinol,
rhaid nodi yma fanylion yr awdurdod yr
ydych yn ei roi i'r atwrnai(eiod).

● gydag awdurdod i
wneud y canlynol ar fy
rhan

yng nghyswllt
● fy holl eiddo a'm
busnes
● yr eiddo a'r busnes
canlynol:

Dilëwch ba un bynnag sy'n amherthnasol
trwy'i groesi allan.

Rhan B: parhad

A6–28 A fyddech gystal â darllen y nodiadau
isod ar ymyl y dudalen sy'n rhan o'r
ffurflen ei hun. Os oes yna unrhyw
gyfyngiadau neu amodau, nodwch y
rheiny yma; os nad oes, croeswch y
geiriau hyn allan os ydych chi'n dymuno
(gweler nodyn 3 ar flaen y ffurflen hon).
Os yw'r ffurflen hon yn cael ei llofnodi yn
unol â'ch cyfarwyddiadau chi:—
● rhaid i'r sawl sy'n ei llofnodi beidio â
bod yn atwrnai nac yn dyst (i Rannau B
nac C).

● yn amodol ac y
cyfyngiadau   a'r
amodau isod:

Fy mwriad yw i'r pŵer
hwn barhau hyd yn
oed os byddaf, un
diwrnod, yn feddyliol
analluog.

- rhaid i chi ychwanegu datganiad sy'n dweud fod y ffurflen hon wedi'i llofnodi ar eich cyfarwyddiadau chi.
- rhaid wrth ail dyst (gweler isod).

Yr wyf wedi darllen, neu darllenodd rywun i mi, nodiadau Rhan A sy'n rhan o'r ffurflen hon, ac yn cynnig esboniad ohoni.

Eich llofnod chi (neu farc).

Llofnodwyd gennyf fi fel gweithred a chyflwynwyd

Dyddiad.

ar

Rhaid i rywun fod yn dyst i'ch llofhod
Llofnod y tyst.

ym mhresenoldeb
Enw llawn y tyst

Ni chaiff eich atwrnai(eiod) fod yn dyst(ion) i chi. Ni chynghorir i'ch gŵr neu'ch gwraig fod yn dyst i chi.

Cyfeiriad y tyst

Dim ond os nad ydych chi'n llofnodi'r ffurflen hon yn bersonol, ond eich bod wedi rhoi cyfarwyddiadau i rywun arall ei llofnodi ar eich rhan, (er enghraifft, os yw anabledd corfforol yn eich rhwystro rhag llofnodi) y bydd yn rhaid i chi gael ail dyst. Llofnod yr ail dyst.

ym mhresenoldeb

Enw llawn y tyst

Cyfeiriad y tyst

Rhan C: I'w llenwi gan yr atwrnai(eiod)

Nodyn:

A6–29

1. Gellir addasu'r ffurflen hon i ganiatáu ar gyfer cyflawni gan gorfforacth.

2. Os oes mwy nag un atwrnai, rhaid rhoi dalennau ychwanegol yn unol â'r ffurf isod, at Ran C.

A fyddech gystal â darllen y nodiadau isod ar ymyl y dudalen sy'n rhan o'r ffurflen ei hun.

Peidiwch â llofnodi'r ffurflen hon nes bod y rhoddwr wedi llofnodi Rhan B neu os oedd y Rhoddwr, yn eich barn chi, eisoes yn feddyliol analluog adeg llofnodi Rhan B.

Deallaf fod gennyf ddyletswydd i gyflwyno cais i'r Llys am i'r ffurflen hon gael ei chofrestru o dan Ddeddf Atwrneiaeth Barhaus 1985 pan fo'r rhoddwr ar fin bod yn feddyliol analluog neu eisoes yn y cyflwr hwnnw.

Os yw'r ffurflen hon yn cael ei llofnodi yn unol â'ch cyfarwyddiadau chi:—
• rhaid i'r sawl sy'n ei llofnodi beidio â bod yn atwrnai nac yn dyst (i Rannau B nac C).
• rhaid i chi ychwanegu datganiad sy'n dweud fod y ffurflen hon wedi'i llofnodi ar eich cyfarwyddiadau chi.
• rhaid wrth ail dyst (gweler isod).
Llofnod (neu farc) yr atwrnai.

Dyddiad.
Llofnod y tyst.

Rhaid i'r atwrnai lofnodi'r ffurflen a rhaid cael tyst i'w lofnod. Ni chaiff y rhoddwr fod yn dyst ac ni chaiff un atwrnai fod yn dyst i lofnod y llall.
Dim ond os nad ydych chi'n llofnodi'r ffurflen hon yn bersonol, ond eich bod wedi rhoi cyfarwyddiadau i rywun arall ei lofnodi ar eich rhan, (er enghraifft, os yw anabledd corfforol yn eich rhwystro rhag llofnodi) y bydd yn rhaid i chi gael ail dyst. Llofnod yr ail dyst.

Deallaf hefyd fod fy mhŵer i ddefnyddio eiddo'r rhoddwr er budd unrhyw un, ar wahân i'r rhoddwr, wedi'i gyfyngu.
Nid wyf dan oed

Llofnodwyd gennyf fi fel gweithred a'i chyflwyno
ar
ym mhresenoldeb

Enw llawn y tyst
Cyfeiriad y tyst

ym mhresenoldeb
Enw llawn y tyst
Cyfeiriad y tyst

Index

LEGAL TAXONOMY

FROM SWEET & MAXWELL

This index has been prepared using Sweet and Maxwell's Legal Taxonomy. Main index entries conform to keywords provided by the Legal Taxonomy except where references to specific documents or non-standard terms (denoted by quotation marks) have been included. These keywords provide a means of identifying similar concepts in other Sweet & Maxwell publications and online services to which keywords from the Legal Taxonomy have been applied. Readers may find some minor differences between terms used in the text and those which appear in the index. Suggestions to *sweetandmaxwell.taxonomy@thomson.com*.

(All references are to paragraph numbers)